GEORGETTE HEYER'S
REGENCY WORLD

A conservatory was the perfect place for a marriage proposal.

GEORGETTE HEYER'S
REGENCY WORLD

Jennifer Kloester

ILLUSTRATED BY

Graeme Tavendale

Published by Sourcebooks, Inc.
P.O. Box 4410, Naperville, Illinois 60567-4410
(630) 961-3900
FAX: (630) 961-2168
www.sourcebooks.com

Originally published in the United Kingdom in 2005 by William Heinemann

Library of Congress Cataloging-in-Publication Data

Kloester, Jennifer.
  Georgette Heyer's Regency world / Jennifer Kloester ; illustrated by Graeme Tavendale.
      p. cm.
  Originally published: London : William Heinemann, 2005.
  Includes bibliographical references.
  1. Heyer, Georgette, 1902-1974—Settings. 2. Heyer, Georgette, 1902-1974—Knowledge—England. 3. Regency in literature. 4. Regency—England. 5. England—In literature. 6. England—Social life and customs—19th century. I. Tavendale, Graeme. II. Title.
  PR6015.E795Z84 2010
  823'.912—dc22

                                    2010017246

Printed and bound in the United States of America
        VP 10 9 8 7 6 5 4 3 2 1

To J. Roy Hay

Contents

List of Illustrations

Introduction

The entries selected for this book are drawn from the history in Georgette Heyer's twenty-six Regency novels. For many years these books have beguiled my leisure hours, affording me enormous pleasure, but also giving me a great deal of useful information about the English Regency period. I hadn't known just how much accurate and factual information there was in the novels until I came to research and write this book, and, although I'd always been under the impression that Heyer was meticulous in her communication of the period, I hadn't appreciated the scope of her research, nor the degree to which she immersed herself in the Regency era.

The aim of *Georgette Heyer's Regency World* is to expand on Heyer's history and to provide for the modern reader an explanation of the people, places and events that made her Regency world so unforgettable. The book is designed as a ready reference for the Heyer fan, the general reader, or for anyone interested in the history of the period. Everything in the book is inspired by a reference in at least one of Heyer's twenty-six Regency novels and, if there is an unashamed bias towards the upper class, this is a deliberate reflection of the characters, plots and action of the books.

Georgette Heyer's novels are stylish constructions with exemplary syntax and faultless punctuation as well as a rhythm and cadence of language that has the power to carry the reader away into the world of the English Regency. Today her dialogue, witty romantic plots and many memorable characters remain the benchmark for the modern writer of the Regency historical novel. Georgette Heyer continues to stand alone, however, not only as the creator of the Regency genre of historical romance, but also as its finest exponent. It is my fervent hope that this book will add to the pleasure of reading hers.

Jennifer Kloester
March 2005

Acknowledgements

I am grateful to many people for their support while writing this book but especially to:

Paul L. Nicholls for his enthusiastic interest in and support for the book, as well as for his careful reading, incisive comments and wise counsel throughout the writing process. Also for sharing with me his appreciation of Georgette Heyer's stylish prose and ironic wit.

Roy and Frances Hay for wonderful friendship, good advice and many congenial lunches. Also for reading the draft chapters, making helpful suggestions, lending me many useful texts and patiently responding to my calls on a miscellany of research questions.

Barry Kloester for his inspiring integrity, love, kindness and support. For sharing so many wonderful adventures with me, for believing I could do it and helping me to get there. To Ben, Christopher and Elanor who endured the writing process, made me laugh, and who give me so much joy. To Lladro, my faithful companion and prince among dogs.

Dianne Tobias and Fiona Skinner for their loyalty, integrity, enduring friendship and for always listening; Dolly MacKinnon for her brilliant insight, inspiration, friendship and advice; Yve Cruickshank for her generosity and kindness in reading the drafts; and Joanna and Andrew Cruickshank for their support. Ro Marriott for her generosity in sharing Georgette Heyer with me, Jean

Strathdee-Cook of the London Library for her kind support and for going above and beyond the call of duty to find elusive original Regency sources. Vija, Kay and the staff at the Baillieu Library, the University of Melbourne, as well as the staff at Deakin University Library, the State Library of Victoria, the London Library, the British Library and Peter Downie and the staff at Barwon Books. Rory Lalwan at the Westminster City Archives; Anne Lewis, David Philips, David Goodman, Ron Ridley and the History Department, the Melbourne Scholarship Office and the School of Graduate Studies at the University of Melbourne; Phillip Warne and Jeff Oxley for fixing my shoulder at the crucial moment; and Dr Claire Darby and Dr Sandor Monostori for their professional advice on gout and other medical questions. Thanks also to Mercedes, Hayley and Nicola at Kwik Kopy, as well as Judith McGinness.

I also owe special thanks to: Frank and Wendy Brennan for past kindness, encouragement and advice. Richard and Judy Rougier, Jane Aiken Hodge, Susanna Rougier, Jeremy and Judith Rougier, and Hale and Eunice Crosse for their hospitality, generosity and support during my research trips to England. Sally Houghton for her wonderful Georgette Heyer website and generous support, Kirsten Elliott for the inspiring tour of Bath, Jennifer Nason and Alex Lipe for their friendship and hospitality, Pauline Parker, Valerie Tarrant and Susan, Peter and Marjorie Johnston, Frank Ford and Günter Gerlach for being there, Hilary McPhee for her continuing encouragement of aspiring writers and her dedication to the pursuit of excellence. Also my agents Bruce Hunter and Jenny Darling and her assistant Donica Bettanin for their tremendous support, interest and enthusiasm, and my editor Nikola Scott for her superb and incisive editing, encouragement and advice. Finally to Graeme Tavendale, illustrator *extraordinaire*, for bringing my vision to life. Thank you.

Up and Down the Social Ladder

REGENCY SOCIETY

The true Regency lasted only nine years. It began on 5 February 1811 when George, Prince of Wales, was officially sworn in as Regent and ended on 31 January 1820 when he was proclaimed King George IV. Yet the term 'Regency' is frequently used to describe the period of English history between the years 1780 and 1830, because the society and culture during these years were undeniably marked by the influence of the man who would become George IV. With the final years of the Napoleonic Wars and the enormous impact of industrialisation the Regency was an era of change and unrest as well as one of glittering social occasions, celebrations and extraordinary achievement in art and literature. Artists such as Thomas Lawrence, John Constable and Joseph Turner created iconic paintings which today constitute a tangible record of some of the people and places of the period, while many of England's greatest writers produced some of their most enduring works during the Regency. The writings of Jane Austen, Walter Scott, John Keats, Mary Shelley, Samuel Coleridge, William Wordsworth, Lord Byron and Percy Bysshe Shelley continue to stand as a testament to the romance, colour and vitality of the times. In many ways the Regency period was also a reflection of

*Known for his flamboyance and high living, the Prince Regent, or 'Prinny',
gave his title to one of the most colourful eras in England's history.*

the character and personality of the Prince Regent himself who was
one of the most flamboyant and cultured of all English monarchs.
His passion for art, architecture, music, literature and hedonistic
living set the tone for the era and caused his Regency to be for ever
linked with the high-living, mayfly class that was the *ton*.

The Regency world was highly structured and the conventions
attached to Regency life were so numerous and intricate that usually
only those born and bred into upper-class circles knew and understood them. Above all, it was intensely class-conscious: the *ton* (from
the French phrase *le bon ton*, meaning 'in the fashionable mode' and
also known as Polite Society or the Upper Ten Thousand) lived a
privileged, self-indulgent life; birth and family were vital to social

acceptance, and social behaviour was determined by a complex set of rules of varying flexibility, with different codes of behaviour for men and women. It was an era of manners, fashion and propriety, and yet, for the upper class, it was also a time of extraordinary excess, extravagance and indulgence. By contrast the middle class was more interested in morality than manners and often found it difficult to follow the distinctive behaviour of the upper class.

THE SOCIAL LADDER

During the Regency the social ladder had a fixed, inflexible hierarchy within the nobility and an almost equally rigid class structure within the rest of the population:

Monarch
Royalty
Aristocracy
Gentry
Middle Classes
Artisans and Tradespeople
Servants
Labouring Poor
Paupers

Class was defined primarily by birth, title, wealth, property and occupation, and there were many distinctions—some subtle, others obvious—within each level of society. While visiting his country seat of Stanyon in *The Quiet Gentleman*, Gervase Frant, seventh Earl of St Erth, met his near neighbour, Sir Thomas Bolderwood, and was at first unsure of this jovial gentleman's exact social standing. Although Sir Thomas's countenance, wealth, title, home and family all indicated good breeding, his manners lacked polish and there was a certain rough quality in his speech, the result—as he informed the Earl—of having spent most of his life in India. Discerning one's own place on the broader social scale was not all that difficult but knowing the exact position in relation to someone else of the same class was not always easy; although Mrs Bagshot in *Friday's Child* was in no doubt about the sudden (and infuriating) elevation in her young cousin Hero's social status after Hero's unexpected marriage to a peer. Ancestry was key, as were property and money (most obviously shown by the number of servants and carriages one had), although wealth became a less reliable guide to a person's breeding after industrialisation and the expansion of the Empire. Acceptance into the *ton* was often a question of degree, as discovered by the villainous Sir Montagu Revesby in *Friday's Child* when his elegant air and address were enough to see him admitted into some fashionable circles but he was still excluded by many of those at the heart of the *ton* who considered him 'a commoner'. During the Regency, the advent of the new rich—those industrialists, financiers, merchants, manufacturers, bankers, nabobs and even admirals of the fleet who had garnered enough wealth to buy their way into the upper echelons of society—created a new complication for the class-conscious aristocrat. An heiress was always an attractive prize but marriage between a member of the peerage and a female whose parents 'smelled of shop' had to be very carefully considered before any commitment was made. A scion of a noble house might find himself cut off from his inheritance if he persisted in marrying into a much lower social class, as Lord Darracott's son, Hugh, discovered after he married a weaver's daughter in *The Unknown Ajax*.

Members of the aristocracy and the gentry might be different in birth and title but between them they *were* the ruling class. A well-bred country squire of ancient lineage but with no more than a baronetcy or a knighthood to his name, if that, might meet a duke or an earl on equal terms (particularly if he was a neighbour) and show him deference only on formal occasions. In *Sylvester*, Squire Orde met the Duke of Salford on his home ground and, while being perfectly polite, did not hesitate to speak his mind or censure the Duke's actions. During the Regency the nobility was made up of members of the royal family, peers above the rank of baronet and their families, statesmen and the prelates of the Church of England such as the more powerful bishops and the Archbishop of Canterbury (who took precedence over all ranks after the royal family). The gentry included baronets, knights, country land-owners (often incredibly wealthy) and gentlemen of property and good birth but no title. Robert Beaumaris of *Arabella* was plain Mister but his family's ancient lineage (his cousin was a duke and his grandmother the Dowager Duchess), his fortune, breeding and address amply compensated for his lack of title and made him one of the most eligible bachelors in England. Apart from manners and breeding, one of the main distinguishing factors between the upper class and the upper levels of the middle class was the need for the latter to actually *earn* their living.

The middle class was growing fast in Regency England as increasing numbers of financiers, merchants and industrialists were added to the wealthy doctors, lawyers, engineers, higher clergy and farmers who, among others, comprised the upper ranks of the class. To be in the middle ranks of society usually meant ownership of some kind of property—land, livestock or tools—and the ability to earn a regular and reliable income. The number of servants employed in a house and the type of carriage(s) and number of horses one owned were also useful class indicators, although some among the new middle class, such as the affluent merchant Jonathan Chawleigh in *A Civil Contract*, tended to mistake opulence for elegance and an excess of food or finery as a sign of wealth and status. But the middle class was a very large and diverse group and it also included shopkeepers, teachers, builders, the lesser clergy, members of the government administration, clerks, innkeepers and even some of the servant class. Property was really the main factor that separated the lowest level of the middle class from the better-off among the labouring poor.

ROYALTY

The English monarchy was an ancient institution based on the principles of heredity and primogeniture, which meant that the eldest male child inherited the throne on the death of the monarch. Where the son predeceased the monarch the right to inherit the throne passed to the son's eldest male child or, if he had no sons, to his daughter. If the heir to the throne had no children, the next

George III's intermittent bouts of madness eventually saw his son made Regent.

eldest brother became the heir and his children moved into the direct line of succession ahead of their father's siblings. In the event of there being no male to wear the crown, the eldest daughter would inherit the throne and become queen. As heir to the throne the Regent's daughter, Princess Charlotte, was a great favourite with the general populace and many people, including the young and beautiful Fanny, Lady Spenborough, of *Bath Tangle*, took great interest in keeping up to date with the Princess's love life and reading accounts of the Princess's engagement, first to Prince William of Orange and then to Leopold of Saxe-Coburg.

The succession became a topic of great fascination during the years of the Regency and George IV's reign. For nearly a century the passage of kings had been fairly straightforward, for the rise of the House of Hanover had seen in 1811 George I ascend the throne in 1714, followed by his son George II in 1727 and his grandson, 'Farmer' George III, in 1760. Then the unexpected appearance of George III's intermittent bouts of madness began to disrupt the sequence. In 1810 his condition deteriorated and George, Prince of Wales, was appointed Regent to rule in his father's place until the King's death, when he would himself become king. When the Regent's heir, his daughter and only child Princess Charlotte, suddenly died in childbirth in 1817 there was a rapid scramble (what Captain Belper in *The Foundling* called 'the Heir-to-the-throne Stakes') among the royal dukes—the Regent's six brothers—to marry and produce a legitimate heir to the throne.

THE ARISTOCRACY

The creation of new peers was usually at the discretion of the sovereign but at different times it could be politically advantageous to win the loyalty of powerful men by the conferring of titles. For much of the Georgian period the peerage had remained

largely unchanged but between 1780 and 1832 George III and
George IV added one hundred and sixty-six new members to the
peerage between them. By 1820 there were three hundred peers in
England: eighteen dukes, seventeen marquises, one hundred earls,
twenty-two viscounts, one hundred and thirty-four barons and
nine peeresses. In addition to this there were many baronets and
knights who stood at the head of the gentry class and could count
themselves among the aristocracy.

A peer could have more than one title but generally used that
of highest rank. Most peers earned a lower ranking title first and
then added the higher titles to their name as they were conferred.
Dukes, for instance, could also hold the titles of Marquis (or
Marquess), Earl, Viscount and Baron with each title having its

*Queen Charlotte was a loyal and devoted wife but she often disapproved of her
pleasure-loving eldest son.*

own separate name and style if desired—as in the 'Most Noble Adolphus Gillespie Vernon Ware, Duke of Sale and Marquis of Ormesby; Earl of Sale; Baron Ware of Thame; Baron Ware of Stoven; and Baron Ware of Rufford'. Titles were hereditary through the male line and, as heir, the eldest son of a duke, marquis or earl could use his father's secondary title as a courtesy title: thus a son of the Duke of Sale would be styled Marquis of Ormesby until he succeeded to the dukedom. Younger sons and daughters of a duke or marquis used their given names preceded by Lord or Lady, while the son of an earl was styled the Honourable (in writing only) and a daughter used Lady followed by her given name. The male and female children of a viscount or baron were also styled Honourable followed by their name and surname but, again, only in writing as Jonathan Chawleigh in *A Civil Contract* was chagrined to discover on the birth of his grandson Giles Jonathan Deveril. Mr Chawleigh thought poorly of 'Honourables' and was disappointed to learn that the son of a viscount had no title of his own.

Duke or duchess was the highest rank in the British peerage outside the royal family. The title was conferred by the sovereign in gratitude for great service to the Crown and always included the words 'of' followed by a place—usually one which had relevance to the duke's seat or history, hence the Duke of Salford. A ducal couple were addressed as Duke or Duchess, Your Grace, His Grace the Duke of Salford or Her Grace, the Duchess of Salford or, more formally, Most Noble.

Dating from the fourteenth century, the title of marquis denoted a man second in rank to a duke. As with a duke's title, that of the marquis was also followed by a place-name, although this was not used in speech. A marquis's wife was a marchioness. He would be the Most Honourable the Marquis of Alverstoke in writing, and together they would be Lord and Lady Alverstoke in speech.

Earl was the oldest title in the peerage, usually followed by a county or city name. The earl would be styled the Right

Honourable the Earl of St Erth in correspondence, and he and his countess would be addressed as Lord and Lady St Erth in person.

The title of viscount was created in 1440 and was the fourth ranking title in the peerage. It was followed only by a name and did not use 'of' after the title—as in the Right Honourable the Viscount and Viscountess Lynton or, simply, Lord and Lady Lynton.

Dating from Norman times, the rank of baron was the most commonly held rank in the peerage and the title Baron was always followed by a place-name or other name. 'Of' may or may not be used—as in Baron Carlyon or Baron of Beauvallet. The wife of a baron was a baroness. In writing he would be styled the Right Honourable the Lord Carlyon and in speech he and his wife would be addressed as Lord and Lady Carlyon.

THE GENTRY

The 'Quality' was a generic reference used by the middle and lower classes to describe anyone deemed to be a member of the upper class. Members of the peerage were automatically included as was anyone recognised as one of the gentry although, unlike the peerage, they might not necessarily retain a title as was the case with the well-to-do Squire in *Sylvester*, Mr Orde, and the impecunious but well-born Stacy Calverleigh of *Black Sheep*. Recognition of the Quality by those further down the social scale was usually immediate although, as Amanda Smith discovered in *Sprig Muslin*, a young lady of good birth travelling alone might not be treated by innkeepers or middle-class women with the degree of deference usually accorded to those of her class. Only the fortuitous arrival of the obviously aristocratic Sir Gareth Ludlow saved Miss Smith from the humiliation of being sent to a much less genteel hostelry down the road. As a group the gentry was less easily defined than the peerage (whose titles clearly set them apart) but it included wealthy landowners who held no title, baronets and knights, esquires and gentlemen. The latter two titles were slightly tricky in that the difficulties associated with determining who held authentic rights to them, together with the changing definition of the word 'gentleman', meant that many more people used the term than the upper class was willing to accept as one of themselves.

Baronet was the sixth ranking title after the five degrees of the peerage and the honour was established in 1611 by James I. A baronetcy was conferred by the sovereign and the title was heredi- tary in the male line (in Scotland it could pass to a female). The title enabled the holder to call himself Sir followed by his full name and his wife Lady followed only by the surname as in Sir Waldo Hawkridge and Lady Hawkridge.

Although lower in rank than a baronet, a knighthood conferred a similar right of title to that of the baronet and enabled the knight to call himself Sir followed by his full name and his wife Lady followed only by the surname, as in Sir Harry Smith. In speech he would be addressed as Sir Harry and she would be Lady Smith. Originally a medieval rank of chivalry, by the time of the Regency a knighthood could be bestowed on a man for a wide variety of services to the Crown or State.

In medieval times the rank of esquire had carried with it a degree of honour almost equal to that of a knight. Over the centuries, however, the title had lost much of its meaning as more and more males outside the gentry attached it to their names in an effort to attain a higher level of respectability. In writing a man could style himself Fred Merriville, Esq., but in speech he was addressed simply as Mr Merriville.

The rank of gentleman was not conferred but rather applied to those who were obviously genteel or not ignoble but who held no other rank or title. By the time of the Regency a gentleman could be almost any man who did not have to work for a living and the term was often assumed by ambitious men or those with pretensions to class. Although there was no formal title for a gentleman it was not uncommon for a man with social ambition to style himself in his correspondence as, for example, 'Swithin Liversedge, gentleman', although in speech there was no distinction and he would be addressed simply as Mr Liversedge.

THE NEW MIDDLE CLASS, NABOBS AND 'CITS'

The term 'middle class(es)' was not actually used until 1832, well after the Regency, but the group of people it came to include were an important and growing force in the early nineteenth

Many clergymen enjoyed a comfortable life while administering to the needs of their aristocratic patrons or their parish.

century. Those in the middle classes ranged from professionals such as financiers, bankers, prominent doctors, engineers and lawyers, government place-holders and bureaucrats, factory owners, wealthy merchants, nabobs and the well-endowed clergy at the upper end of the scale; to teachers, innkeepers, artists, master craftsmen, smaller merchants, shopkeepers, lesser clergy, and small freeholders at the lower end; while the doctors, lawyers and merchants of moderate means, yeoman farmers, prosperous builders, small manufacturers, chicken-nabobs and university dons took their places somewhere in the middle. A more elastic entity than the upper class, the middle class was forever shifting and changing, its boundaries and inner distinctions difficult to define. The vulgar but endearing Mrs Floore in *Bath Tangle* clearly belonged to the new middle class for, although her fortune was large and she had married above her station, her birth was humble and her manners would never be genteel.

From the late eighteenth century, men returning from India or the Far East with a large fortune made abroad began to be referred to as 'nabobs'. During the Regency, nabobs were known for buying estates or a seat in parliament, or marrying their daughters into the aristocracy in a (frequently successful) attempt to enter society at a higher level than may have been open to them when they had left England. Unless they were of acceptable birth, like Miles Calverleigh in *Black Sheep*, most nabobs would climb only as high as the upper reaches of the middle class, and remain there, watching their children and grandchildren eventually become accepted as part of the aristocracy—as was the case with Jonathan Chawleigh of *A Civil Contract*. Chicken-nabobs were the much less well-heeled adventurers whose exploits in foreign parts had earned them a minor fortune—usually no more than fifty or sixty thousand pounds—or at least a competence, while overseas. They were called 'chicken' nabobs because their fortunes were smaller than those of the nabobs who returned home with enormous wealth.

Wealthy merchants, such as Jonathan Chawleigh in A Civil Contract, *often aspired to see their children marry into the upper class.*

The term 'cit' referred to the citizens of the City of London—those who ran or worked in the financial heart of the City and who were often of plebeian origins like Hannah Plymstock's brother who so strongly disapproved of the aristocracy in *Cotillion*. Cits were also the merchants and shopkeepers who lived in the City, necessary individuals, but generally kept at arm's length from the *ton* unless they were extremely wealthy.

FURTHER DOWN THE LADDER

Artisans and tradespeople were skilled workers who had a high level of expertise as well as labour to offer in return for an income.

Some artisans were descended from a long line of master craftsmen and used their skills to build successful businesses, make their fortune and climb their way up the social ladder. By the time of the Regency it was not unknown for newly established peers of the realm to have had grandfathers (or even fathers) who had started life as artisans. Not all artisans were well off, however, and many managed to earn little more than the most successful among the labouring poor.

Servants could be difficult to place in the overall class hierarchy as there was great variation in earnings and living conditions depending on their role, the attitude and status of their employer, their wage and board arrangement, the opportunity for promotion or, in some cases, for lining their own pockets. A minority—mainly butlers, chefs, stewards and head gardeners working for royalty or

Maids were among the hardest working of all domestic servants.

the upper ranks of the nobility—earned large salaries, often at the rate of £100 or more per year. Most servants, however, earned from as little as £6 a year (scullery maids, maids-of-all-work, and stable boys) to approximately £40 a year for a Groom of the Chambers or a butler.

A rigid hierarchy was strictly observed within the servant class and its proprieties were often more closely adhered to by its members than was the case among their employers. Domestic servants were classed as either upper or lower servants and in large households the two groups ate separately, sitting in strict order of rank around the meal-table:

THE UPPER SERVANTS

Steward	Housekeeper
Groom of the Chambers	Head Housemaid
Butler	Lady's Maid
Valet	

THE LOWER SERVANTS

Footman	Housemaid
Coachman	Kitchen maid
Groom	Scullery maid
Stable boy	Laundry maid

The cook (or male chef in a great house) was usually employed directly by the master or mistress of the house and paid more than the steward, and as such was often regarded as separate from the rest of the domestic staff. In *False Colours*, the great hedonist and gourmand Sir Bonamy Ripple had three cooks—headed by his French chef Alphonse—all of whom were 'indispensable to his comfort'.

A servant's standing was determined by his or her role in the household and the place of the master or mistress both in the family line and in society—a position which could change instantly in the event of a birth, death or marriage. The heir's valet, for example, took precedence over a younger son's valet. A family reunion in *The Unknown Ajax* brought two mature valets to Darracott Place, their places at table in the servants' hall determined by their masters' positions in the family line. When the new heir arrived at the house his youthful and inexperienced valet automatically took precedence over the two older men for, despite his young age, as the heir's valet he outranked them both. A servant's social position and standing were often jealously guarded and it was not uncommon for the upper servants to hold themselves aloof from the lesser servants or even to be snobbish about their employers' guests or relatives deemed to be socially inferior. Miss Clara Crowle, as dresser to Lady Bridlington in *Arabella*, was allowed a good deal of licence with her mistress but when she dared to criticise her mistress's young guest she stepped over the line and was chastised by her employer.

The Bottom of the Ladder

The largest of all social classes during the Regency, the labouring poor, were those who struggled on a daily basis to survive, from labourers to pedlars, chimney sweeps and climbing boys, ordinary soldiers and naval men, vagrants, paupers and those too old, too sick or too unlucky to find work. Although some found employment as itinerant or seasonal workers many among the labouring poor were driven to crime, prostitution or an early grave. Young Ben Breane, the gatekeeper's son in *The Toll-Gate*, having found himself without relatives to care for him, was terrified of being thrown on the parish or sent to work in the foundries in Sheffield; while the urchin rescued by Patience Chartley in *The Nonesuch* was one of many who eked out an existence among the dyeing-houses and manufactories in the back-slums of Leeds.

Climbing the Social Ladder

The quickest way up the social ladder was through marriage and, failing that, by the accumulation of great wealth, a landed estate, and the acquisition of a title. In *Frederica* it was the heroine's great ambition to see her beautiful sister, Charis, successfully launched into the *ton* in the hope that she might contract a good marriage— for with only their brother's small estate to support them this was the best hope for seeing Charis and her younger siblings comfortably and independently established for the rest of their lives. In the middle and lower classes—where hierarchy was not distinguished by title, and birth and money were often merely indicators rather than deciding factors in determining an individual's position on the social scale—knowing one's exact place depended on a number of things. In *A Civil Contract* a potential feud between the housekeeper, Mrs Dawes, and her mistress's personal maid, Miss Pinhoe, was averted once it was discovered that the two women were from the same county and the social pecking order was made clear from Mrs Dawes's superior standing as the daughter of a prosperous farmer. The myriad of levels within each degree of class and the subtle distinctions that pushed one person ahead of another constantly shifted as people jostled for a better social position, and overt signs of superiority such as clothing, manners, speech, dwelling, income, personal property and numbers of servants (if any) became increasingly available to a growing number of people. In general, however, most people knew their place and, accordingly, showed deference or a marked superiority in their dealings with others. For those already titled, gaining a higher title was the most obvious means of social advancement.

For some families, scaling the social heights was a climb which could take several generations. A man might make his way in the world of trade or commerce, gain financial independence, buy an estate and earn himself a baronetcy or a seat in the House of Commons. From there he could aspire to the lowest rank of the peerage (baron) or marry his daughter (or, less likely, his son) to a member of the nobility. If he could not himself rise through the ranks, his children, grandchildren or even great-grandchildren might well achieve such honour through marriage, increased wealth, political influence or great service to the State. Although the aristocracy could be ruthless in excluding from its ranks those new entrants deemed to be of inferior birth, the passage of time was an effective panacea and it usually took, at most, two generations before the descendant of a commoner became an accepted member of the upper class.

2

At Home in Town and Country

MAYFAIR

Mayfair, that fashionable district in the West End of London that housed most of Georgette Heyer's London characters, was bounded by Park Lane to the west, Piccadilly to the south, Bond Street to the east and Oxford Street to the north. The original May Fair, for which the area was named, began in 1689 and was an annual fête, hugely popular but so riotous that, by 1720, land developers had started planning the construction of 'a large square and several fine streets and houses'. Grosvenor Square was the centrepiece of a planned eight-acre estate with Brook Street and Grosvenor Street as the two main east–west arteries. Green Street, Duke Street, South Audley Street and Mount Street, among others, were all part of the development with many fine houses and mews (stables) constructed there in the first half of the eighteenth century. Throughout the 1700s other streets and squares were also built in the increasingly exclusive area as more and more of the upper classes sought to rent or buy impressive residences west of the City, away from the fumes and foul air of the 'easterly pile', and closer to Hyde Park, Westminster and the Court of St James. By the time of the Regency many of the newly constructed mansions, classically inspired villas and rows of tall, elegant town houses in such desirable locations as

A London town house was the place to live during the Season.

Berkeley Square, Half Moon Street and Curzon Street had become home to the titled, rich and fashionable. Mayfair was for ever established as the place to live in London.

THE LONDON HOUSE

Although upper-class houses varied in architecture, size and style, they shared several common elements which offered their wealthy owners or leaseholders grand, spacious living in elegantly appointed, well-lit rooms and as many of the modern conveniences as possible—depending on the age and design of the house. Most quality London houses of the Georgian period were made of stone and during the Regency were often rendered with stucco and painted. The majority of these houses were constructed with at least four floors plus a basement, cellars and an attic. On finding the grand family mansion in Grosvenor Square too large and dreary for their taste, the newly married Lord and Lady Sheringham in *Friday's Child* decided they needed a 'snug little house' in Mayfair and eventually found a suitable town house in Half Moon Street. In the early nineteenth century, increased prosperity enabled many among the wealthy classes to extend and enlarge their London houses or build entirely new ones with five, and sometimes six, storeys.

Whether a house was old or new, the layout was fairly uniform, with the main living areas on the ground and first floors, the bedrooms, schoolroom and nursery on the two floors above that, the kitchen, scullery, housekeeper's and butler's rooms and a sleeping area for the footman in the basement, the housemaids' quarters in the attic and the wine and coal in the cellars. The living areas usually included, on the ground floor, an entrance hall, saloon, dining room and possibly a library or book-room. It was the Marquis of Alverstoke's book-room rather than the saloon or

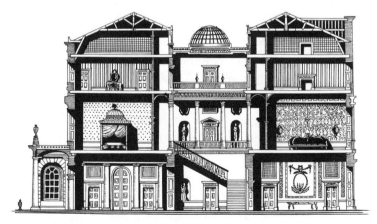

Cutaway of a London house.

drawing-room to which Frederica was escorted when she arrived at his town mansion in Berkeley Square in the company of two park-keepers and a shrill, 'hatchet-faced' woman. The drawing-room was on the first floor and was often a double room or adjoined by a saloon with double doors which could be opened to create one large room. On the next floor were the (usually separate) bedchambers used by the master and mistress of the house and, in more progressive households, possibly a bathroom like the lavish one installed by Jenny Chawleigh's father in *A Civil Contract*. A dressing room adjoined each bedroom (although a man might sometimes have his dressing room located rather inconveniently on a separate floor) and ladies sometimes used their dressing room as a small daytime sitting room. Children's bedrooms, the nursery and schoolroom were on the floor above and older boys and girls often had separate rooms. Very large houses sometimes had a ball-room on the ground floor at the back of the house which could accommodate several hundred people. Lord and Lady Ombersley of *The Grand Sophy* were hosts at a grand ball for five hundred invited guests which was held in the ballroom of their house in Berkeley Square. Lit by a magnificent candle-filled chandelier and decorated with flowers, the Ombersley ball was one of the great successes of the Season.

The living areas of most London town houses were furnished with large and small tables, various kinds of chairs, couches, foot-stools, chandeliers, candelabra, carpets, curtains, paintings, tapes-tries, *objets d'art* and the other accoutrements that enhanced the occupants' comfort and were a way of subtly (or not so subtly) demonstrating degrees of wealth and status to one's guests. Bedrooms were generally well-appointed suites, though more sparsely furnished than the living rooms with just a bed, wardrobe, chair, dressing table or washstand, a floor rug and a free-standing mirror. In *April Lady* Nell Cardross's husband had her bedroom transformed into a romantic boudoir with rose-silk curtains around

*Gracious living was the order of the day in the drawing-rooms
of many London town houses.*

a magnificent tent bed and the adjoining dressing room hung with
blue and silver brocade. Ladies sometimes had a *secretaire* or writing
desk in their bedroom or small sitting room and a couch or daybed
there as well for the occasional daytime repose.

Every bedroom had its chamber-pot (placed discreetly under
the bed for easy access during the night), and water-closets were
becoming increasingly popular in upper- and wealthy middle-class
houses. It had taken centuries to develop an efficient, workable toilet
but in 1778 Joseph Bramah had patented his valve-operated water-
closet and by 1797 had reportedly sold some 6,000 of them. In 1813
the Earl of Moira's country house in Leicestershire boasted two bathrooms and six water-closets and his wife even had her own elegantly
appointed personal bathroom and WC adjoining her dressing room.
Jonathan Chawleigh's passion for new inventions in *A Civil Contract*
caused him to have the latest Bramah water-closet installed under

a staircase in Adam and Jenny's Grosvenor Street house. In houses without the modern conveniences, use of the chamber-pot (emptied out the window) or privy (a seat over a hole in the ground and located out the back of the house) continued to be used.

Lighting was gradually improved during the Regency and from the early 1800s many upper-class houses used oil-lamps in addition to the traditional tallow and wax candles by which most homes were lit. Chandeliers and candelabra of all sizes used hundreds of candles to light ballrooms, drawing-rooms and dining rooms, while a single candle in a holder might be enough to light a bedroom. Gas lighting was introduced during the period and, although in 1821 the Prince Regent had gas installed at the Brighton Pavilion in order to light the decorative glass windows at night it was to be many years before the system was refined enough for widespread domestic use. Peregrine Taverner in *Regency Buck* was awestruck by the magnificent central chandelier above the dining table when

In Arabella *the heroine rescued Jemmy the climbing-boy from his ruthless master.*

he was one of several guests invited to the Pavilion for one of the Regent's famous bachelor dinner parties.

Keeping warm, even in the grandest houses, could be challenging. Most rooms had a fireplace and fires were usually lit in the early morning in the bedrooms and after breakfast or, as required, in the main living rooms. Coal was the main form of fuel in the cities but fires were a most inefficient form of heating as much of the heat went straight up the chimney. In some houses fires were kept burning throughout the day only in the winter months and then only in the main living rooms of the house. In *Cotillion* miserly Mr Penicuik allowed only the smallest fires to be lit in the main rooms at Arnside even in the coldest weather which caused his ward, Kitty Charing, to be especially grateful for the unexpected luxury of a fire in her bedroom when she visited London. Winter temperatures often extended into autumn and spring and it was not uncommon in wealthy (and less penny-pinching) households for fires to be lit nine months of the year. In houses with several main rooms, chimneys had to be swept at least every three months and the narrow flues (about a foot in diameter) meant that small boys, known as climbing-boys, were often sent into the chimneys to clear out the accumulated soot. When a climbing-boy fell down the chimney in *Arabella* the heroine was horrified to discover the exact nature of the abuses endured by the seven-year-old Jemmy. An appalling practice, this form of chimney-sweeping saw many children under the age of eight abused, injured and killed, and from 1817 humanitarians intensified their efforts to make the use of climbing-boys illegal and have the custom abolished.

ON THE FRINGE: HANS TOWN AND RUSSELL SQUARE

Although in the eighteenth century Mayfair had still been home to builders, tradespeople and shopkeepers as well as the upper class they serviced, by the time of the Regency the area was felt by many to be the exclusive preserve of the acknowledged leaders of fashionable society and members of the aristocracy. For those families with fortunes made in commerce, trade or one of the professions and possessed by a burning ambition to enter polite society, the next best thing to a house in Mayfair was an address in one of the districts adjacent to that exclusive quarter. Upper Wimpole and Harley Streets to the north, Russell Square in Bloomsbury to the north-east and Sloane Street and Hans Town to the south were often chosen as suitable residential areas by those on the social fringe. Such a move could also be slightly problematic, however, as the Merrivilles discovered in *Frederica*, for in upper-class circles the revelation that a person had an address in Upper Wimpole Street, or one of these new estates—Russell Square and Hans Town were often stigmatised as new rich—could lead to social exclusion.

MORE MODEST DWELLINGS

Social standing within the middle class, where ranking was subtle and complex, was largely determined by the extent to which a household employed domestic help, purchased luxury goods and increased the amount of time free from work. Middle-class houses varied greatly in size and furnishings but even the smallest and most modest households were usually distinguished from those of the poorer classes by having more than two main rooms, a separate kitchen close to a water supply, and a single family with at least one servant as occupants. Furze Farm, owned by the young and handsome Mr Mudgley in *The Foundling*, was a moderately sized dwelling set in freehold land, large enough to house a family comfortably but decidedly middle class with the occupants doing much of the domestic and farm work assisted by a servant girl and a number of hired hands. Further up the middle-class ranks, houses could be as large as any of those owned by the upper class and with as many (or more) servants to ensure that the upwardly mobile master and mistress of the house never did anything in the way of manual labour. The ability to hire servants and maintain a carriage and horses was an important indicator of social status— although it was not necessarily a reliable guide to a person's class as evidenced by the huge retinue of servants and the several carriages and liveried footmen employed by the vulgar Jonathan Chawleigh in *A Civil Contract*. Industrialisation and overseas trade saw a marked increase in the range and availability of consumer goods and many among the growing and increasingly prosperous middle class became eager purchasers of clothes, household items, accessories, furnishings, utensils and furniture with which to enhance their houses.

During the Regency an income of £10,000 a year was enough to enable a member of the upper class to maintain both a country estate and a town mansion and afford all the pleasures of life that went with them. Hugo Darracott in *The Unknown Ajax* teased his cousin Anthea about her (expensive) desire to own, rather than rent, a London house in the event that she moved to the metropolis. A moderately sized town house in Mayfair could be rented for £1,000 a year and between 1810 and 1814 a comfortable town residence and the life to go with it cost approximately £3,000 for the year with half of that spent on food and wine, and about £500 each on servants, carriages and horses. In *Frederica* the opportunity to rent out their home in Herefordshire enabled the Merriville family to afford a London Season and, by practising careful economy, Frederica was able to ensure that she and her lovely sister Charis were as well-dressed as any in the *ton*. By the end of the period a family with an income of £1,000 a year could afford to keep five servants and a carriage and pair, while a family on £400 a year could employ two housemaids and keep a groom and a horse.

Domestic Staff

A great house owned by a member of the aristocracy, such as the Duke of Sale in *The Foundling* or the late Earl of Spenborough in *Bath Tangle*, might employ an enormous number of servants with (in addition to maids, footmen, coachmen, grooms, stable boys and gardeners) a personal household staff of a steward, butler, Groom of the Chambers, under-butler, housekeeper, dresser or lady's maid, nursery or young ladies' maid, chef or cook, agent-in-chief, valet, chaplain, governess, tutor-companion, head keeper, head gardener and even a confectioner or pastry-chef. Most upper-class families, however, managed with fewer servants than the number required for service in a ducal mansion. And a more usual retinue might include a butler, cook, valet, lady's maid, several general maids, footmen, a scullery maid, possibly a page-boy, and the stable staff. Hero and Sherry in *Friday's Child* decided that they could manage quite comfortably with just a cook, a butler, a valet, a personal maid, two abigails, a footman, a coachman, a couple of grooms and his lordship's tiger, Jason. For a young man living in chambers in London—such as Captain Gideon Ware of *The Foundling*—a pleasant bachelor existence could be achieved with the services of just a cook, a valet, a maid and a groom.

Servants were an integral and essential part of Regency upper-class life, and their continual presence in almost every aspect of it was, at times, quite difficult for their employers. In *April Lady* Nell Cardross had to quell her brother Dysart's irrepressible urge to discuss her personal affairs while they were travelling in an open carriage with both the coachman and the footman within earshot, and, in *The Reluctant Widow*, Lord Carlyon and his guests waited until the servants had left the dining room before they discussed a relative's scandalous behaviour. Although a servant's presence was largely taken for granted on waking, while dressing, at mealtimes, at social events and when travelling, it could also be a constraint as employers sought to keep their personal affairs to themselves or at least within the family or between friends. Lord Dolphington in *Cotillion*, aware that his coachman Finglass invariably reported his activities to the Countess, often had to resort to subterfuge to prevent the servant passing on information which might have incurred his mother's displeasure. But there was little that went on within the walls of a large estate, a London town house or a suburban villa that was not known by at least one of the retinue of servants employed to run them and it was a rare employee who did not discuss an employer's affairs—if not with everyone in the servants' hall then at least with his or her peers among the staff. Items of interest overheard or discovered by one servant could quickly spread through the house, and frequently beyond, with interesting gossip almost always shared amongst the staff of London's elite homes. In *Sprig Muslin*, the Earl of Brancaster's pronouncement to his daughter, Lady Hester Theale, that she had received an offer of marriage from Sir Gareth Ludlow was quickly spread among the servants by the butler, the valet and two footmen.

Domestic staff were usually required to work long hours to ensure their employers' comfort and the smooth running of the household, and valets and personal maids frequently had to wait up in order to attend to their master or mistress late at night. Some servants, such as Evelyn Fancot's valet Fimber in *False Colours* and Sophy Stanton-Lacy's personal maid Jane Storridge in *The Grand Sophy* often chose to stay up in order to attend their master and mistress on their return from a ball or night on the town. A wealthy employer might keep a large staff, all of whom were expected to be neat, clean, punctual and efficient in the performance of their duties and on hand around the clock or at their employer's pleasure. Most servants' work was hard, repetitive and boring. Footmen were constantly expected to fetch and carry, run errands and wait at table, maids toiled up and down multiple flights of stairs carrying coal scuttles and linen, grates had to be cleared, cleaned and polished and fires lit before breakfast, while general cleaning, polishing, mending and making were never-ending tasks.

Food and cooking were a major preoccupation during the Regency and it required a sizeable kitchen staff to provide throughout the day and evening the varieties and quantities of food which wealthy families had come to expect. Connoisseurs such as Sir Bonamy Ripple of *False Colours* were passionate about food and took great delight in trying new dishes, planning extravagant menus and selecting the best wines to accompany even a minor meal. Breakfast and dinner were considered the most important meals and it was customary to serve a large evening repast with several removes over a number of courses. Kitchen staff were confined to the basement with its bare stone floor, where they began work early and spent their day preparing food in Spartan conditions over a labour-intensive wood- or coal-fed open range and oven or—in more fortunate, modern households—a new closed stove such as the Bodley installed at Fontley Priory in *A Civil Contract*. After each meal the vast numbers of dishes, pots, pans and utensils had to be cleaned and scoured—often without the convenience of running water—then dried and put away ready for the next meal. Food had to be bought, prepared, cooked, served and cleared all without drawing any aspect of the work involved to the attention of the servants' employer.

Many servants began life in domestic service at a young age, starting as a scullery maid or an odd-job boy and working their way up the ranks, with some of them reaching the exalted heights of butler or housekeeper. A strong sense of loyalty to a long-term employer was not unusual and personal servants, such as a lady's maid or valet, often developed close relationships with their mistress or master. Lord Damerel's valet in *Venetia* had stood by his master through many adventures and remained in his employ for years despite the erratic salary and Damerel's wild moods and often scandalous behaviour. For many in the upper class there was a strong sense of *noblesse oblige*; an ability (held to be innate in anyone born into the aristocracy) to interact with the servant class in a way that allowed a degree of respect, friendship, and even affection, between master and servant. Even so, clear divisions between the classes were maintained in the relationship. In *Bath Tangle* there was a stark contrast between Lady Serena Carlow's ease of manner when dealing with servants and the estate staff and that of her cousin Hartley who had unexpectedly inherited the earldom but was neither born nor bred to the role. It was not uncommon for servants to remain with one family for their lifetime, growing old in their service until they were eventually pensioned off or, in some cases, retired to a cottage on the estate to live out the remainder of their lives as did the twins' old nurse, Mrs Pinner, in *False Colours*.

As the commander-in-chief of the general domestic staff, the steward was responsible for employing all the male servants in the house, with the exception of his master's valet. He kept the household accounts, ordered necessary household items, paid the bills, servants' wages and expenses, and dealt with the local tradespeople. He earned about £40 a year, had his own room and did not wear livery but instead dressed in a dark coat and trousers, with a waistcoat and neckcloth.

The Groom of the Chambers was second in rank to the steward among the male servants. Although the role of Groom of the Chambers was becoming less common during the Regency he remained an important figure in many of the great houses where his main responsibility was to take charge of the guests and their servants during their stay. He ensured that visitors were properly attended to, knew the daily programme, and knew where they needed to be and how to get there. In *The Foundling* the Groom of the Chambers, Mr Turvey, relished the idea that the young Duke of Sale, having attained his majority, might fill the house with guests and thereby grant him the opportunity to demonstrate his talents.

The butler was in charge of the footmen and responsible for the wine and wine cellar, the plate and the silverware, of which he kept an inventory. He welcomed guests at the front door (which had been answered by the footman) and announced them to the master or mistress of the house. He ensured that the house was always kept in good order, decanted the table wine, oversaw the serving of meals, carved the meat and stood behind his master's chair until the meal was over, at which time he led the other servants from the room, returning when the gentlemen had finished their port to oversee the clearing of the table and lock up the plate and silver-ware. A good butler was expected to be able to recognise class and good breeding and was extremely knowledgeable in all matters of etiquette and propriety—he was also aware of everything of importance that went on inside the house. In *The Toll-Gate* the butler, Huby, had been in service to the Stornaway family for many years and it was only his strong sense of loyalty to them that enabled him to commit the appalling (for a good butler) act of watering the wine in a bid to get rid of an unwelcome guest. A butler earned between £25 and £35 per year, had his own room (usually near the pantry and the silver or plate safe) and, like the steward, did not wear livery.

As the personal attendant to the man of the house a valet was always employed by him directly rather than by the steward. The valet's main occupation was the care of his master's wardrobe, including his boots and shoes, but he could also shave him each day and generally accompanied him when travelling. An upper-class valet took enormous pride in seeing his 'gentleman' properly turned out in the latest fashion, knowing he had helped him into his exquisitely cut, skin-fit coat, proffered a perfectly starched neckcloth for tying, or eased him into a pair of boots polished to a high gloss with blacking made from the valet's own secret recipe. In *Arabella*, Mr Painswick was a peerless valet to the hero,

Mr Beaumaris, and such a master of his craft that many gentlemen of fashion had sought to acquire his services. Valets were on call around the clock and often sat up into the early hours waiting for their masters to return home (even when instructed, as was Painswick by Mr Beaumaris, to go to bed) at which time they would retire to their own room.

The housekeeper was the steward's equivalent in charge of the female staff (with the exception of the personal staff such as the nurse, lady's maid and cook), and was one of the busiest servants in the house. She directed the maids in their work and oversaw the running of the house in terms of its cleaning, linen, store-room, still-room and china closet. She also kept the household accounts (submitted weekly) and met regularly with her mistress to take her orders. The housekeeper was expected to know about home remedies and basic first aid and was also required to turn her hand to sewing, mending, and bottling, preserving and drying the excess fruit, vegetables and herbs from the kitchen garden. It was the housekeeper, Mrs Gurnard, in *Venetia* who organised a large hamper to be carried to the Priory when Aubrey was thrown from his horse, and she who refused to take orders about the running of Undershaw from the social-climbing Mrs Scorrier. Although they did not wear uniform, most housekeepers were plainly dressed in dark colours and were usually paid about £25 a year, with their own room or set of rooms. With the steward, the housekeeper presided at the table in the servants' hall and in the housekeeper's room where she ate with the rest of the upper servants.

The lady's maid was also known as an abigail or dresser, and was the personal attendant to the lady of the house who directly employed her. She was required to wait on her mistress before breakfast to ensure that she had hot water and was ready to rise. She then laid out her lady's clothes, helped her dress, did her hair, attended to any clothes that needed mending, special cleaning or ironing, tidied things away and made sure her mistress was looking her best before going downstairs. During the day she attended to her lady's wardrobe and other household tasks, such as making lotions and cosmetics, or accompanied her mistress while shopping or walking. A lady's maid had to be well dressed, quick, efficient and discreet as she was often in her employer's confidence as well as her company. Some lady's maids developed a close personal relationship with their mistresses and, while they remained respectful, took on the role of confidante and advisor. In *Lady of Quality*, Annis Wychwood's formidable abigail, Jurby, had attended her mistress since childhood and knew her better than her own family.

Starting at 6.30 a.m. in summer and 7.00 a.m. in winter, the footman began his day filling the coal scuttles in the main rooms, cleaning the household's shoes and boots, polishing plate and laying the breakfast table. In *The Corinthian* it was the under-footman who discovered, as he went about his morning duties in Sir Richard Wyndham's library, the shawl, the cravat and the telltale strands of guinea-gold hair that set Sir Richard's family in such a bustle. At every meal it was the footman's job to lay the table, carry in the food, wait at table, stand while the family ate and then clear away. Back in the kitchen, they washed the glasses and silverware before starting the whole routine again. In houses with more than two footmen, the third footman and below did the rougher jobs such as fetching wood, coal and water and cleaning the boots, while the first and second footmen cleaned plate, trimmed lamps and candles, answered the door (after midday) or went out on carriage duty (sitting or standing behind the carriage). As Frederica discovered, a footman could also be required to attend a member of the household on a walk or shopping trip, following on foot at an appropriate distance. Footmen slept in the basement or cellar and wore a formal livery of knee-breeches, tail-coat, stockings and a powdered wig.

Next to the kitchen, scullery and laundry maids, the housemaid was one of the hardest workers in the house. She was up by 6.00

a.m. to light the fire in the kitchen, open the shutters and start sweeping, cleaning and dusting the hallways, living rooms and stairs and polishing the banisters, grates, fenders and furniture. Before her master or mistress got up she lit the fires in their bedrooms and, after they had gone down to breakfast, made their beds, dusted and swept their rooms and emptied the chamber-pots and wash-basins. Maids were expected to fulfill their duties as quietly and unobtrusively as possible and were often so good at moving quietly about the house while they worked that in *Arabella* the sound of fire-irons crashing in the hearth was so unusual that it woke the heroine from a sound sleep. The kitchen maid mainly worked as an assistant to the cook, preparing food, cleaning utensils and sweeping the kitchen. The scullery maid rose at dawn to clean the kitchen range and start the fire so that the cook could prepare breakfast, and spent the day washing the dishes and cleaning, scrubbing and scouring any pots, pans, bowls and utensils not dealt with by the kitchen maid. She also scrubbed the floors. The laundry maid did most of her work in the wash-house at the back of the main house. If there was more than one laundry maid then the more skilled of the two was usually responsible for the family's personal linen while the other maid did the general washing and the servants' laundry. Maids earned between £6 and £8 a year, slept on the top floor of the house and were each provided with a close gown, stockings, cap and apron to wear while they worked.

Servants were often able to augment their income through tips and other perquisites such as cast-off clothing or household items. The lady's maid and valet had first entitlement to their employers' unwanted clothes, shoes and accessories which they would often sell, and the cook and butler in some households were not above fiddling the books or helping themselves to extra food or wine as did the Groombridges—and later the Bradgates—in *Friday's Child*. At Christmas time servants could expect a gift of money and when visitors stayed in the house it was expected that they would tip the staff according to their station and the degree of service. These tips, known as vails, were an important addition to many servants' wages and, in houses where employers failed to entertain, servants often felt compelled to seek a place where tips were more likely to be forthcoming. Charles, the new footman at Darracott Place in *The Unknown Ajax*, was so unimpressed by his employer's ill temper and parsimony that he had decided to leave his lordship's employ at the end of a year and seek a position in London where the potential for tips and 'extra gelt' was far greater.

GREAT ESTATES AND COUNTRY LIVING

Although many wealthy families came to London for the Season, most spent a large part of the year at their homes in the country. Land had long been the foundation of wealth and power in Britain and, although the nation was still largely rural in the early nineteenth century, industrialisation had begun to make its presence

The upper class had many beautiful houses set in rolling parklands or surrounded by landscaped gardens.

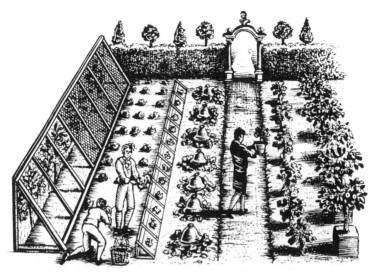

A kitchen garden was an important part of any great estate.

felt with improvements in agricultural techniques and transport, the growth of towns and many new technologies. For those new to the peerage or to positions of wealth and power, a great estate was essential for consolidating their social position and, it was hoped, the means of establishing a dynasty. Stacy Calverleigh in *Black Sheep* understood fully the social cachet attached to being 'Calverleigh of Danescourt'. Landed families were careful to protect their estates through a system of primogeniture and entail whereby the house and lands were bequeathed to the eldest son or next male heir and he was prevented from selling any part of the estate during his lifetime. Many upper-class families considered it their duty to enlarge the family estate with each new generation (often through marriage to the heir or heiress of a neighbouring property) and encouraged interaction between the sons and daughters of local landowners. In *Lady of Quality* Lord and Lady Iverley had long held hopes of a match between their son Ninian and Lucilla, the daughter of an old friend and heiress to the neighbouring estate.

Country houses varied enormously in size, style and layout, and castles, manor houses, converted priories and even palaces—some dating from as early as the fourteenth century—were home to many of England's noble families. Usually built beside or in the midst of the owner's tenanted farm land, the great houses, such as Stanyon Castle in *The Quiet Gentleman*, were often architectural showpieces kept separate from their more mundane agricultural acres by beautiful landscaped gardens, lakes or wooded parkland. The private land immediately surrounding the house (known as the demesne) was often laid out with formal garden beds, topiary hedges, rose gardens, rolling lawns and magnificent stands of trees. Many houses had a ha-ha on the edge of the manorial lawn to divide the garden from the surrounding parkland. This was a ditch or escarpment, designed to be invisible from the house, with a vertical wall on the inner side and a shallow slope on the park side designed to keep out wandering livestock. In addition to the ornamental garden, a country estate also had a well-stocked kitchen garden that supplied the main house with most of the fruit, vegetables and herbs necessary for its day-to-day running. A very wealthy estate often had a whole series of rectangular walled gardens linked by lockable wooden doors as well as several succession houses which could produce such desirable fruits as melons, grapes, peaches and nectarines, and exotic blooms, such as orchids and carnations. Succession houses enabled gardeners to cultivate a range of fruit and ornamental trees and plants by bringing them on in stages and re-potting or re-bedding them in protected conditions. A few of the great houses also had a pinery for growing pineapples and during the Regency these exotic fruits were highly prized. It was considered a great honour to receive one of the coveted fruits from a noble friend or relative. Lord Charlbury in *The Grand Sophy* had some of the finest succession houses in the country and the Ombersley family were grateful for his gift of grapes and honoured by the promise of the first ripe pineapple from his famous pinery.

Architecturally, the great houses varied in design from the medieval priory to the Elizabethan hall or the newer Gothic buildings which had become fashionable by the time of the Regency. Sometimes houses were a mix of architectural styles, the result of several centuries of additions. Staplewood in *Cousin Kate* had been home to succeeding generations of the Broome family from the time of James I and the ensuing two centuries had seen each new heir enlarge or embellish the original manor house with its Great Hall and Grand Stairway. Magnificent from the outside, the interiors were frequently designed for breathtaking beauty as well as habitation and housed many priceless works of art including sculptures, paintings by the great masters, weapons and armoury, tapestries, rugs and furniture.

Life in the country tended to be lived at a slower pace than life in London and, for the upper classes, the months spent on the family estate could be either a wonderful escape from the demands of city living or a period of intense boredom to be endured until the return to the metropolis. Houses were generally large with spacious rooms, high ceilings and large fireplaces in the main hall and living rooms. Most great houses had several wings, at least one of which was reserved for the family. The rest of the house usually comprised a main entrance hall, drawing-room, dining room, breakfast room and library on the ground floor, with the bedrooms, dressing rooms and bathrooms upstairs. Many houses had a grand ballroom and, increasingly during the Regency, a billiard room. Richmond Darracott in *The Unknown Ajax* preferred to challenge his sporting cousin Vincent to a game of billiards rather than spend the evening playing cards with his mother and grandfather in the long drawing-room. The master of the house usually had a study and his wife had a small sitting room or boudoir next to her bedroom. Conservatories were also popular during the period and were generally built on the south side of the house to catch the sun. Many aristocratic houses had their own private chapel, either in the house or as a separate building.

While the master and mistress of the house had certain responsibilities and duties to perform to ensure its smooth running as well as that of the estate, unless they took an active interest and physically involved themselves in the farming or household work (as a few of them did), they mainly spent their time in recreational pursuits. With a large contingent of servants to ensure there was always plenty of good food, cosy fires, pleasant rooms and personal service, the country house was ideal for playing host to large numbers of guests. For several months of the year the family and their guests spent their days enjoying (or enduring) the rituals of country living. In *False Colours* a house party at the Denville family's country seat of Ravenhurst was enjoyable for those among the guests who appreciated the quiet entertainments of country living. For women this usually meant taking pleasure in the garden or going for a walk, ride or drive in the countryside or parkland belonging to the estate. If they preferred being indoors, or if the weather was inclement, they could read, write, embroider, paint or indulge their musical tastes on the pianoforte or harp. Men had a wider range of activities available to them and could spend entire days out of doors with their dogs tracking game, shooting or fishing, with fox-hunting in the winter. Visits between local landowners were also an important part of rural life and evenings were often spent conversing over the dinner table with friends and neighbours and their families, followed by cards, music, or an impromptu dance. In *The Nonesuch* Sir Waldo Hawkridge's extended stay at Broom Hall was the signal for the local gentry and other well-to-do families to embark on a series of increasingly lavish dinner parties, dances and balls with Sir Waldo and his cousin as the honoured guests.

Regency society was largely a land- and property-based entity and the upper class drew its base income mainly from the rent paid by urban and rural tenants. Land was a precious and jealously guarded commodity and a son and heir who exploited his estate for his sole benefit (instead of maximising its productivity for the benefit of his family, his tenantry and the wider community), or who lost any part of his holdings through waste, mismanagement or profligate behaviour, was often looked down upon or even despised by the *ton*. Even for those landowners, such as Stacy Calverleigh in *Black Sheep*, who took no direct interest in their estates—leaving their management to an agent or bailiff—the idea of having to sell part of their land to fund debt was abhorrent. Some members of the aristocracy took an active interest in the management of their estates, ensuring that the land was worked effectively, tenants cared for and improvements made. In *A Civil Contract*, Adam Deveril was keenly interested in agriculture and making the most of his acres. He travelled from Lincolnshire to Norfolk to attend the famous Holkham Clippings at Thomas Coke's pioneering estate and there meet with other farmers and learn as much as he could about new crops and methods of farming. Most landowners' primary interest, however, was not in how their land was farmed but how much it paid them. To some it did not matter whether the income from their land came from the rents paid by tenant farmers, mining leases and the royalties paid on the coal, iron, tin or other metals dug from their land, from building leases or from the money paid to cut a canal through their estate. While the Regency lasted, land still equated to wealth, to power and to status and as such it remained an essential part of upper-class Regency life.

3

A Man's World

UPPER-CLASS REGENCY MEN

In Regency England men determined the legal, social and political order of things, and for many men in the moneyed upper ten thousand it was a hedonistic time devoted to entertainment, merriment and debauchery. Etiquette and protocols were often a mass of contradictions both within and between the classes. A man could marry for love or convenience or money or power, but he was not bound to be faithful. Discretion was hoped for, even expected, but if he failed in its delivery a man could still be accepted into the heart of the *ton*. Given the nature and indulgences of the Prince Regent himself, this was not surprising. So much of the grand self-indulgence, the immorality, the gambling, the ornamentation and the waste perpetrated by the upper class and condemned by the middle and lower classes was to be found in the actions of the once-loved, but now increasingly despised, Royal Prince. Although often well intentioned and with an eye for beauty and a love of the arts, the Prince Regent and his royal brothers (in particular the Dukes of Clarence, Cumberland and York) seemed to lead the way in almost every area of vice. Practically nothing was too extreme or too opulent or too expensive, making it difficult for criticism to be effectively levelled at

*Fashionable gentlemen could often be seen tooling a curricle down Piccadilly
or St James's Street in London.*

those who followed their example. Lord Ombersley in *The Grand
Sophy* was a particular friend of the Duke of York's and, like him,
pursued a life of pleasure which was marked by debt, mistresses
and a sublime disregard for many of the proprieties laid down by
the *ton*.

In his daily life the Regency man enjoyed a much wider
range of entertainments than his female counterpart. Whereas
a female's reputation was among her most important assets, a
male's reputation was far more resistant to scandal. Married
or single, a well-born and well-heeled man could frequently
indulge in quite shocking behaviour on the streets and in the
bars, brothels and gaming hells of Regency London without
becoming a social outcast. Nell Cardross's reprobate young
brother Dysart engaged in all manner of outrageous pranks and
even joined Lord Barrymore's infamous Beggar's Club without
seriously endangering his social standing. When in society,
however, he was bound to abide by the protocols and etiquette

of his class, like most well-bred gentlemen who adhered to an unwritten code of honour that determined their behaviour in a range of social situations.

In elite social circles a man was expected to be elegant in both dress and manner when in public and to pay due deference to women and his social superiors. A man's behaviour in private, when among other men or 'in his cups' (never in front of a lady), could be determined by a completely different set of much looser moral standards. In public a man was expected to adhere to the modes and manners of polite society in which, for example, open shows of affection were considered inappropriate and a kiss between a man and a woman denoted an intention to marry— assuming they were of the same class. Class was a powerful factor in determining a man's behaviour, for a 'gentleman' might kiss or make up to a servant girl or country maid with a fair degree of impunity—although in *Sprig Muslin* the rakish old uncle sends a young servant girl, 'unused to the ways of the Quality', into hysterics. In general, the lower classes were expected to understand this sort of behaviour as the way of the Quality and accept that no serious relationship could be expected to result from it. In *The*

Well-bred men were often seen enjoying the company of loose women, or Cyprians, in the foyer of Covent Garden.

Unknown Ajax, dandified Claud Darracott exemplifies this attitude by engaging in a series of flirtations with serving girls, dairymaids and, in the nearby town, the blacksmith's daughter without any serious intention. Attitudes of the upper class to the middle class were very different, however, and only a scoundrel such as Sir Montagu Revesby in *Friday's Child* would stoop to seducing a respectable girl of good family and subsequently deserting her and their bastard child. Paradoxically, upper-class society perceived his sin not in having fathered an illegitimate infant or having multiple affairs but in his not providing for the child. It was, after all, perfectly acceptable to be a rake but not to disregard one's moral duty. The upper class, despite its insistent demands for propriety, was extraordinarily inconsistent in its responses to the excesses of behaviour by the *ton*.

A man's first responsibility was to his name and to the enhancement of his family's wealth, power and prestige. On leaving school or university he was usually taken by his father or other well-born male sponsor to a levee (an all-male affair) at St James's Palace where he would be presented to the monarch or his representative after which he could take his place in society. If he were an eldest son and the heir to an estate he was expected to marry before he was too old to father a son to carry on the family name. It was this responsibility that compelled Sir Gareth Ludlow in *Sprig Muslin* to seek a suitable bride after his brother Arthur was killed at Salamanca. If a man was a younger son, once he had completed his education it was incumbent upon him to make his way in the world by living within any allow-ance provided for him or by entering one of the professions. A married man was expected to support his wife and children materially and be discreet in managing his extramarital affairs or in keeping a mistress.

As a father, a man's interaction with his children could be extremely limited but he was expected at least to teach his sons the ways of the world, to educate them in manly pursuits such as hunting and shooting, and to impart a sense of duty to the family. For his daughters he was required to enable his wife to 'fire them off' into society and to provide a dowry in the event of their marriage. Some chose to involve themselves more fully in their children's upbringing but society did not usually look askance at those men, like Adam Deveril's father Bardy Lynton in *A Civil Contract*, who did little more than father his offspring, provide them with life's necessities and introduce them into society when they came of age.

A formal education was considered essential for the upper-class man and he began learning his letters at an early age. At five or six he usually entered the home schoolroom where he was taught by a governess, or a tutor if he had no sisters. A proper education was one grounded in the Classics and most boys were sent away after the age of eight to one of the well-established public schools such as Eton, Harrow, St Paul's or Winchester. There they were taught Latin, Greek, languages such as French or Italian, history and mathematics in a large schoolroom in the company of several hundred other boys. School life was often extremely harsh and many boys endured meagre servings of poor food, freezing conditions, physical, sexual and emotional abuse, rats in the dormitories, loneliness and anxiety. Parents such as Gerard Monksleigh's mother in *Bath Tangle* frequently worried over the rigours and privations of boarding-school life. There were happy moments, however, and many pupils greatly enjoyed the freedoms that life away from home offered and engaged in all manner of pranks and activities both inside and outside the school grounds. Many boys forged friendships during their school years which continued at university and beyond. At the age of sixteen or seventeen boys went up to either Oxford or Cambridge or, like Hugo Darracott in *The Unknown Ajax* or Adam Deveril in *A Civil Contract*, went straight into the military.

*Although many young men opted for a life of pleasure while at
university some students chose an academic life.*

University was considered important, not so much for its
academic opportunities (serious study was an option rather than
a requirement) but for the social life and the friends and contacts
which could be made there. Viscount Pevensey and his devoted
and foolish friend, Cornelius Fancot, met at Harrow and embarked
on a riotous career of pranks, dares and wagers which, in *April
Lady*, continued during their time at Oxford and became the highlight of their bachelor life in London. The nature of university
life, with its emphasis on high-spirited behaviour and apparent
acceptance of young men as being naturally inclined to engage in
all manner of pranks, dares and other reckless deeds, meant that
it was not uncommon for students to find themselves rusticated
(sent down or suspended) for at least part of a term as a result of
activities deemed unacceptable even by the university authorities,
such as riding a horse up the college stairs or, as Nicky Carlyon
does in *The Reluctant Widow*, borrowing a bear to chase a couple

of university dons up a tree. Some students did engage in academic life, however, and serious-minded young men such as Aubrey Lanyon in *Venetia*, who was entered at Trinity College Cambridge, aspired to be scholars and win a fellowship. Young men usually spent two or three years at the university before entering society as fully fledged adults.

A Bachelor's Life

During the Regency the life of the well-bred and financially independent bachelor was often one of unalloyed pleasure. After a pleasant spell at either Oxford or Cambridge the sons of the nobility would frequently remove to London and take rooms in one of the many gentlemen's lodgings in the West End of town. Duke Street, St James's Place, Clarges Street, Ryder Street or any of the streets in the area of St James's were popular, as was a set of

In April Lady Dysart, *Viscount Pevensey, was famous at Oxford for leaping his hunter over a dining table and engaging in many of the outrageous pranks and escapades that were an accepted part of university life.*

*Many a young Regency blade aspired to spar with 'Gentleman'
John Jackson at his famous boxing saloon in Bond Street.*

chambers in Albany. The chambers, or 'sets' as they are still called
within Albany, were available only to single men and consisted
of comfortable bachelor apartments with two spacious main
rooms, an entrance hall and two or three smaller rooms which
could house the kitchen, bathroom and either a study or second
bedroom if one of the main rooms was used as a master bedroom.
Each set also had space allocated to it in the basement and attics
for servants' quarters and storage. Lord Byron lived in Albany in
1814–15 as did *The Foundling*'s Gideon Ware who, as a captain in
the Lifeguards, appreciated its close proximity to his headquarters.
Albany's central location just west of Piccadilly made it popular
with many a Regency bachelor who wanted easy access to the
clubs, pubs, hells, pleasure haunts and glittering social life available
to the well-bred man of leisure.

As long as he had some form of income, a dedicated bachelor (such as those younger sons of the aristocracy not subject to family expectations and the need to provide an heir) could spend his life indulging his various whims and fancies. His day often did not begin until after noon, when he arose, ate a leisurely breakfast, and spent considerable time dressing before setting off for his club around three. He could take a look in at Tattersall's and get the latest sporting news or engage in a sparring match at Jackson's Saloon. At five he might join the promenade in Hyde Park, there to admire the ladies, converse with friends or show off his riding or driving style if he was an accomplished equestrian or whip. In *Arabella* young Bertram Tallant, on his first trip to London, eagerly anticipated the pleasure of an evening spent with friends going to the theatre or the opera, eating supper at the Royal Saloon or the Piazza, or visiting popular haunts such as the Daffy Club, Limmer's Hotel or Cribb's Parlour, where he might smoke a pipe, listen to the conversation of the sporting men and even handle the Champion's silver cup.

A well-bred bachelor, such as Freddy Standen in *Cotillion*, was a favourite among society hostesses who could rely on him to make up the numbers at a dinner party or be an agreeable guest at a ball. Some bachelors took pleasure in escorting married ladies to the theatre or Almack's club, safe in the knowledge that no demands of a matrimonial nature would be made of them. A bachelor was also more at liberty than most married men to extend an evening spent at a ball, party, masquerade or the opera, into an all-night affair and thought nothing of drinking at his club, visiting a gaming hell or imbibing rough liquor in the seedier parts of town until after sunrise. Outside of the Season, a personable bachelor like Felix Hethersett in *April Lady* might join the fashionable set at a seaside resort or accept an invitation to stay at a country house where he could begin shooting in late August and (if he could afford it) join the hunt from November. Even for those single men compelled to

Like many young men of his day Bertram Tallant in Arabella *wanted nothing more than to join a Hussar regiment.*

earn a living and exercise their talents in the army, the navy, the Church, parliament or the law, it was possible for those dedicated to sport or the pursuit of pleasure to minimise the demands of their profession and dedicate a large part of their daily life to the delights of a bachelor existence.

Although the younger sons of the nobility did not have to fulfill the expectations and responsibilities incumbent on the eldest son, neither did they enjoy the wealth and power that came with his inheritance. Although in some cases younger sons like Claud Darracott in *The Unknown Ajax* inherited land or money from their mothers or other relatives, most relied on the income (usually a competence only) supplied to them by the family estate and which could sometimes be paid at the discretion of the heir. While such an allowance might enable them to live a pleasant bachelor existence it was rarely enough to support a family. As a result, many younger sons were compelled to find employment and generally found themselves restricted by the conventions of the period to the handful of professions considered suitable for the sons of the upper class.

They could enter the navy—and gain a suitable position through patronage of the kind Mr Beaumaris planned for Harry Tallant in *Arabella*—or join the army by buying a commission into a regiment. During the Regency a pair of colours in a Hussar regiment cost approximately £800 pounds and automatically made a man an officer regardless of his capability or qualifications. Intermittent conflict with the former American colonies, and Napoleon's campaigns in Europe in the early years of the Regency, made the military an attractive occupation for many adventurous or romantically minded young men. For the less bold, taking Holy Orders and becoming a beneficed clergyman was generally an undemanding way of life which enabled many practitioners to continue to enjoy the popular activities of the period—riding, hunting, drinking and gaming—without censure, and, for those who wished to marry, a well-endowed living provided ample means for supporting a wife and family. The Reverend Hugh Rattray in *Cotillion*, while conscientious in the performance of his clerical duties, was also a sporting man and prided himself on his athletic prowess. A desire to enter the Church did not necessarily have to spring from a strong religious conviction or a passion for the calling; for many younger sons it was a position which could ensure a reasonable degree of comfort based on an income derived from one or more livings which were frequently made available from the family estates (known as 'livings in the gift').

The other main occupation for an upper-class man was in politics, either as a member of the House of Commons, or through service in the diplomatic corps or the Foreign Office. In *The Reluctant Widow*, of Lord Carlyon's three younger brothers one was an army officer, one was at Oxford and the third, John, was secretary to Lord Sidmouth at the Home Office. For some men it was also possible to acquire a government sinecure or subsidy through appointment to public office. Sinecures were a form of government patronage often used by the King or his ministers to secure political support from powerful families or individuals. There were many positions in the gift of the government which could be bestowed on the men and women of the aristocracy and their dependants and they often paid handsomely. Carlyon's uncle, Lord Bedlington, although a close friend of the Prince Regent and honoured with a barony, was not (unfortunately) the recipient of such a grant although he tended to live as though he were the beneficiary of a generous government stipend. During the Regency, parliament was made up of the monarch, the House of Commons and the House of Lords. Whigs and Tories were not political parties in the modern sense of having a defined organisation but were two entities loosely held together by common philosophies, shared interests and the desire for power. Individual MPs were free to move between the parties and vote according to their conscience or personal interest, although family allegiances, traditional beliefs, friendship and patronage all played a part in determining where their loyalties lay. Although they had their differences, both Whigs and Tories came from the upper class and whether they were an aristocrat, member of the gentry or rich financier, they had many things in common—including an allegiance to the Church of England, a desire to protect their interests and a belief in a natural social order which placed them firmly at the top of the heap. Although his father had been a Whig, Adam Deveril, the new Viscount Lynton in *A Civil Contract*, shocked his friends by choosing to take his seat in the House of Lords as a Tory so that he might better support the Duke of Wellington in his fight against Napoleon.

The Tories were traditionally the more conservative of the two parties and were often identified as supporters of the Crown and allies of the Church of England. They were derogatorily referred to (by the Whigs) as the 'King's Friends'. After the Napoleonic

Wars the Tories were inclined to be reactionary in government and generally resisted moves for reform. During the Regency two Tory prime ministers held office: Spencer Perceval from 1809 until his assassination in 1812 and Lord Liverpool from 1812 to 1827. The Whigs tended to be identified with the great landowners, and with parliamentary rather than kingly authority. Although they were, like the Tories, mostly conservative, the Whigs were more tolerant of religious dissent and more likely to favour (cautious) reform. During the Regency the Whigs struggled for political unity but were constantly put at a political disadvantage by internal divisions and a failure to find one leader among the various Whig factions—all of whom had their own interests to promote. In *The Unknown Ajax*, Matthew Darracott's defection from his father's Whiggish beliefs to his wife's Toryism earned him many parental snubs but also saw him rise steadily up the political ladder.

MARRIAGE

Not all men chose to marry, but for those who sought to become leg-shackled, marriage could be a serious business with the potential to materially affect a man's social standing, wealth, power and influence. An eldest son with a title and expectations of a considerable inheritance usually had a wide choice of potential wives and it was expected that he would marry for the good of the family. In *Sylvester*, the hero startled his mother when he asked her advice about the list he had made of well-born ladies from which he planned to choose his wife since he seemed to assume that any of the ladies under consideration would be his for the asking. For the upper-class man, marriage usually meant finding a partner from within his own social sphere and, if possible, selecting a bride with a large dowry. An eldest son with lands to inherit but no fortune to go with them would often seek an heiress or a bride with a sizeable dowry or marriage portion—even if it meant stepping down the social ladder to find her. Stacy Calverleigh in *Black Sheep* was determined to win himself a bride with a large fortune and was quite prepared to marry a female from a lower social class to do so, while, despite her merchant-class origins, the possession of a large fortune made Tiffany Wield of *The Nonesuch* an attractive prize to many better-born men. During the Regency many daughters of the new wealthy merchant class married into the aristocracy and (both genetically and financially) brought new lifeblood to the upper class.

For a younger son of noble birth but modest means, the hope was that he would marry an heiress or at least a well-born woman of property. The difficulty was that younger sons were considered, for the most part, a very poor bargain when compared with the eldest son and heir, and they often married those younger daughters of the nobility who had not managed to find a wealthier husband. As the elder of aristocratic twin brothers, Evelyn Fancot of *False Colours* was deemed a far more desirable *parti* than his equally handsome and charming sibling, Kit. Although arranged marriages were less common during the Regency than they once had been, among the aristocracy and the royal family they were considered an important way of safeguarding or strengthening bloodlines, family fortunes and inheritances. The Duke of Sale felt compelled to offer for the hand of Lady Harriet Presteigne when it was made clear to him in *The Foundling* that his uncle had arranged the marriage and Lady Harriet was expecting his proposal. Sometimes parents (especially fathers) exercised a right of veto over their offspring's choice of marriage partner, although such injunctions were not necessarily adhered to and determined sons and daughters would flout parental authority and either marry by special licence or elope to Gretna Green as Gerard Monksleigh persuaded his young love to do in *Bath Tangle*. It was rare, however, even for an eloped couple to marry outside their social circle or where there was no fortune on at least one side.

Bucks, Beaus and Dandies

The buck: The term generally referred to the bloods or sporting types, but could also mean a man of spirit. The buck usually stood out from the crowd and a 'buck of the first head' was a man who pursued every kind of pleasure and often surpassed his friends in debauchery.

The beau: Despite the literal meaning of the word, a man did not have to be handsome to be a beau. Although several of the Regency beaus had pleasing countenances, the epithet was applied more on the basis of a man's place in the fashionable world rather than his looks or dress. A beau was a leader in society like Sir Richard Wyndham of *The Corinthian* and while he was often an arbiter of fashion, he could also acquire the nickname as a result of his manners, eccentricities, noble rank, clever wit or some other trait that set him apart or made him notorious. To be a beau, a man needed either vanity, idiosyncrasy, a desire for attention or remarkable good looks and town polish but, above all, he had to have 'Presence'.

The Corinthian: This term described the well-dressed athlete. A Corinthian was a man who, as Mr Beaumaris told Arabella in *Arabella*, 'besides being a very Tulip of Fashion, is an amateur of sport, a master of sword-play, a deadly fellow with a pistol, a Nonpareil amongst whips'. He generally excelled in all the sporting pursuits including fencing, single-stick, boxing, hunting, shooting and tooling his carriage—usually a curricle—preferably with the kind of skill that would see him admitted to the Four-Horse Club. He would also be a man of good character addicted to all forms of sport, at home among all classes and able to cut a dash at Almack's or blow a cloud with the roughest pugilist at Cribb's Parlour.

The dandy: The word 'dandy' came into fashion in about 1813 and was used to describe any man who paid particular attention to his clothes and appearance. The Regency was the great age of the dandy and they were the leaders of fashion during this period. Until 1816 Brummell was their king; it was he who ordained that a well-dressed man concentrated on clean linen, exquisite tailoring, a perfectly tied neckcloth, a dark, well-cut coat and a general air of understatement. The elite circle of men who gambled, drank and played together set the fashion for a host of eager imitators, many of whom aspired to join their ranks. Mere clothes could not make a man a dandy, however, nor grant him admission to the inner ranks of the dandy set. A true dandy, such as Gervase Frant, seventh Earl of St Erth, esteemed not just the cut of his coat, but also wit, learning, artistic appreciation, a reserve of manner that seemed like arrogance to lesser mortals, and a demeanour so calm that nothing could impair it. A dandy was generally uninterested in sporting ventures, although he might be proficient in some or all of them.

The Nonesuch or Nonpareil: He was the incomparable man, one who excelled in all the manly pursuits but was also an arbiter of fashion and a leader in all things aesthetic. He was a man of taste, a person people deferred to, watched and often slavishly copied. He was a setter of fashion, not merely a follower, and, as Sir Waldo Hawkridge explained to Miss Trent in *The Nonesuch*, his appellation was applied by those who admired his handling of the ribbons, his manners, dress and his athletic ability.

Pinks and tulips: These names of beautiful flowers were used by the Regency sporting journalist Pierce Egan to denote exceptionally well-turned-out gentlemen. A pink was a man at the height of fashion and a tulip was a fine fellow who dressed well.

The fop: Like the dandy, the fop took an absorbing interest in his clothes. Unlike the dandy, however, the fop dressed for show, adorning his person with clothes of bold or unusual design or hue and embellishing them with ostentatious jewels, frills and furbelows. The fop craved attention and did everything in his power to draw the eye of the passer-by. He was frequently a chatterer and usually deemed a vain fool by his peers. Sir Nugent Fotherby in *Sylvester* was the epitome of a fop with his rings, diamond pin, fobs and seals, his extravagant neckcloth, exotic waistcoats and specially designed boots. Many fops aspired to set a trend or create a new fashion and some took their clothes to extraordinary extremes—such as wearing their shirt collars so high that they could not turn their heads or wearing voluminous trousers or coats with overlong tails.

A fop such as Sir Nugent Fotherby in Sylvester *drew every eye with his extravagant dress and accessories.*

A fribble: An effeminate fop, derived from a character in David Garrick's eighteenth-century farce *Miss in her Teens*.

A Bartholomew baby: A person dressed in tawdry or gaudy clothes like the dolls on sale at Bartholomew Fair.

A coxcomb: A particularly foolish and conceited fop.

4

The Gentle Sex

THE REGENCY WOMAN

To be born an upper-class woman during the Regency meant being raised to a particular expectation of what that role entailed. As 'the gentle sex', women were meant to be both ignorant and devoid of the various vices of the more 'natural' man and were generally not expected to have opinions or ideas of a political nature. In *Black Sheep,* Abigail Wendover's brother was appalled to learn that she not only knew all about the hero's rakish past, but had been informed of it by the hero himself. For the most part, a woman's life was a domestic one and, whether or not she was married and regardless of class, it was accepted that her primary talents were all associated with running a household, bearing children, and being 'ornamental'. Innocence was also held to be a virtue in the female—both in knowledge and experience—and the fact that many women were extremely knowledgeable and aware of life's realities was often disguised or kept below the surface veneer of respectable and acceptable behaviour.

Beauty, taste, modesty, manners, a strong sense of duty and a desire to make a good marriage were esteemed as the most desirable female attributes and girls were trained from birth to abide by the restrictions placed upon them and to conform to their parents'—and later their husband's—expectations. In *The Foundling*, Lady Harriet's mother made it quite clear that, once married, her daughter should turn a blind eye to her husband's *affaires* but that she too could take a lover once she had given birth to an heir. That many upper-class women stepped outside the boundaries once they were married, and especially once they had produced an heir, is clear and the lives of society women such as Lady Cowper, the Duchess of Devonshire, Lady Oxford, Lady Hertford and even the Regent's wife, Princess Caroline, all bear witness to the flexible morality and often dynamic choices that these women made. Upper-class Regency women understood their world and its often contradictory rules, and frequently chose not only *not* to play by them but also to manipulate and use them to their advantage. While the general expectation was that a woman should be docile and tractable and look to the man for leadership, in many cases women found their own paths to some form of independent thought or behaviour. Lady Hester Theale in *Sprig Muslin*, at twenty-nine and still unmarried, was regarded by her father and her family as an 'encumbrance'. When she turned down an offer of a brilliant marriage, they were furious and tried to persuade her to do otherwise, but Hester's mind and inner life were very much her own and she responded to their demands through a mist of vague responses and an apparent acquiescence that disguised a strong will and a delightful sense of humour.

Within the highly structured class system of England during the Regency, one of the ways in which the aristocracy kept themselves apart from the masses was by creating their own rules, restrictions and a system of etiquette that enabled them to recognise and connect with those of their own order. This system of behaviour was instilled into young women from an early age and they quickly learned that to forget propriety or step outside the rules was the prerogative only of the royal, the very rich, the eccentric or the outcast. In considering her future, Venetia Lanyon in *Venetia* was aware that some women—like Lady Hester Stanhope and the Ladies of Llangollen—chose to renounce the world and live free of social convention, but she also recognised that it was not a choice available to her. A woman's reputation was among her most important assets, along with her breeding, her fortune and her looks. Propriety demanded that emotions be kept tightly controlled in public, and it was expected that most situations would be met with composure and an appropriate degree of gravity. Displays of temper or too much humour or levity were considered quite unbecoming, 'funning' being acceptable only within certain subject boundaries and in appropriate situations and environments. Anthea in *The Unknown Ajax* was 'too-lively' for absolute propriety and had a ready tongue which her mother constantly tried to curb. Ironically, however, hysterics, fainting fits and swooning were accepted—even expected—where a woman, such as Mrs Dauntry in *Frederica*, was known to have an 'excess of sensibility'.

Language was also carefully regulated since a young woman could quickly be stigmatised as a 'hoyden' if she showed herself to be too familiar with the language of the stables, spoke her mind or showed herself to be knowledgeable about male pursuits such as gambling, boxing and the muslin company. Hero, the youthful and disastrously innocent bride in *Friday's Child*, was chastised by her husband for asking about his 'opera-dancer' and had to be instructed in the ways of the world by a brotherly friend. The social, cultural, economic and intellectual restraints imposed on Regency women—and single girls in particular—repressed many of their natural inclinations and life could be tedious for an upper-class lady faced with a limited number of activities with which to occupy her time and mind. The death of a family member, even a distant connection, could restrict her activities still further as society expected dutiful females to be in mourning and observe the proprieties by absenting themselves from dances, balls and most other social events, usually for quite some time. Lady Serena

Sophy Stanton-Lacy in The Grand Sophy *outraged
Miss Wraxton by driving her down the exclusive
male precinct of St James's Street.*

Carlow of *Bath Tangle* chafed at the restrictions imposed on ladies in
mourning after her father's tragic death, and found the limitations
of life in Bath almost intolerable. For some women these limits on
behaviour and occupation often resulted in bouts of illness and the
regular use of opiates such as laudanum.

Although a woman was denied the freedoms available to a man,
there were some significant exceptions to the apparently rigid rules
of etiquette and manners, but only for those firmly established
within the *ton*. Much might be forgiven the lady of impeccable
lineage, and a great deal allowed to the girl of vast fortune, although
London society could be ruthless in excluding anyone judged to
have stepped outside the bounds of propriety. It was Sophy's position as the popular Sir Horace Stanton-Lacy's daughter that, in *The
Grand Sophy*, enabled her to drive her carriage down the men-only
precinct of St James's Street without creating a scandal. Although
Sophy's independent ways, forthright speech, dashing appearance

and mastery of horse and pistol shocked some among society's elite, her personality, social connections and breeding enabled her to do things which would have seen other, less well-positioned women instantly ostracised. As the centre of the Regency world, London had its own particular set of rules which differed—mainly by degree—from the rules directing behaviour in rural England or in the family home. Some activities (such as waltzing) that were severely frowned on in more rural regions, might be permissible, even fashionable, in London; yet sometimes the reverse was true—a young woman, for instance, might indulge in certain activities in her home district (such as carriage-racing or riding alone) that, if repeated in the metropolis, would see her frowned upon or even ostracised in polite circles. Marianne Bolderwood was warned against waltzing by her mama when she attended a ball at Stanyon Castle in *The Quiet Gentleman* for she had yet to make her London debut and any hint of such forward behaviour from a girl not yet out ran the risk of being censured by the patronesses of Almack's. For those bred to its rules and expectations, however, the social whirl of the London Season could be a glittering, exciting, romantic world full of promise and possibilities.

ALL THE ACCOMPLISHMENTS

Beyond learning to read and acquiring enough arithmetic to manage the household accounts, girls were not expected to acquire an education in the same way as boys. Although it was not uncommon for upper-class women to learn French or Italian this was perceived as a useful social skill rather than an intellectual endeavour. In addition to the reading, writing, arithmetic and basic general knowledge imparted in the schoolroom, girls were mainly instructed in the domestic arts and expected to acquire a number of accomplishments such as singing, watercolour painting,

Circulating libraries such as Hookham's in London, Donaldson's in Brighton and Duffield's and Meyler's in Bath were especially popular with young ladies during the Regency.

fine embroidery and an ability to play the pianoforte or the harp, and a girl's leisure time was generally spent engaged in one of these activities. In *The Toll-Gate*, Lady Charlotte Calne was prevailed upon by several of the assembled company to show off her accomplishments by playing the harp and singing for them as part of the evening's entertainment (although there were some who wished she hadn't). Children of both sexes participated in physical games with friends or siblings, but young women were expected to become less boisterous as they approached adolescence and confine their main physical activities to walking or riding.

Although many well-bred young women were educated at home, during the Regency it was not uncommon for the daughters of gentlemen to attend a ladies' seminary as either a boarder or a day student. Cherry Steane in *Charity Girl* was a student at Miss Fletching's school in Bath where she spent several happy years before being sent to live with her Aunt Bugle in Hampshire. Such institutions were often established in a private home by an impoverished gentlewoman with enough capital to set up a small school, or by one of a handful of progressive female educators with a vision of women as being something more than purely ornamental. Most seminaries offered what was described as 'a comprehensive education' which included languages, the womanly arts, music and acceptable outdoor leisure activities. Correct posture and deportment (with use of the backboard) were also taught, as were manners, etiquette and the kind of elegancy of mind considered essential to a prettily behaved girl. As the rise of industry saw a corresponding increase in the wealthy merchant class, the desire to see his daughters creditably established (preferably wed to a member of the aristocracy) led more than one ambitious and affluent tradesman to send them to one of London's or Bath's more exclusive seminaries in the hope that they might establish advantageous connections with the daughters of the upper class. In *A Civil Contract*, wealthy merchant Jonathan Chawleigh sent his daughter Jenny to Miss Satterleigh's Seminary for the Daughters of Gentlemen in Kensington for precisely that reason.

In addition to knowing how to behave it was also vital for a debutante to demonstrate her prowess in at least one of the accepted female accomplishments. Singing, watercolour painting, fine embroidery, dancing, sketching and the ability to play an instrument, such as the harp or the pianoforte, were considered essential skills for the young lady about to make her come-out. Grace, elegance, poise and good posture were deemed evidence of good breeding, and simplicity of presentation—without affectation, simpering or false modesty—when singing, reciting poetry or playing an instrument was applauded as entirely becoming to a virtuous young woman. Judith Taverner won approval for her unaffected performance on the piano during her week-long stay with the Duke and Duchess of Rutland at Belvoir Castle in *Regency Buck*, and Charis Merriville in *Frederica* was judged to have a simplicity of manner which only enhanced her beauty. In addition to practical skills, books and magazine articles encouraged well-bred women to cultivate a manner which was charming yet simple, amiable though reserved, sensitive but not overmuch and expressive yet refined. Thoughts and opinions (on appropriate subjects) were expected to be elegantly expressed in a well-modulated voice and with just the right amount of deference to one's social superiors and the exact modicum of condescension to lesser mortals. In *The Spanish Bride*, Juana's limited English made communication with her new sister-in-law difficult, but Mrs Sargant's uncertainty about her brother's young wife was somewhat allayed by Juana's low, musical voice and evident good breeding. During the Regency the art of conversation gradually became more valued as a womanly accomplishment among the upper class, as arranged marriages became less common and women came to be seen more as companions and less as mere adjuncts to their husbands.

MAKING A COME-OUT

By seventeen, and sometimes earlier, a girl was able to begin spreading her social wings and might attend certain sorts of smaller parties, family dinners and minor assemblies in places such as the resort towns of Bath or Harrogate. She was precluded from attending London assemblies or any sizeable occasion until she had made her debut, and grand social events hosted by royalty, such as the Prince Regent's magnificent fête at Carlton House, were out of the question unless she had been formally presented at Court. In spite of her experiences as a society hostess while living overseas with her diplomat father, Sophy Stanton-Lacy in *The Grand*

Sophy was ineligible to attend this grand affair because she had not yet been presented at one of the Queen's Drawing-Rooms. This centuries-old tradition was available to daughters of the aristocracy and to those who had married into the upper class, and a young woman was not considered to be fully 'out' in society until she had been presented. A strict protocol was enforced prior to presentation, requiring the lady's name to be put forward and approved before a date for presentation could be set. A woman attended a drawing-room in full Court dress in the form of a *grande toilette* consisting of a magnificently embroidered or ornamented silk, satin or lace dress over a hooped skirt, her finest jewels, and a head-dress with as many as eight ostrich feathers. In *Cotillion*, Meg, Lady Buckhaven, bought a magnificent satin dress with a lace overskirt to wear to Court but had to persuade her loving husband to pay the £300 bill for it sent by the dressmaker.

Presentations took place at St James's Palace and a debutante was always escorted by her mother or other female sponsor—often

A Court presentation was a magnificent occasion with the ladies wearing their finest gowns and most beautiful jewels, and the gentlemen resplendent in full Court dress.

a member of the aristocracy whose connections or influence at Court might see her protégée favoured by royal attention for slightly longer than the minute or so it took to be introduced and to make her curtsy to the Queen. The haughty but elegant Lady Nassington of *A Civil Contract* kindly chaperoned Jenny Chawleigh to her presentation and enabled Jenny to feel more confident about meeting the Queen and the Princesses. Most girls came out into society by eighteen and hoped to be married within their first Season, or at least receive an offer as Letty proudly told her cousin John she had done in *The Toll-Gate*.

MOTHERS, WIVES, WIDOWS AND DAUGHTERS

From the moment of birth, an upper-class Regency child would be shared to varying degrees between parents and servants. Although a mother might choose to breast-feed her baby, as Jenny Chawleigh did in *A Civil Contract*, it was not uncommon for well-born ladies to engage a wet-nurse to attend the infant. Some mothers were more actively involved in their children's upbringing, taking an interest in their lessons and helping to nurse them in times of illness, but their greatest involvement in their children's lives was when they entered society. An upper-class mother's first duty was as a marriage-broker; she was responsible for finding eligible partners for her offspring and for a mother of several daughters (such as Lady Bugle in *Charity Girl*) this could become the main focus of her life.

A good upper-class mother would ensure that her daughter had at least one London Season with a presentation at Court, and that she was exquisitely gowned and thoroughly schooled in the ways of the world. Once in London it was imperative to be seen in all the right places and hopeful mothers would make visits of ceremony and leave calling cards at the homes of influential women in the hope of reciprocal visits or an invitation to their next ball or party. Lady Bridlington in *Arabella* considered how best to bring her protégée to the notice of the most powerful and well-disposed ladies of the *ton*, and spent a great deal of time planning her ball and thinking of who to invite in order to ensure that Arabella had the opportunity to meet the cream of London society. If possible, vouchers for Almack's were obtained and a mother would escort her daughter to evenings in the hallowed rooms as well as to every other acceptable social event to which they had been invited. It was not unknown for ambitious mothers to plot ways in which their daughters could attract the attention of an eligible bachelor, or to devise a lavish ball or daring alfresco breakfast in order to entice the London elite into their homes and bring their daughters into direct contact with the *ton's* most attractive men. Lady Laleham in *Bath Tangle* was a well-known social climber who contrived to visit the Spenborough home when she knew the rich and eligible Marquis of Rotherham was also visiting.

In the early nineteenth century marriage meant that in a legal as well as a practical sense a woman, and any money or assets she might own, including jewels, personal possessions, household items and clothing, came under her husband's control the moment the knot was tied. Even betrothal meant she had to have her fiancé's permission to dispose of her own property. In the case of Tiffany Wield, the spendthrift heiress of *The Nonesuch*, this was held to be a good thing but for many women the loss of autonomy was unpalatable. As a wife she was viewed by the law as being one with her husband, and consequently she lost her legal status as a separate individual and with it the considerable legal rights available to her as a single woman. Her real property, including land, houses, livestock, chattels and church livings could become his if he claimed them but by the time of the Regency it had become increasingly common in upper-class circles for these holdings and any income derived from them to be placed in a separate trust for a wife's use and benefit. If a husband predeceased his wife her property reverted to her and if she died childless it would revert to her heirs. If her husband was alive and she died leaving children, he held her property until his death when it passed to her heirs. Any children born during a marriage (whether his or not) were legally his and in the event of a divorce or separation a husband could take the children, his wife's money and personal property (unless it had been set apart legally) and refuse her access to them.

The only offset to the injustices meted out to wives under Common Law was the provision of another type of law known as Equity. For those who could afford to implement its benefits, the court of Equity could enforce trusts and legal arrangements (often included in the marriage settlement) made to safeguard women's property; it could also secure property left to her for her own use and it could enable her to sue where she had a right to do so—a right she was denied as a wife under Common Law. A wife's loss of legal rights carried a few advantages, however, for on marriage a husband became responsible for all of her debts, including those incurred before their wedding. In *Friday's Child* Hero's mounting debts forced her husband to sell some of his investments in order to meet the costs and Nell Cardross of *April Lady* fretted over a sizeable dressmaker's bill which she dared not reveal after her husband had paid her other debts. A husband was legally bound to support his wife so long as they shared a bed and board and if she committed a crime (other than murder or high treason) while her husband was present, under the law he was held to have coerced her and she was automatically deemed innocent.

On becoming a widow a woman regained the legal rights she had enjoyed as a single female and, in some cases, benefited greatly from her husband's death. Lady Barbara Childe revelled in her freedom as a dashing young widow and, in *An Infamous Army*, vowed never to remarry. If she had owned property prior to her marriage, on her husband's death it reverted to her; if her husband died intestate (without a will) she was entitled to a third of his personal property; if no arrangements for a property settlement or jointure had been made at the time of marriage she had an automatic right to claim support from one third of his estates for life. In some cases a widow was also provided with a dower house, usually set at a small distance from the main house on the principal estate. Elinor Rochdale in *The Reluctant Widow* was entitled to an income from her deceased husband's estate and the young and beautiful Lady Spenborough of *Bath Tangle* moved to the dower house on the edge of the family estate several weeks after her husband's death. By the time of the Regency a widow with property and an independent income was in a better position to protect her assets from the possibility of them being dissipated by a second husband in the event of a remarriage. The freedom enjoyed by those financially independent widows meant that they were often cautious about re-entering the marriage state.

Upper-class daughters were thoroughly schooled in what was owed to their family and the family name, and love was not considered an essential requirement for a good match. In some families, if the parents were able to arrange an eligible match, they hoped that the girl might feel affection for the chosen bridegroom; but if not, she was expected to swallow any aversion and marry him anyway. Some parents, such as Lady Ombersley in *The Grand Sophy*, held in abhorrence the notion of compelling a loved daughter to marry against her will; on the other hand, a girl who found herself in love would be able to contemplate marriage with a man only if he were of good birth or had a substantial estate or fortune. Love alone was not enough within the upper class. Isabella Milborne, the 'Incomparable' of *Friday's Child*, clearly understood what was expected of a woman with her looks and breeding and dutifully encouraged the attentions of the Duke of Severn instead of those of the rakish but handsome George, Lord Wrotham. Obedience, decorous behaviour and an avoidance of any action that might make her appear 'fast' or forward were essential for social acceptance, and a well-bred daughter knew that any untoward behaviour would likely see her whisked off to the family's country estate to rusticate and reconsider her feelings or to wait for scandal or rumour to recede. In *Sylvester*, Phoebe Marlow's grandmother was convinced that Paris was the ideal place to take her granddaughter while her friends endeavoured to quash the rumours about Phoebe that had set the *ton* on its ears.

On the Marriage Mart

Marriage was a vital issue for upper-class Regency women. It offered the possibility of a degree of freedom and independence that was not generally available to them as single women and could also save them from the stigma of spinsterhood. Once they had made their debut, most girls expected to be married or at least betrothed in their first Season and certainly by the second or third. After that a family's hopes of suitably disposing of a daughter (considered to be no longer in her first bloom of youth) began to fade and by their late twenties most women despaired of finding a suitable husband. At twenty-nine Annis Wychwood in *Lady of Quality* was unusual in having decided she had no wish to be married and rejecting every eligible offer made to her since her come-out.

In upper-class circles the main marriage mart was London during the Season, where the constant round of social events and activities provided ample opportunity to mingle with eligible men and find a suitable partner for an unmarried daughter. Entry to the exclusive Almack's club was considered the height of social attainment, with admission obtainable only by a voucher bestowed on a young woman by one of its seven powerful patronesses, two of whom discussed whether or not to bestow the coveted vouchers on Judith Taverner in *Regency Buck*. Known during the Regency as the

'Marriage Mart', Almack's was *the* place for the new debutante to be seen and to meet the cream of eligible Regency bachelors, many of whom made obligatory appearances at the rooms in King Street despite finding both the entertainment and the refreshment rather dull. One of the main aims of the London Season was for families of the same class to interact in a range of social settings and for their children to contract suitable alliances. For women, a creditable marriage was the great aim, a brilliant marriage was the great hope.

TO GRETNA GREEN

The tiny village of Gretna Green was situated just over the English–Scottish border on the main road from Carlisle. The village was made famous after 1754 when Lord Hardwicke's Marriage Act took effect, precluding anyone in England from being married under the age of twenty-one without parental consent and also compelling couples to marry in a parish church building before an ordained minister. Scottish law, however, made no such demands and Hardwicke's edict had little effect over the border where a man and woman could be married without notice. Sixteen was the legal age to marry in Scotland and parental consent was not needed. For those in love and below marriageable age, for older men seeking a younger bride or for a rake or fortune-hunter dangling after a rich young heiress, Gretna Green was the obvious destination.

Many couples made the journey along the Great North Road from London. It was a long drive by coach and, even under-taken at speed or in fear of pursuit by outraged relatives, took several days. It was also a costly venture as Gerard Monksleigh discovered in *Bath Tangle* when he calculated the post-charges for a journey of over three hundred miles. Under Scottish law a couple wishing to marry needed only to commit to one another in the presence of at least two witnesses to make their union

Faced with parental opposition to their marriage, a desperate young couple might consider a flight to Gretna Green.

legal. Although young couples could be and were married in the smithy or over the anvil by the blacksmith, most marriages were performed by 'anvil priests' in the inns of Gretna Green. The idea of being married over the anvil has passed into folklore since then and may originally have been a matter of convenience. In Gretna Green the blacksmith's shop was located in the centre of the village at the intersection of five coaching roads known locally as 'Headless Cross'. It was therefore easy to find and the blacksmith, used to being awoken at all hours for shoeing, was possibly more amenable than most to being disturbed by anxious couples wishing to tie the knot.

A BRILLIANT MATCH OR A DISASTROUS ALLIANCE

A good match required good birth; wealth was also important but a rich man of greatly inferior birth would not be considered except in times of dire financial need or when such an offer was clearly the only chance for a daughter to be married—and even then too lowly a birth could preclude such a mismatch. A disastrous alliance was perceived as one in which a woman married a man of inferior birth with no fortune or expectations— an eventuality which, in *Sprig Muslin*, led Amanda's well-bred grandfather to forbid her engagement to a mere captain in the 43rd Regiment. The possibility of such an unequal match was one against which heiresses, especially young debutantes such as Fanny Wendover in *Black Sheep*, had to be continually guarded and known fortune-hunters, rakes or impecunious younger sons with no hope of inheriting the title were generally held at arm's length or avoided completely.

Most inappropriate matches could be circumvented as long as the correct protocols for arranging a marriage were followed. A man wishing to offer marriage approached the parents first, sought an interview with the father (or the mother if a widow) and made his intentions known. These would then be conveyed by her parents to the young woman who might be given the opportunity to respond. Or, if the parents were happy with the match, they would give their permission for the man to approach his intended himself and endeavour to persuade her to accept him. As Kit Fancot discovered in *False Colours*, men were sometimes compelled actively to seek approval from the prospective bride's extended family as well, and were even subjected to a period of assessment before consent could be given. This was especially so in cases where the bride was bringing a fortune or estates to a less well-heeled but impressively well-born suitor.

Once a couple had agreed to wed a notice was sent to the papers announcing the betrothal. From this point it was virtually impossible for a man to withdraw without committing breach of promise (for which he could be sued) or worse, damaging his honour and reputation. The right to cry off or end an engagement was the woman's prerogative and she could generally do so with impunity

*During the Regency many of society's fashionable elite were married
at St George's, Hanover Square.*

provided it was not too close to the wedding date. A woman who
gave back her ring after the wedding arrangements were finalised
(as Lady Serena Carlow did in *Bath Tangle*) risked being branded
a jilt and could suffer socially as a consequence. An engagement
period was usual and it was necessary to call the banns on three
Sundays in a row before a marriage could proceed. Where a couple
was determined to marry quickly, as was the case in *Friday's Child*, a
marriage licence enabling an immediate wedding could be bought
from the bishop.

A good marriage was the primary goal for most women; failing
that, almost any marriage was preferable to the single state, the
exception being an inappropriate match which could result in

a daughter being cut off from her family. Marriage afforded a degree of independence and a freedom not available to the single upper-class woman as Lady Buckhaven was pleased to discover in *Cotillion*. A married woman could go out unchaperoned; she could have a range of male friends; she could go out with another man socially; she could even take a lover—provided that she was discreet and had already done her duty by presenting her husband with an heir. Most upper-class women were conscious of the elasticity of morality once they were married, and of the fact that this could and would very often apply—although often unequally—to both husband and wife. Nell Cardross in *April Lady* was well aware that her husband might have a mistress or conduct an affair for that had been her mother's experience—it was she who had carefully instructed Nell in the importance of never asking difficult questions or communicating that one knew anything about such things. An aristocratic mother might counsel her soon-to-be-wed daughter that her future husband's extra-marital activities simply did not concern her. For many women it was far better to marry a man who had no thought of fidelity or for whom they had no particular affection and be mistress of their own household, than to remain for ever a dependant in the parental home. For Melissa Brandon of *The Corinthian*, marriage to the very rich Sir Richard Wyndham was her 'duty' and in *The Grand Sophy* Cecilia's older sister Maria felt compelled to marry the blockish James in view of his respectable offer, her papa's financial difficulties and the reality of there being four other sisters to provide for. And if they were unhappy, there was always the hope that their husband might die on the battlefield, the hunting field, in a duel or from an excess of drink. Although arranged marriages were often successful, during the Regency love-matches became increasingly common as more and more men and women sought the fulfilment to be found in a relation-ship based on genuine affection, mutual respect and love.

OTHER OPTIONS

There were limited roles for the well-bred single woman over the age of twenty-two or -three when she was considered past her prime. If she were wealthy in her own right or possessed of a comfortable 'independence', she might set up house with a suitable female companion although, as Venetia Lanyon recognised in *Venetia*, this would probably see her stigmatised as an 'eccentric' and result in her being ostracised by elite circles. If independent living was not an available option—more often the case owing to the extremely limited means by which a woman could obtain an income during the Regency—then she would probably become a dependant in the household of a family member. Maiden aunts, distant cousins, nieces and unmarried older daughters often took on the role of companion, governess or nurse to a more prosperous family member in return for lodging, board and a socially accepted position. It could be an unenviable position, however, for spinsters were generally considered inferior beings and the maiden aunt, sister or daughter denied marriage often found herself an object of pity to be shunted between relatives and treated little better than a domestic servant.

For those gently born women without family upon whom they could depend, one of the few paid occupations available to them was that of companion or governess. For women forced into this position there was usually little to look forward to beyond a lifetime of drudgery, submission and what Kitty Charing in *Cotillion* perceived as 'the slights and snubs which were a governess's portion'. A few women, such as Ancilla Trent in *The Nonesuch*, deliberately chose to support themselves through teaching rather than burden their families, but for those women of good birth such a decision generally placed them outside their accustomed social circle. Ancilla knew only too well that by becoming a governess a woman automatically reduced her social standing. Apart from teaching, the only other genteel occupations available to an upper-class female were that of dressmaker or milliner, neither of which would allow her to retain her place within society. Although there were a few exceptions, the many constraints placed upon women during this period and social expectations in general made it very difficult to aspire to any status other than that of wife and mother regardless of intellect or scholarly interests. For those women unable to marry the prospects could be bleak.

5

On the Town

THE SEASON AND THE LITTLE SEASON

Running from late January to early July, for the upper class the Season was the social high period of the year. Parliament began sitting in January—the signal for the move to town to commence—but many families delayed their return to the metropolis as the Season did not get into full swing until March or April. Centred in London, it took place during the (ideally) pleasant spring months and consisted of an endless round of balls, assemblies, theatre parties, military reviews, masquerades, dances, routs, alfresco breakfasts and any other gay or dashing entertainment that an ambitious host or hostess could conceive of within the bounds of propriety. For those upper-class families with a country seat and children to marry off, the Season was the time to return to London and take up residence in an owned or rented town house somewhere in Mayfair in order to play the 'marriage market'. Arabella, growing up in the very restricted society of Heythram in Yorkshire, longed to visit London where she might enjoy the balls, assemblies, theatre parties and other pleasures of the Season. For those on the social fringe, the hangers-on, the genteel and the well-bred but impoverished, the Season was also an opportunity to catch a rich husband or wife.

Parliament rose in June and families would retire to their country estate or to a seaside resort such as Brighton. London could be unbearable in the summer months and was thought by many to be fetid and unhealthy. In *The Spanish Bride*, Harry Smith's young wife Juana watched the city grow thin of company in late June and endured many hot, dull days in the capital while waiting for news of her husband. A return to town in September was considered acceptable, however, and many among the upper class came back to London for the Little Season, which lasted until early November when the fox-hunting began and there was a general retreat to the country. The Little Season also provided an opportunity for some girls to be brought out in advance of the Season proper and to try their social wings a little before embarking on the intense round of engagements that made up the Season. If it hadn't been for old Lady Bugle's untimely death in *Charity Girl* which meant the family were in mourning, her granddaughter Oenone might have come out during the Little Season in the autumn rather than having to wait until the following year.

ALMACK'S

Of all the venues in Regency London, Almack's was undoubtedly the most exclusive. Founded in 1763 by a Scotsman, William Macall, it derived its name from a simple reversal of the two syllables of Macall's surname. Macall became known as William Almack and the original Almack's was a gambling club in St James's Street which eventually became the famous Brooks's club. In 1764 Almack commissioned the building of a magnificent set of rooms on a site in King Street, behind St James's Square, in the centre of fashionable London. Almack's opened on 20 February 1765 with a subscription price of ten guineas which admitted the purchaser to the three rooms where a ball and a supper were held once a week for twelve weeks. In its early years, Almack's also provided the venue for a ladies' gambling club where those fashionable and aristocratic women who gained admission to the rooms could meet over cards and engage in deep play. In 1781 Almack's niece inherited the rooms and her husband, the keen-eyed and knowing Mr Willis, oversaw the running of the club and became famous as its imperturbable and ever-courteous doorkeeper. Not every visitor to Almack's was favoured with the attention of the great Mr Willis but Freddy Standen in *Cotillion* was an agreeable guest and a graceful dancer and was well-liked by the powerful doorkeeper.

Determined from the outset to make the club sought-after and exclusive, Almack set up a management committee of high-born ladies responsible for administering the vouchers which were the only means of gaining the tickets required for entry to the rooms. Thus were the patronesses established, and their autocratic rule quickly gained a hold over upper-class society, to the extent that one aspirant likened the pursuit of tickets of admission to Almack's to the Quest for the Holy Grail. Undoubtedly, part of the attraction was the difficulty in acquiring the necessary voucher. With the number on the list never exceeding two thousand, only those ladies and gentlemen who met with the approval of one or more of the lady patronesses would be so honoured. The challenge lay in determining what might win their approbation. As Eugenia Wraxton warned Miss Stanton-Lacy in *The Grand Sophy*, neither birth nor fortune could guarantee a voucher, although beauty, wit and careful dressing could open the doors, and a graceful dancer or person of taste might win approval and thereby gain admittance to the hallowed rooms.

The allocation of vouchers was decided in a weekly meeting during which the committee determined who, in addition to those already in the visiting books, would receive the coveted honour. Self-elected to their roles as arbiters of taste and fashion, the patronesses were frequently despotic in their rule and arbitrary in the selection of attendees. Offending any one of them could mean permanent exclusion from the club. Even the most nobly born persons were subject to their whims and idiosyncratic rules and many among the aristocracy sought their approval in vain. Even with the most eligible connections Gussie Yarford, Lady Appleby, in *Friday's Child*, could not get a voucher to Almack's. For those fortunate enough to gain admittance a set of strict rules was laid down and even the most notable in society were required to abide by them. The Duke of Wellington was turned away from the doors on two occasions: once, for arriving after eleven o'clock, at which time the rooms were closed to all newcomers, and again for attending in pantaloons instead of the requisite formal evening wear of knee-breeches. Peregrine Taverner in *Regency Buck* was another who discovered to his chagrin just how inflexible were the rules and how despotic the patronesses.

It was the very exclusiveness of Almack's and the extraordinary power and influence of the lady patronesses that made it so desirable. For many in the upper class it was *the* place to find a marriage partner, for, although the dancing was carefully regulated and the supper unremarkable, the company to be found there was guaranteed to be of the highest order. To receive a voucher was the ultimate in social *cachet*. As Frederica Merriville so clearly recognised in *Frederica*, to attend a ball at Almack's was to announce to the polite world that a person had arrived, that they too belonged, by right of birth or fortune or personality. Acceptance by the *ton* was for many the ultimate goal and the ultimate achievement.

THE PATRONESSES

The lady patronesses who ruled Almack's during the Regency differed as much in looks and temperament as they did in their roles in high society. No more than six or seven women formed the committee at any one time and in 1814 five were well-born English ladies and two were foreigners. Lady Jersey, Lady Sefton, Lady Cowper, Lady Castlereagh, and Mrs Drummond-Burrell were all born into aristocratic English families while Countess Lieven was Russian and Princess Esterhazy was of German birth. Between them these women formed a cabal that wielded an extraordinary influence in London society for years.

Lady Jersey was born Lady Sarah Sophia Fane, the daughter of the tenth Earl of Westmorland. She married George, Viscount Villiers, and became Lady Jersey when her husband inherited the title and became the fifth Earl of Jersey. Her mother-in-law was the notorious Frances, Lady Jersey, mistress of George, Prince of Wales, later Prince Regent. Though not considered to be a great beauty, Sarah was intelligent and energetic, with a sense of

Lady Jersey.

Lady Cowper.

humour appreciated by many but which evaded the notice of
some in society. In certain circles she was ironically referred to as
'Silence' because of her propensity to talk non-stop, and also as
'Queen Sarah', although she was neither arrogant nor vain, despite
being heiress to her grandfather's substantial fortune. Considered
by some to be affable and kind, and by others to be ill-bred, rude
and something of a tragedienne, Lady Jersey was, above all, strict in
maintaining the exclusivity of Almack's. In *Frederica*, her powerful
position as 'Queen of London's most exclusive club' was a source
of anger and humiliation to Lady Buxted, who needed a voucher
for her plain daughter Jane from the woman to whom she had
in earlier years been rude and condescending. A high-stickler,
Lady Jersey would admit only those known to dance well and was
rigorous in upholding the club's unbending rules, although it was
she who was credited with bringing from France a new dance, the
quadrille, to Almack's in 1815.

Lady Sefton was considered the kindest of the patronesses, with
an amiable disposition which made her rather more approachable

than the rest. She married the well-known dandy William Philip Molyneux, 2nd Earl of Sefton, and she and her husband became notable society hosts with a wide circle of friends among members of the aristocracy. The Seftons were very fond of house parties, balls, the theatre and the opera where they had a box which they kindly lent to friends and acquaintances (including Sherry and Hero of *Friday's Child*).

Mary Lamb became Lady Cowper when she married the fifth Earl Cowper in 1805. She was the daughter of the first Lord Melbourne and of Lady Melbourne, the great Whig hostess. Neither as powerful as Lady Jersey nor as exclusive, Lady Cowper was the most popular of the patronesses. She was admired for her wit, her tact and her affability. It was Lady Cowper who was most likely to smooth over quarrels among the patronesses or smile

Lady Castlereagh.

Countess Lieven.

approval on a new bride or debutante; in *Frederica*, though, the Marquis of Alverstoke was advised not to apply to Lady Cowper for vouchers for his wards on account of her deep distress over the death of her mother.

Heiress to the second Earl of Buckinghamshire, Lady Castlereagh was one of the most formidable of the Almack's patronesses. Born Lady Emily Anne Hobart she married Robert Stewart, Viscount Castlereagh, and quickly became known for her elegance and hauteur. She was not as powerful a patroness as Lady Jersey or Lady Cowper but to win her approval, as Jenny Chawleigh did in *A Civil Contract*, could ensure acceptance by the *ton*.

When Clementina Drummond married one of the minor dandies, Peter Robert Burrell, he appended his wife's surname to his own and she became Mrs Drummond-Burrell. As heiress to the great Drummond banking fortune, Clementina Drummond-Burrell was renowned for her haughtiness and for keeping her distance from all but the most socially acceptable. She was the most difficult of all the patronesses to please, with an icy demeanour that tended to thaw only in the company of other strait-laced women (such as Eugenia Wraxton of *The Grand Sophy*).

Countess Lieven was born Dorothea Christorovna Benckendorff in Riga and, at fifteen, married Lieutenant-General Count Christopher Andreievitch Lieven who became Russian Ambassador to the Court of St James. Countess Lieven was a determined woman, clever, haughty and arrogant, and she counted among her friends some of the great political leaders of the day including the Duke of Wellington, George Canning and Earl Grey. Sir Horace Stanton-Lacy in *The Grand Sophy* was a friend of the Countess, calling her the 'great *intriguante*' and flirting with her whenever he was in London. A strong sense of her own importance gave her a decided air of superiority and she was ruthless in excluding from the hallowed halls of Almack's any who did not meet her approval. It was Countess Lieven who introduced the waltz to Almack's, most probably in 1813.

Although she was a great-niece of George III's wife, Queen Charlotte, Princess Esterhazy's standing in London society came more from her husband's role as Austrian Ambassador to the Court of St James and her own powerful position as a patroness of Almack's than it did from her royal connections. A pretty woman, she was short and plump but with an animated personality, an occasional propensity for spite, a penchant for etiquette and a disdain of social climbers. It was Princess Esterhazy who angered Judith Taverner in *Regency Buck* with her mocking look and untimely laughter, and it was to the Princess that Mr Beaumaris applied for permission to ask Arabella to dance the waltz with him in *Arabella*.

The Best Circles

Often referred to as the Upper Ten Thousand, the *ton*, the *Beau Monde*, or Polite Society, those in the best circles lived a privileged and indulgent life. Birth and family were vital for social acceptance, although close connections and approval by those already in the upper echelons could pave the way for a few in society who were neither well-born nor well-heeled but whose wit or elegance set them apart. Most people in society came from the ranks of the landed aristocrats. Those of royal blood, members of the great houses, those of ancient lineage—with or without a title—and members of well-born families, could all take their place in the elite inner circle.

Society could be a ruthless arbiter of who was in and who was out, and its rules varied enormously depending on an erring individual's status, wealth and family connections. A double standard was usually applied wherever royalty or the upper echelons of the aristocracy were concerned. To have an illegitimate child or an adulterous relationship in the ranks of the gentry or the middle and lower classes was considered scandalous behaviour and usually resulted in the ostracism of the offender by both friends and family, as poor Ruth Wimborne discovered in *Friday's Child*. In the upper classes, however, such conduct, while giving rise to gossip and creating a degree of scandal, was frequently overlooked. The Prince Regent himself had numerous affairs, contracted an illegal marriage and treated his wife and daughter with rough disdain. His brother, the Duke of Clarence, was renowned for his ten illegitimate children but the FitzClarences, as they were known, were received everywhere, whereas illegitimacy below the rank of earl generally excluded an individual from the best circles. Lady Oxford, Lady Melbourne and the Duke and Duchess of Devonshire, among others of the nobility, all had affairs, produced illegitimate offspring or ran up huge gambling debts without serious consequence in terms of their social standing.

Individuals could find themselves excluded from the polite world, however, if their social position was not high enough to grant them immunity or if their conduct was deemed so scandalous as to put them beyond the social pale. Even women of the *ton* could find themselves ostracised if they cuckolded their husband by running off with another man—particularly if their lover was of a lower social standing. In *The Quiet Gentleman*, the first wife of the sixth Earl of St Erth had her name obliterated from the family records after she ran away with a well-known libertine. A man could be excluded from society for dishonourable behaviour such as failure to pay his gaming debts or other debts of honour, cheating at cards, attacking an unarmed opponent, improper conduct in a duel, or for running off with a married woman. The irrepressible Wilfred Steane in *Charity Girl* was forced to flee England when it was discovered he had been cheating at cards, and Sir Montagu Revesby in *Friday's Child* was threatened with public exposure after he stepped over the line. Bankruptcy, the loss of one's estates, criminal activities, murder and treason were all guaranteed to see a person permanently excluded from the *ton*.

Depending on the offence, people who committed certain social solecisms could find themselves gradually frozen out of society. Being refused the essential vouchers to Almack's, finding themselves without an invitation to particular events, or being the recipients of the 'cut direct' were sure signs of social transgression. The cut direct was generally used sparingly as it was a powerful weapon in the social armoury, always done in public and always after making eye contact with the person to be cut, at which point the person making the cut would slowly and deliberately turn his or her head away. Phoebe Marlow in *Sylvester* felt the effects of society's displeasure in this way, when she was suspected of having written a novel satirising several influential members of the *ton*. Excluding social transgressors by deliberately refusing to speak or associate with them was a socially devastating way of dealing with those who had crossed the social bounds. Beau Brummell was probably unique in maintaining his position in society even after receiving the cut direct from the Prince Regent. In the end it was Brummell's gambling debts and not the Regent's displeasure that forced him into exile in Calais.

RULES AND ETIQUETTE

Rules and etiquette were particularly prevalent among the upper classes with some kind of protocol laid down for every social situation. Very few of these rules were written down, however, and variations could apply depending on the circumstance. The most rigid protocol was applied at Almack's club under the beady eye of its patronesses. Attendees had to enter the rooms before eleven o'clock or be barred from the door. Formal evening dress was essential: the ladies in their most beautiful gowns and jewels and

Only those who had been approved by the patronesses and presented with a suitable partner could dance the waltz at Almack's.

the men in long tail-coats, white cravats, knee-breeches and stockings, and carrying a chapeau-bras. As Mrs Scattergood sternly told Perry in *Regency Buck*, under no circumstances were men to be admitted wearing ordinary breeches, trousers or pantaloons. Once the waltz was introduced into the clubrooms a young lady could only participate in it with the patronesses' approval and on their presenting her with a suitable partner.

In society there were a great many other rules and points of etiquette which were understood and generally observed. In addition to the more deep-seated social structures that dictated the mating game, the choice of spouse and the conduct of married couples, many of the rules governed the behaviour between men and women and between the various ranks in the social hierarchy.

- Social connections were usually formed through a series of meetings, usually beginning with morning calls to the homes of those in fashionable society.
- Morning calls were generally undertaken in the afternoon.
- A morning call did not usually exceed half an hour.
- In London, a woman paid morning calls to her social equals or inferiors but not to her social superiors until they had called on her or left a card.
- A person new to the city or country area waited for calls of ceremony to be made to them by those already established before they made a call of their own.
- In the country it was acceptable for a man to make a call or leave a card with someone of higher social standing if they were new to the neighbourhood.
- A gentleman calling on a family asked for the mistress of the house if the visit was a social one, and the master if it was a business call.
- A card was left if the lady of the house was indisposed or not at home. It was acceptable for a gentleman to call on a daughter

of the house if she were well above marriageable age or a long-standing friend.

- Callers were received by men in their business room or library, by women in the morning room or in their drawing-room.
- A lady, either married or single, did not call at a man's lodging.
- A lady was permitted to drive her own carriage, but only about the town attended by a groom, or by herself on the family estate.
- A lady never drove on the open road or engaged in any kind of public contest or race.
- It was acceptable to go out riding or driving with a man as long as a groom or other chaperone was in attendance.
- It was acceptable to go out driving or riding with a man without a chaperone if he was a relative or close family friend.
- A lady could ride a horse and even hunt as long as she was correctly attired and rode side-saddle.
- Galloping in Hyde Park was prohibited.
- During the season it was essential to be seen in Hyde Park during the promenade hour of 5.00 to 6.00 p.m.
- Servants and social inferiors were always kept at a proper distance but without arrogance, pride or aloofness.
- Servants were spoken to with exactly the right degree of civility and never with the casual informality with which a person would speak to an equal.
- Neither a lady nor a gentleman discussed private business in the presence of servants.
- Servants were generally ignored at mealtimes.
- It was essential to dress for dinner.
- When going in to dinner, the man of the house always escorted the highest-ranking lady present. The remaining dinner guests also paired up and entered the dining room in order of rank.
- Dinner guests were seated according to rank, with the highest-ranking lady sitting on the right-hand side of the host, who always sat at the head of the table.

- When dining informally it was acceptable to talk across or round the table.
- At a formal dinner one did not talk across the dinner table but confined conversation to those on one's left and right.
- Ladies were expected to retire to the withdrawing room after dinner, leaving the men to their port and their 'male' talk.
- A hostess should never give the signal to rise from the table until everyone at the table had finished.
- It was acceptable to offer one's snuff-box to the company but not to ask for a pinch of snuff from anyone else.
- Overt displays of emotion were generally considered ill-bred.
- Laughter was usually moderated in polite company, particularly among women.
- Men could give themselves up to unrestrained mirth, provided they were in the company of other men or among women of low repute.
- Well-bred persons controlled their features, their physical bodies and their speech when in company.
- A lady always spoke, sat and moved with elegance and propriety.
- A bow or curtsy was always made when meeting or speaking to royalty.
- Children always bowed or curtsied on meeting their parents for the first time each day.
- A bow or curtsy was executed according to the status and relationship of the person encountered and with regard to the particular circumstance.
- A bow was made on entering or leaving a room, at the beginning and end of a dance, and on encountering any person one wished to acknowledge.
- Debutantes did not stand up for more than two consecutive dances with the same partner.
- Only those young ladies who were 'out' danced the waltz and then only with an acceptable partner, usually someone she already knew, or to whom she had been formally introduced.

- Full mourning dress was worn for an appropriate period, which varied depending on the mourner's relationship to the deceased. A person did not go into society while in full mourning. Half mourning (usually grey or lilac) could be worn after an acceptable period of mourning had been observed and the mourner could choose to attend social functions but not fully participate in them.

Every well-born lady and gentleman also knew the unwritten rules and understood the social niceties that set them apart from the less 'cultured' masses. These were often the tiny details and nuances of socially acceptable behaviour that were instilled from an early age and which were often only discussed in private.

- To be thought 'fast' or to show a want of conduct was the worst possible social stigma.
- A lady never forced herself upon a man's notice.
- No lady was to be seen driving or walking down St James's Street where several of the gentlemen's clubs were located.
- No lady was to walk or drive unattended down Piccadilly.
- No female was to refer to any of those male activities about which a lady should feign ignorance.
- A husband was expected to keep his indecorous activities and less cultured friends separate from his marriage.
- A wife was expected to be blind to her husband's affairs.
- A married woman could take a lover once she had presented her husband with an heir and so long as she was discreet about her extramarital relationships.
- Women were expected to be ignorant of any proposed duel.
- A lady did not engage in any activity that might give rise to gossip.
- Subjects of an intimate nature such as childbirth were never discussed publicly.
- When out socially a lady did not wear a shawl for warmth no matter how cold the weather.

- A gentleman was expected to immediately pay his gambling debts, or any debt of honour.
- It was unacceptable to owe money to a stranger.
- It was acceptable to owe money to a tradesperson.
- It was considered bad form to borrow money from a woman.
- A female did not engage in finance or commerce if she had a man, such as a husband, father or brother, to do it for her.
- A lady did not visit a moneylender or a pawnbroker.
- Extremes of emotion and public outbursts were unacceptable, although it could be acceptable for a woman to have the vapours, faint, or suffer from hysteria if confronted by vulgarity or an unpleasant scene.
- A well-bred person behaved with courteous dignity to acquaintance and stranger alike, but kept at arm's length any who presumed too great a familiarity. Icy politeness was a well-bred man's or woman's best weapon in putting 'vulgar mushrooms' in their place.
- A well-bred person maintained an elegance of manner and deportment.
- A well-bred person walked upright, stood and moved with grace and ease.
- A well-bred person was never awkward in either manner or behaviour and could respond to any social situation with calm assurance.
- A well-bred person was never pretentious or ostentatious.
- Vulgarity was unacceptable in any form and was to be continually guarded against.
- Indiscretions, liaisons and outrageous behaviour were forgivable but vulgarity never was.

Scandal!

For many in the Regency, and particularly the upper classes, reputation was everything. Scandal was the means by which most errant individuals lost their social standing but it was also the life-blood of high society; the delight of both ladies and gentlemen who exchanged crim. con. stories on the dance floor, over a hand of cards or even at Almack's, as Meg did with her brother Freddy in *Cotillion*. Criminal conversation (crim. con.), a euphemism for adultery, was common practice among the *haut ton* during the Regency, and the Prince Regent and several of the royal Dukes were among the worst offenders. Their various affairs, monetary embarrassments, debaucheries and excessively hedonistic behaviour were frequently scandalous and the delight of many of the great caricaturists of the day. Satirical cartoons by Rowlandson, Cruikshank and Gillray would appear en masse in London print-shop windows, drawing huge crowds of appreciative onlookers. In 1785, while still the Prince of Wales, the Regent had married his mistress Mrs Fitzherbert. The marriage was illegal because, as a Catholic, Mrs Fitzherbert was ineligible to wed a future English monarch, and the Prince was not yet twenty-five and therefore in breach of the Royal Marriage Act. Yet they lived together for several years until the Prince's extravagance forced a change. In 1795, huge debts saw the Prince contract a hasty marriage to his cousin, Caroline of Brunswick, in return for the payment of his debts and a larger allowance from parliament. The couple separated soon after the wedding, but not before Caroline had conceived a daughter and heir to the throne, Charlotte. Never comfortable in his role as either husband or father, throughout the Regency the Prince behaved in a way that remained a constant source of scandal. His high-handed behaviour after his daughter had broken her engagement to the Prince of Orange was a source of eager gossip at Lord and Lady Lynton's first assembly in *A Civil Contract*. Ever self-indulgent, despite his many attributes, the Prince engaged in a series of affairs with older women, spent vast sums on cosmetics, clothes, food, wine and entertainment, and on pet projects such as Carlton House and the Brighton Pavilion.

Money was a constant problem for the royal Princes, most of whom spent lavishly and were continually in debt. The Regent's brother, the Duke of York, became embroiled in a huge monetary scandal when it was discovered that his mistress, Mary Anne Clarke, had been profiting from the illegal sale of military commissions and promotions. As Commander-in-Chief of the army the Duke signed off the lists of new commissions and it was alleged that his mistress could not have engaged in selling these without his cooperation. The Duke was forced to face a parliamentary inquiry and was eventually cleared of the charge but not before his love letters had been read out and reprinted in a series of best-selling scandal sheets which eventually forced him to resign from the army. Another brother, the Duke of Clarence, well known for his dalliances and in particular for his ten illegitimate children with his long-time mistress, the actress Mrs Jordan, sought relief from his debts by proposing to the very rich Miss Taverner in *Regency Buck*. Even more outrageous was the Duke of Cumberland's reputation—he was thought by some to have committed incest with his sister Sophia and to have murdered his valet.

Outside the royal family, society was constantly abuzz with the latest on-dits, discussing every sordid or delicious detail of the newest infidelity, elopement, illegitimate offspring, bankruptcy, social faux pas or other dishonourable act committed by a member of the *ton*. Whether society forgave or tolerated indiscretions mainly depended upon the birth and circumstances of the perpetrator. Society looked with disapproval on many of Lady Barbara Childe's escapades in *An Infamous Army* but her birth and her relationship with her grandfather, the Duke of Avon, saw her invariably accepted as a member of the *ton*. As long as the proprieties were met on the surface, what went on behind the scenes was often overlooked. Dalliances, affairs, mistresses and lovers could be acceptable as long as they were discreet; one could commit adultery, and it could be public knowledge, so long as the relationship was maintained in private and neither philanderer flaunted their affair in public. It was the very conspicuous and often hysterical manifestation of Lady Caroline Lamb's passionate obsession with Lord Byron that society deplored and which brought about her social downfall. Above all, high society disdained open displays of emotion and any form of vulgarity. By indulging her feelings for all to see and publishing a scandalous novel, *Glenarvon*, in which she satirised those in society whom she perceived to be her enemies, Caroline committed the ultimate social sin. One of the main characters in the book and the object of her desperate passion, Lord Byron, was himself the subject of several scandalous reports which engrossed and titillated society for several years. Having been society's darling after the publication of *Childe Harold* and *The Corsair* (although Judith Taverner in *Regency Buck* preferred the poetry to the poet!), Byron's rumoured incestuous relationship with his half-sister, Augusta Leigh, his treatment of his wife Annabella Milbanke, his bouts of extreme behaviour, his debts, and his eventual separation from his wife, led society to turn their backs on the once-adored poet and he left England in 1816, never to return. Many young Regency men, including Oswald Denny in *Venetia*, aspired to achieve the dark passion of Byron's *Corsair* by wearing their hair wildly ruffled, knotting a silk handkerchief around their necks and adopting a brooding, soulful look intended to arouse the romantic longings of any well-read or romantic female.

DANCING

Whether at a ball at Almack's or a masquerade at the Opera House or Covent Garden, a Vauxhall Gardens fête, a private party or a public assembly, dancing formed an important and integral part of Regency life. All classes of society engaged in the dance in both private and public venues and frequently in celebration of an important event such as a birthday, a coming-of-age or a marriage. Dancing was one of the few social activities in which men and women could participate together. For an upper-class debutante, balls and assemblies were one of the primary places to meet a potential husband and to demonstrate the grace, deportment, musicality and ability to master the intricate steps of the most popular dances of the day that were the characteristics of a 'proper' education. In *Cotillion*, for example, Lady Buckhaven prevailed upon her brother Freddy to teach their cousin Kitty the steps of the waltz and the quadrille in order to further her chances of making a good match.

During the Regency the four principal dances were the country-dance, the cotillion, the quadrille and, more commonly after Tsar Alexander had danced it at Almack's in 1814, the waltz. The English country-dance had been popular since the seventeenth century and allowed for a large number of dancers in each set. Men and women formed two lines, facing each other, with the couple at the top of the set being 'first'. As the dance progressed, the top couple would move one spot further down the line after each figure and eventually take their place at the bottom of the set, by which time the original last couple had become the first. The cotillion was a form of French *contredanse* which was itself a version of the English country-dance. Performed by eight dancers in a square formation, the cotillion was executed using a series of 'figures' and 'changes'. A regular cotillion consisted of ten changes with a figure performed between each change. The changes were generally the same within each cotillion, but the figures between them were different for each dance. Similar to the cotillion, the quadrille was introduced early in the Regency and consisted of five figures and no changes using the same square formation of eight dancers. When it was first introduced the quadrille proved difficult for many unwary dancers and so cards were produced with directions for the correct execution of the various figures and changes. Almack's provided dance cards for those less expert dancers but, although a useful device, it was also an unwieldy one when used during the actual dance. The steps of the quadrille were French and at some assemblies the master of ceremonies or the band leader would call out the figures to the dancers to make it easier for the less experienced members of a formation to perform the steps correctly. Executing steps such as the *chassé, jetté, coupe balote, glissade* or the *pas de basque* with elegance and grace required a high degree of skill. Marianne Bolderwood at her first ball in *The Quiet Gentleman* found that she had to concentrate carefully on the steps of the quadrille while her partner, Gervase, executed even the most difficult steps with considerable grace.

As the less difficult country-dances gradually made way for the cotillions and quadrilles, dancing masters or 'caper-merchants' were frequently employed to teach the steps and sequences in private homes, prior to the lady or gentleman attempting them in public. Some of the great ladies of the day, such as the Duchess of Devonshire, organised morning classes in their homes where several young women could learn the dances together. It was the Duchess's example that convinced Mrs Chartley, the rector's wife in *The Nonesuch*, to grant permission for her carefully brought up daughter Patience to participate in the planned morning dances at Staples where the young ladies would learn the waltz and practise the other fashionable dances. After its introduction at Almack's, the waltz had become generally popular by 1815 and was danced in most English ballrooms, despite the disapproval of some who held it to be too intimate and strenuous a dance for delicate debutantes. The enormous change from dances performed in sets to one danced by a mere couple, and in such close proximity to each other, meant that many young women only danced the waltz at private balls or at assemblies when they had been formally introduced to a 'suitable' partner.

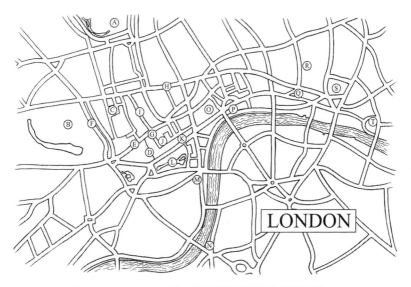

A: REGENTS PARK B: HYDE PARK C: GROSVENOR SQUARE D: GREEN PARK
E: PICCADILLY F: PARK LANE G: ST. JAMES'S STREET H: OXFORD STREET I: BOND STREET J: ALMACK'S
K: CARLTON HOUSE L: ST JAMES'S PARK M: WESTMINSTER ABBEY N: VAUXHALL GARDENS
O: COVENT GARDEN / DRURY LANE P: SOMERSET HOUSE Q: St. PAUL'S CATHEDRAL
R: GUILDHALL S: STOCK EXCHANGE T: TOWER OF LONDON.

THE THEATRE

The theatre was enormously popular during the Regency and
most large towns had at least one playhouse. In London, the two
great theatres of the period were Covent Garden and the Theatre
Royal, Drury Lane, both of which held a monopoly on the
production of straight plays as a result of a royal patent granted by
Charles II in 1660. Most theatres only opened for six months of
the year and, apart from Drury Lane and Covent Garden, were
restricted by their licences to presenting pantomimes, musicals
and farces. This did not prevent them from drawing large crowds,
however, and the attraction of continually changing programmes
and new and enticing 'spectaculars' saw as many as twenty thousand people attending the various theatres each night during
the Season. Tickets for the pit at the Haymarket theatre sold

for 10s. 6d. while a hired box could cost as much as £2,500 for the Season. Members of the upper class frequently rented a box, to which they could invite friends or family, promote a suitable match for a son or daughter, or simply take the opportunity to show off their jewels and other costly attire while enjoying an evening's entertainment.

Theatre-going was remarkably informal and it was perfectly acceptable to arrive part of the way through a performance, to talk loudly throughout or to leave at any point as Edward Yardley's evening party chose to do in *Venetia* after Mrs Hendred was distressed by unexpected events. The pit was a favourite venue among the dandy set as a place to meet with friends, converse, show off the latest fashion, take snuff and ogle the ladies, both on stage and in the audience. It was quite normal for members of the audience to express loudly their disapproval of any aspect of a performance and they would call out, stamp their feet or throw things at the actors if they were unhappy. Opera was very popular during the Regency—although Bertram Tallant in *Arabella* confessed that he wanted to go to a night at the opera not for the music but for the fun of strolling in Fops' Alley. One of the most notable evenings at the opera was 11 June 1814 when the Prince Regent, Tsar Alexander, his sister the Grand Duchess Catherine of Oldenburg, and King Frederick of Prussia attended Covent Garden theatre as part of the Peace Celebrations. The defiant arrival of the Regent's estranged wife, Princess Caroline, during the singing of 'God Save the King' was especially satisfying to the many lovers of real drama present in the theatre and was the highlight of the evening for Lydia Deveril of *A Civil Contract*, who was at the theatre that night attending her first public function as a debutante. Both Covent Garden and Drury Lane staged operas and ballets, though less often than the more traditional theatre programme, which usually consisted of a straight drama followed by a farce. Evenings at the theatre could take as long as five hours and often did not end before midnight.

The farce was generally the most popular part of the evening and so compelled patrons to stay to the end.

Many of the great names of the theatre performed for Regency audiences. Mrs Siddons came out of retirement to perform briefly in 1812, her brothers Charles and John Kemble were major theatrical figures and the brilliant, but difficult, Edmund Kean became a huge hit after his London debut at Drury Lane in 1814 where he appeared as Shylock. He was probably most famous for his Hamlet, a performance to which Freddy Standen of *Cotillion* had once escorted his mother and which had Lydia Deveril in *A Civil Contract* in raptures. The great clown Grimaldi, whose costume, make-up and comic style created a tradition (and whose performance was fondly remembered by the Duke of Sale in *The Foundling*); the 'bewitching debutante' Vestris with her 'divine legs', her wit and her singing; and the opera singers Catalani and Naldi, all drew huge crowds and the favours and attention of the nobility.

IN THE PARKS

Hyde Park was a favourite destination for people from every walk of life during the Regency. Beginning at the western end of Piccadilly, with three hundred and fifty acres of green lawns, groves of shady trees, meandering pathways and the Serpentine river, it was a delightful place to promenade and play. For the men and women of the *ton* it was *the* place to be seen during the Season between the hours of 5.00 and 6.00 in the afternoon. Ladies often walked with a friend or female companion, wearing the latest style of walking costume or promenade dress and their most fetching hat or bonnet, all the while hoping to catch the eye of some eligible bachelor. The dandies loved to promenade or 'go on the strut', ogling the ladies and observing other bucks and beaus to ensure that they too were wearing the very latest in fashionable attire. This was the place for lovers to meet and for those of the *demi-monde*—fair Cyprians and richly dressed courtesans—to make assignations with interested gentlemen. Hyde Park was the great crossroads at which all classes of Regency society arrived and jostled, admired, ignored, mimicked, mocked and avoided each other.

Hyde Park was originally the site of the ancient manor house of Hyde, owned by the monastery of St Peter's, Westminster, but which was taken over by Henry VIII in 1536. At the end of the seventeenth century, when King William III moved his court to nearby Kensington Palace, he regularly had to make his way through Hyde Park from the Palace to St James's. Finding it to be dark and dangerous, the King ordered the way to be lit. Three hundred oil lamps lined the highway which was known for a time as the '*Route de Roi*' (Way of the King) but which eventually came to be known more familiarly as 'Rotten Row'. Just inside the perimeter of Hyde Park, Rotten Row was a broad roadway that ringed the entire park and on which visitors were able to walk, ride a horse or drive a carriage. During the Regency, riding and driving were the exclusive domain of the upper classes and those with the means to aspire to membership in it. Young Lady Cardross in *April Lady* could often be seen driving around Rotten Row in the stylish barouche drawn by a pair of perfectly matched greys and given to her by her husband on the occasion of their marriage. Only those who could afford to wear the correct attire and keep a horse in London (with all the attendant expenses) or hire a hack from one of the large commercial stables could afford to ride in Rotten Row. People from every section of society would throng to Hyde Park during the hour of the promenade to watch the well-heeled of society dash past on a magnificent thoroughbred or showy hack or drive by in a high-perch phaeton, a stylish barouche or a smart sporting curricle.

*It was considered the height of fashion to be seen riding in Rotten Row,
and men and women often agreed to meet there and ride together.*

The Prince Regent was a regular visitor to the park. A keen
rider throughout his life, his growing corpulence saw him less
on horseback and more frequently tooling a phaeton, tilbury or
curricle drawn by one or more pairs of beautiful high-stepping
horses. The Prince was well known as a skilful whip and had been
acknowledged since his youth as a top sawyer and for his ability to
drive a carriage-and-six (a feat matched by few men of the day).
Men and women frequently rode together on Rotten Row, the
women riding side-saddle and wearing the latest thing in elegant
riding habits, and the men in leather breeches, top-boots, a well-cut
coat and the compulsory starched neckcloth. Moving at a sedate
walk, a stylish trot or a graceful canter (galloping was forbidden),
riders wended their way between the many carriages, pedestrians
and onlookers that crowded the Row during the promenade hour,
bowing to acquaintances, stopping to talk to friends or comparing
notes on the horses and owners that surrounded them. In *The
Grand Sophy*, Sophy Stanton–Lacy attracted great admiration when

riding her beautiful horse Salamanca in Hyde Park although she was chided for galloping there.

Situated twelve miles from St Paul's Cathedral, Richmond Park was a favourite destination for Londoners eager for a day away from the city. The perfect distance from London for keen riders, and ideal for a gentleman wishing to take a lady out in his carriage, Richmond offered a beautiful sylvan setting for walks, rides and picnics. Rolling hills, grassy slopes, woodland gardens, groves of ancient trees and herds of red and fallow deer made it an enticing spot for visitors, and the varied landscape was especially tempting to those energetic riders and accomplished equestriennes, such as Phoebe Marlow in *Sylvester*, who, after the constraints of Rotten Row, yearned for a gallop across the two and a half thousand acres of this largest royal park.

The Peace celebrations were a grand affair enjoyed by thousands.

During the Regency visitors to London's parks witnessed several grand spectacles including military reviews, parades and grand celebrations. The Prince Regent had a great love of ceremony and spectacle and throughout his Regency there were many opportunities for the people to read about or see some of the splendid celebrations devised by or for the pleasure-loving Prince. Perhaps the most memorable series of spectacles staged during the Regency was the Visit of the Allied Sovereigns and the grand jubilee celebrations held between June and August 1814, which excited the interest of Lady Lynton and her guests in *A Civil Contract*. Napoleon had accepted defeat, abdicated and gone into exile on Elba that year, the Peace had been declared and the sovereigns were meeting in London to mark the occasion. In addition to a lavish programme of banquets, balls, parades and gala nights at the theatre, the Regent ordered a series of extravagant celebrations in London's three main parks. This public celebration of the Peace which Jenny, Lady Lynton, was so keen to see, began on 1 August 1814, and lasted for nearly two weeks, ending on the Regent's birthday on 12 August. As Jenny's husband, Adam, had predicted, huge crowds filled the parks, and traditional Bartholomew Fair booths and refreshment stands were set up all around the perimeter, with many alehouses also erecting tents. The highlight of the celebrations was the Grand Spectacle commencing in Hyde Park just before 6.00 p.m. with a manned balloon ascent and a naumachia, or naval battle, on the Serpentine. Purpose-built small-scale ships with both men and guns aboard fought each other in a re-enactment of Nelson's great victory at the famous Battle of Trafalgar. In St James's Park a Chinese bridge and seven-storey pagoda had been built over the canal and at dusk this was lit with a mass of lanterns to the great delight of the crowd. In Green Park a hundred-foot-high fortress had been built to represent the 'Castle of Discord' and at a given signal a huge fireworks display, organised by the famous scientist William Congreve (inventor of the Congreve rocket), was set off from the fortress, while on the Serpentine the enemy ships were set alight, and in St James's Park rockets were shot from the top of the Chinese pagoda. As the fireworks ended a wondrous transformation took place as the Castle of Discord was engulfed in smoke to be revealed as a magnificently illuminated Temple of Concord. This symbol of peace marked the end of the evening's events but at midnight the pagoda caught fire and crashed to the ground, to the delight of many in the crowd who thought it was part of the celebrations. For days after the grand display, revellers lingered in Hyde Park, enjoying the refreshment booths and all the attractions of the fair which had sprung up, but drunkenness and debauchery quickly took hold and on 6 August the Secretary of State, Lord Sidmouth, ordered the crowd dispersed and the parks closed.

Balloon ascensions were another popular spectacle which drew wondering crowds to London's parks during the Regency. The first manned balloon ascension in Great Britain took place in Edinburgh in August 1784 when Mr Tyler travelled half a mile before landing. The first ascent in England was achieved a month later, by the Italian, Vincent Lunardi, whose thirty-three-foot-wide, pear-shaped balloon was made of oiled silk and had no valve. Painted red and blue and covered with a rope net, from which hung long cords for attaching the basket, the balloon was filled through the neck with hydrogen gas made from a mixture of zinc and diluted sulphuric acid. Lunardi took a dog, a cat and a pigeon on his first voyage and, after unloading some sand ballast, rose to a great height before landing in South Mimms to unload the near-frozen cat. In 1785, Mrs Sage accompanied Lunardi on a flight and became the first Englishwoman to ascend in a balloon. By the time of the Regency, however, balloon ascensions had become a popular sight and aeronauts would take off from Hyde Park or other London parks in front of huge crowds. Despite the popularity of balloon ascensions they were often extremely dangerous undertakings—as young Felix Merriville and his family discovered in *Frederica*. Flying at the mercy of the wind and weather a balloon could tear, capsize or be blown out to sea. Fire was always a risk and gas explosions a real possibility if an overfilled balloon rose too high, and it was the freezing temperatures of high altitude that made Felix's hands so cold that he was unable to stop himself from falling after the balloon he was travelling in landed in a tree.

6

The Pleasure Haunts of London

CARLTON HOUSE

Acquired by the Prince of Wales on his coming of age in 1783, Carlton House was a small but exquisitely beautiful palace situated

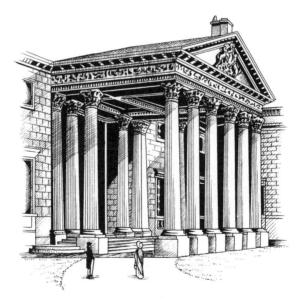

Carlton House was the Regent's private palace and the scene of many grand dinners and private bachelor parties.

at the eastern end of Pall Mall. For many years it remained the Regent's principal residence in London, where he played host to so many of his close friends and intimates that they became known as the 'Carlton House set'. The Earl of Worth in *Regency Buck* was a member of the Regent's set as was the irrepressible Bardy Lynton in *A Civil Contract*. The Regent was famous for his parties and private dinners with their extravagant meals and opulent decorations. Arabella Tallant, the heroine of *Arabella,* attended a dress party at Carlton House and was dazzled by the magnificent rooms and elegant decorations although she was less impressed by the extraordinary vaulted glass-and-cast-iron conservatory to which Mr Beaumaris kindly escorted her. After the French Revolution the Prince had acquired many superb pieces of French royal furniture and priceless artworks including ornaments, paintings, clocks and candelabra, and during his Regency he spared no expense in decorating and redecorating Carlton House to create the opulent interior that so impressed Jenny Chawleigh in *A Civil Contract* when she attended the Regent's famous fête held in honour of the Duke of Wellington in 1814. Although some among the *ton* felt that Prinny's whims were often vulgar—as when he played host at a sit-down dinner for two thousand in 1811 and the main table had a stream flowing down its centre (complete with bridges, mossy banks and live goldfish)—most agreed that Carlton House with its magnificent chandeliers, draperies, furniture, elegant staircase, statuary and crimson, gold and blue interior was one of the most exquisite palaces in Europe.

CLUBS, PUBS AND PLEASURE

The pursuit of pleasure was undoubtedly encouraged by the club culture of Regency London. Most upper-class men belonged to one or more of the exclusive gentlemen's clubs established in the

Lord and Lady Lynton in A Civil Contract *attended a magnificent fête at Carlton House and Jenny thought it exquisitely beautiful.*

previous century with Watier's (also known as 'the Great-Go'), White's, Boodle's and Brooks's the most famous of them all. Membership was gained by nomination and ballot, with birth and family connections the most important prerequisites for admission. In the early part of the Regency (prior to his being forced to go abroad in 1816 because of gambling debts), George 'Beau' Brummell had the power to determine whether a man was accepted as a member at Watier's or excluded—as was Sir Montagu Revesby in *Friday's Child*—via the 'blackball' system. Brooks's and White's were the most political of the clubs with Brooks's being well known as a Whig stronghold whereas during the Regency White's had a definite Tory leaning. White's was also famous for its bow-window in which the dandies, led by Brummell, were wont to sit and ogle passers-by.

Situated on or around the exclusive male precinct of St James's Street, the clubs were the first point of refuge for the Regency man who wished to escape, as Lord Ombersley often did in *The Grand Sophy*, from the exigencies of domestic life and the company of women. They were popular venues, with gambling very much to the fore and bets of any kind—no matter how frivolous or outrageous—engaged in and often recorded in White's famous betting book as Mr Liversedge pointed out to Captain Ware in *The Foundling* when offering him a most unusual wager. Card and dice games were a favourite form of gambling: faro, Macao, whist and hazard were all played for high stakes with many fortunes won or lost on the turn of a card or the roll of the dice. But the clubs were also a meeting place for those who wished to discuss business, politics, the latest sporting news or hear the most recent information from the Continent—it was in the clubs on St James's Street that many men first heard the news of Wellington's victory at Waterloo—and they were the place to form important business and social connections.

White's club (37 St James's Street) was established in 1697 and remains the oldest club in London. Originally opened by Francis White in 1693 as White's Chocolate House, it occupied several locations in St James's Street, including the site of what is now Boodle's. From its inception, White's attracted the cream of England's upper class although neither wit, wealth nor birth guaranteed one's election to the club. Members were elected by ballot in which at least twelve clubmen had to participate by dropping either a white ball, signifying approval, or a black ball to indicate exclusion. A single black ball was all it took to deny a man admission to the club. White's flourished during the Regency and was renowned as the 'home of the dandies' with a dandy set led by Beau Brummell, elected a member in 1789. White's was also, for a time, a Tory stronghold—although men of both parties continued as members—but after 1832 it became apolitical. As Peregrine Taverner in *Regency Buck* was aware, membership

Beau Brummell was one of the most famous members of White's club where he made the bow-window his particular preserve.

of White's bestowed a certain distinction on a man and was an honour coveted by many among the upper class which made it a great relief when his guardian, the Earl of Worth, agreed to have him made a member.

Established in 1762, Boodle's (28 St James's Street) had originally been started as a club at 50 Pall Mall by William Almack, the founder of Almack's. Originally known as the 'Savoir Vivre' it was eventually named after the manager Edward Boodle. In later years Boodle's moved into a fine Adam-style building in St James's Street on the original site of White's club. Although it was a political club at its inception, Boodle's shed its political inclinations early on and its members were content to gamble, partake of fine food, sit in the bow-window and enjoy the club's calm and uneventful environment. Boodle's was one of the clubs to which Lord Lionel Ware went to hear the gossip about his son and nephew in *The Foundling*.

Established in 1764, just two years after Boodle's, Brooks's (60 St James's Street) was another of William Almack's early clubs and was located for a time at 49 Pall Mall, next to the original Boodle's site. Initially, it was a club inside a tavern until the members agreed to employ William Brooks to manage it and the club soon took on his name. Like White's, Brooks's was well known for its high-stakes gambling and during the Regency many fortunes exchanged hands at the tables in Brooks's Great Subscription Room. Originally a young man's club, and a meeting place for men of no particular political persuasion, by the end of the eighteenth century Brooks's had become a noted Whig stronghold with the great orator and hedonist, Charles James Fox, as its leader. Fox's death in 1806 did nothing to diminish the club's Whiggish bent and many of the club's noble members sat on the Opposition benches in the House of Lords although some, such as Adam Deveril of *A Civil Contract*, had Tory leanings but remained members of Brooks's out of respect for their family tradition.

Watier's (81 Piccadilly) appears to have been established originally as a venue for harmonic meetings but, in 1807, the Prince of Wales invited his chef Watier to start a club which would provide a cuisine superior to the more mundane fare offered at White's or Brooks's. Watier took over the rooms at 81 Piccadilly and offered such magnificent food that the club quickly became the talk of the town, drawing to it all the well-born young bucks and bloods of the day who initiated the high play and wild gambling for which Watier's soon became notorious. Known as the 'Great-Go' and called by Byron 'the Dandy Club', Watier's attracted members who were mostly men of fashion addicted to gaming and ready to throw a fortune away on a brief moment of chance. In *April Lady*, Watier's was a favourite haunt of Nell Cardross's pleasure-loving brother, Dysart, who enjoyed the fine dinners and high play. Beau

Brummell was designated the club's perpetual president until 1816 when his debts forced him into exile in France, and by 1819 most of the club's leading members had sustained such enormous gambling losses that Watier's closed its doors for ever.

The clubs made it easy for any well-bred man—whether married or single—to spend time away from home, and wives, sisters, mothers and daughters frequently accepted men's need to escape from their female relatives from time to time. It was tacitly understood by many women that, in order to retain any respect for their menfolk, it was essential either to feign ignorance or to refrain from discovering exactly what men did do when they had escaped. Alcohol was an accepted part of Regency life and all classes imbibed huge quantities of wine, spirits and ale, the latter often drunk at breakfast. Among the upper class Madeira, sherry and brandy were the drinks of preference throughout the day and into the evening, while port was generally reserved as an after-dinner drink. Sir Richard Wyndham in *The Corinthian* imbibed a large enough quantity of brandy to become quite drunk the night before his planned proposal to the aristocratic Melissa Brandon, and on leaving the club felt compelled to go for a long walk to clear his head. Drunkenness was common, particularly among young men for whom it was deemed an acceptable condition. Enthusiastic youths bent on having fun, and possibly in London for the first time, could think of no occupation more desirable than to throw off a third of daffy (gin) at Limmer's Hotel in the company of the fancy, or to drink beer while mixing with the sporting set at Cribb's Parlour. To engage in a revel-rout or wine party and spend the night carousing, engaging in pranks (such as boxing the watch) and finishing the night in the watch-house was, for some, the height of ambition.

Other less salubrious venues popular with men during the Regency were the Daffy Club (a pugilistic setting), the Cock-pit Royal in Birdcage Walk, the Royal Saloon in Piccadilly, the Peerless Pool, and the Westminster Pit where men of all classes gathered to watch dog-fights. Boxing enthusiasts such as Sir Waldo Hawkridge in *The Nonesuch* or the Marquis of Alverstoke in *Frederica* could take themselves off to Gentleman John Jackson's Boxing Saloon at 13 Bond Street where athletic men of fashion (known as Corinthians) could take lessons from the great man himself. Devotees of pugilism generally revered Jackson and eagerly attended his sparring matches at the Fives Court in London or the illicit bouts between the pets of the fancy which were usually set up within a couple of hours' drive of the city.

Even those entertainments which men and women could enjoy together, such as the theatre, music and the opera, had an exclusively masculine side to them. Strolling in Fops' Alley (the walkway between the pit and the stalls) at the opera, or lingering to admire the prostitutes known as Cyprians in the saloon at Covent Garden, was considered famous sport, while flirting with opera dancers or ogling the ladies in the audience were activities to which a man's female companions were expected to turn a blind eye as Hero quickly learned in *Friday's Child*. In addition to the theatre, concerts, opera, soirées, balls, parties and assemblies which were the usual evening activities for the *ton*, Regency men would often seek out the grog shops and brothels of Tothill Fields where they could drink quantities of cheaply distilled spirits and become blind drunk for just a few pence, or have their way with a prostitute for not much more. All the pleasures of the flesh were available to a man with money, and the elasticity of upper-class morality during the Regency meant that there was little that he could not do. For some, however—such as the Honourable Beverley Brandon in *The Corinthian*—years of debauched and dissipated living left them both financially and morally bankrupt.

THE BOW-WINDOW SET

So famous was the bow-window at White's club that Sophy Stanton-Lacy in *The Grand Sophy* dared to drive down the exclusive male precinct of St James's Street in her high-perch phaeton in the hopes of seeing it. The bow-window came into existence in the first year of the Regency. For the club, 1811 was a year of change with the entrance fee doubled from ten to twenty guineas and subscriptions raised to eleven guineas. It was at this time, too, that the original front entrance was moved from the centre of the front façade to its present position nearer to the southern end of the building, with a new entrance created by converting the second window into a door. Where the old entrance had stood, a bow-window was built above the original steps into the club and this and the old entrance hall together served to enlarge the morning room. A new Master of the House, in the person of the efficient Mr Raggett, took over in 1812 and it was at about this time that George Bryan 'Beau' Brummell made the window his domain. In company with three of the noted dandies of the day, Lord Alvanley, Sir Henry Mildmay and Henry Pierrepoint, he would sit in the window where, as the leader of the 'Unique Four', he would freely discuss those passing by. The Earl of Worth, hero of *Regency Buck*, belonged to Brummell's set and was one of those who famously adhered to the Beau's rule that no one sitting in the bow-window should ever acknowledge a greeting from the street. So great was Brummell's influence that no ordinary member of White's would ever have dared to sit in the Holy of Holies!

Vauxhall Gardens

First opened as the 'New Spring Gardens' in 1660 on a twelve-acre site near Lambeth on the south side of the Thames, Vauxhall Gardens was originally a landscaped public garden with an orchard, long walks, arbours and hedges. Referred to by the great diarist Samuel Pepys as 'Fox Hall', the site had originally been that of a house built in the reign of King John known as Vauke's

Hall—hence Vauxhall. In 1728, Jonathan Tyers leased the old Spring Garden and completely redesigned the site, establishing tree-lined promenades and putting in gravel paths, fountains, artificial ruins, illuminated transparencies, statues, platforms for musicians, and lighting the whole with a thousand lanterns. A pavilion, a rotunda and supper-boxes provided places to sit and eat, to dance, watch the passers-by or listen to the orchestra.

Visitors could reach Vauxhall either by crossing the Thames in a boat and passing through the water entrance, as Mr Beaumaris's guests did in *Arabella*, or by way of Westminster Bridge and Kennington Road and there to the lane that gave access to the land entrance. The gardens were enormously popular and open to all classes of society, but between April and June they became the particular pleasure haunt of the upper class. It cost three shillings to enter Vauxhall where visitors could marvel at the many thousands of lamps illuminating the gardens, hanging in festoons from the trees and between the cast-iron pillars of the vaulted colonnade. They could wander the walkways, watch the fireworks or the mechanical Cascade which so delighted Arabella, dance, or even sing along with one of the bands placed around the gardens. Pandean minstrels entertained the guests and an orchestra gave a two-part concert in the rotunda each evening at eight o'clock. Masquerades, *ridottos*, performances by famous singers and gala nights continued at Vauxhall throughout the Regency. It was a favourite haunt of the Prince Regent and in 1813 he was host at a grand fête to celebrate the Battle of Vittoria. The gala event drew such vast numbers that many of them did not get into the gardens at all due to the press of people and carriages outside. In 1814 a naumachia or sea-battle enactment was presented in the gardens and, in 1816, the famous Parisienne acrobat Madame Saqui, adorned with spangles and feathers, enthralled her audience with her rope dancing and tightrope walking. Vauxhall was also famous for its wafer-thin slices of ham and its intoxicating arrack-punch which could be bought for eight shillings a quart but which was notoriously potent. In *Friday's Child* Lord Sheringham took his new bride to Vauxhall for the evening soon after their wedding, and the young couple thoroughly enjoyed the dancing, fireworks and the famous supper. More than a hundred supper-boxes were available for hire, many of them still decorated with eighteenth-century paintings by William Hogarth and Francis Hayman, and each holding six or eight guests. Waiters attended the boxes and guests could order chicken or ham, mix their own salads, sip on burnt-wine or blend their own brew of arrack-punch. The Regency witnessed the last great phase of Vauxhall's popularity and the gardens eventually closed in 1859.

Vauxhall Gardens was the place to see and be seen during the Regency.

Ladies of the Night, Brothels and Gambling Hells

As in every age, prostitution was rife during the Regency. From the high-class courtesan to the streetwalker, women were available to satisfy the lusts of even the most amorous, debauched or hedonistic man. Although they could be found across the city, one of the best-known areas for prostitutes was that comprising the streets and lanes around Covent Garden, also known as the 'stews'. Here, certain inns and taverns were notorious for their sexual offerings and were known to be visited by fashionable women as well as men. The theatres, too, were popular with the Cyprians who could be seen parading their wares in the foyers and the green rooms of Covent Garden and Drury Lane. A box at the Royal Opera House was a favoured venue for those courtesans wanting to display their attributes or throw out a lure to a possible paramour. In *Friday's Child*, the incorrigible Lord Sheringham took his wife to a Covent Garden masquerade where he enjoyed pursuing a masked female or 'bit of muslin' who he was sure was an old paramour known as Flyaway Nancy. For those among the 'Fashionable Impures' who won the favour of an affluent gentleman it meant a life of wealth, luxury and indulgence for as long as they held his favour. To win carte blanche from a lover was the ultimate aim but the harsh reality for many of the women and girls selling themselves on the street was that it was about survival more than luxury or comfort.

Brothels operated across the city and some former courtesans went into business for themselves, running high-class bordellos in elegantly decorated houses and using their wiles, or even a little blackmail, to draw former lovers to their rooms. In *Black Sheep*, Miles Calverleigh sought out an old acquaintance who had risen from the ranks of the Cyprians to become the proprietor of a high-class brothel. Dolly (once known as 'the Dasher'), having been funded by a rich lover, drove a stylish barouche in Hyde Park and carried herself like one of the aristocracy—although she was always willing to oblige an old friend. One of the most famous brothels of the Regency was the White House in Soho Square, formerly an aristocratic mansion before its conversion into a house of ill-repute. It was a large, square building of many rooms, each of which was individually decorated and named according to its style, including the Grotto, the Coal Hole, the Skeleton Room, the Painted Chamber and the Gold, Silver and Bronze Rooms. The house was splendidly decorated with mirrors embedded in the walls and an array of accessories—both mechanical and manual— to gratify the most lascivious visitor. Elegant brothels existed throughout Mayfair and the West End, often standing cheek by jowl with the homes of London's most respectable citizens. Many brothels, though, were simply squalid rooms where pimps and procuresses sold the services of those enslaved to them, and every kind of sexual desire could be gratified for a price.

The other great temptation for men and women drawn to the seamier side of Regency life were the gambling hells. These were often run as 'clubs' and were open to anyone with money to bet on the roll of the dice or the turn of a card. They were especially popular with those gentlemen refused admittance to the more reputable clubs of St James's such as White's, Brooks's and Boodle's, and many of the hells were set up in the St James's and Pall Mall area. By 1820 more than two dozen gambling hells were operating in this part of London with houses in Jermyn, King, Bury and Bennett Streets as well as at 4 Pickering Place (Peregrine Taverner in *Regency Buck* gambled at a hell at number 5), 12 Park Place, 3 Cleveland Row and at numbers 6, 32, 55, 58 and 71 Pall Mall among the best-known. The gambling hell in Bennett Street was also known as 'the Dandy House' and was popular among officers of the Guards and the fashionable men of the day who enjoyed the elegant suppers and high play. The stakes in most hells usually ranged from 5s. to £100, but almost any amount could be covered if a player was confident, or desperate, enough. Many of the hells were notorious for drawing in young, inexperienced players and letting them win before turning the luck in favour of the bank, by which time the gambler was usually caught up by the excitement of winning or, later, the need to recover from his losses. Bertram Tallant in *Arabella* was delighted by the amazing run of luck which he enjoyed on his first night at a 'discreet house in Pall Mall' and felt sure his friend Felix Scunthorpe's dire warnings about sharps and loaded dice had been quite wrong. The elegant surroundings of the gambling hells of St James's and Pall Mall were often a cover for the ruthless play and unfair practices of the houses, which were frequented not only by the rich and fashionable, the clergy and the nobility, but also by cheats and swindlers known as 'black-legs', 'Captain Sharps' or 'ivory-turners'.

Ivory-turners were so-called because of their ability to make the dice (ivories) 'turn' to the numbers they needed to win the game. Dice cheats generally used loaded or 'cogged' dice—known during the Regency as 'fulhams' from the town of Fulham where they were originally made (it also sounded appropriately like 'fool 'em'). Loaded dice were specially made to roll in favour of particular numbers, with those rolling towards the high numbers known as 'uphills' and those rolling to the lower numbers called 'downhills'. Some false dice had only three numbers instead of the usual six, with two sides each with four, five and six pips. These were known as 'dispatchers' for their ability to dispatch a man's money from his pocket with great efficiency. Gambling cheats were known also as sharks, sharps and sometimes as 'Greeks', but the beautiful Olivia Broughty in *Cotillion* assured Kitty Charing that in the best gaming houses Greeking methods were only used as a last resort and loaded dice never! Card-sharps usually cheated by changing the pack (known as fuzzing the cards), marking cards or hiding winning cards or hands up their sleeves or on their person. Sharps and ivory-turners mostly operated in the gambling dens and hells around Pall Mall and St James's, although they sometimes arranged private games with unsuspecting or gullible men (known as 'flats') whose trusting and naive demeanour made them easy to dupe.

CONVIVIAL EVENINGS

For those sports enthusiasts in pursuit of an evening of merriment, sporting conversation and serious drinking, there was no better place to be than the Daffy Club at the Castle Tavern, Holborn. Owned by Tom Belcher, himself a respected pugilist and brother of the great boxer Jem Belcher, the Castle Tavern was the ideal venue for the sporting man. Here he could rub shoulders with the champions, take a glass of daffy with the patrons of the sport or try and get the inside running on a likely contender in a forthcoming match. Ferdy Fakenham in *Friday's Child* was an enthusiastic patron of the Daffy Club and enjoyed getting drunk there. Belcher became landlord in 1814 and under his patronage the well-known boxing aficionado, referee and stakeholder, James Soares, set up the Daffy Club with the support of the Regency journalist and writer, Pierce Egan. Those admitted to the club met in a long room, decorated with pictures of famous fighters and other sporting subjects, and sat at a long table known as the 'ring'. Every kind of sport was discussed by the 'Daffies' and although there were no written rules or formal meetings, high spirits were essential and drinking was the order of the day. The best time to go to the Daffy Club was the night before a big fight when Tom Belcher played host to a great party of enthusiasts and many famous retired fighters could be seen. This was the place to get the whisper on where the next day's match was to be held and to get a look at the contenders. Every aspect of the match would be discussed, bets laid, odds shortened or lengthened and arrangements made for transport to the bout.

A great many boxers became innkeepers after their retirement, setting up 'sporting houses' throughout London and its environs, but the most famous of them all was Tom Cribb, the Champion of England in 1809, and renowned for his stunning defeats of the great American boxer, Tom Molyneux, in 1810 and 1811. Cribb's first tavern was the Golden Lion in the Borough, but he soon moved to the King's Arms on the corner of King and Duke Streets, St James's. Here he established 'Cribb's Parlour', a congenial gathering place for pugilists and the fancy alike, in which they could talk, smoke, drink and admire the Champion's magnificent silver cup. Only those approved by the great Cribb himself could gain admittance to the Parlour and it was the aspiration of many a sporting buck to win the Champion's approval. It was to Cribb's Parlour that Charles Rivenhall was going when he met his sister Cecilia in *The Grand Sophy* and she teased him about what he would do there. Another popular destination with sporting young men, pets of the fancy and their noble patrons was Limmer's Hotel on the corner of Conduit Street in Hanover Square. This was a more fashionable venue than either Cribb's Parlour or the Castle Tavern and the hotel's famous coffee-room still retained something of the atmosphere of the eighteenth-century coffee-house. It was at Limmer's that Bertram Tallant went with his friend Mr Scunthorpe to meet and mingle with the Corinthians and the pets of the fancy, and where he met Mr Beaumaris and found himself telling the Nonpareil about his experiences and ambitions. Limmer's was the place for pugilistic patrons and their stakeholders to meet, plan fights and discuss and organise the workings of the Fives Court. Here the names of promising young novices were put forward with requests for training by a retired champion or boxer of renown, and bets were laid on the likely outcome of a bout between an experienced pugilist and an up-and-coming challenger with little experience but plenty of 'bottom'.

Another evening pleasure haunt favoured by the *ton* was the Royal Saloon located in Piccadilly. With its Turkish-style exterior and famous suppers of lobster and *bucellas* (Portuguese white wine) the Saloon drew large crowds from midnight till dawn. Here, members of the upper class ate in one of the booths or cavorted with the Cyprians and demireps against a painted backdrop of palm trees and eastern architecture. A popular haunt with gamblers, the Royal Saloon was lively, colourful and dissipated and the ideal place to meet with friends or to enjoy supper after an evening at the theatre or opera. Sherry in *Friday's Child* was the life and soul of many a party at the Royal Saloon but was shocked when he found his young wife Hero there enjoying supper with several of his more outrageous friends.

Around the Town

In addition to the more adult entertainments available in the great metropolis, Regency London boasted a range of attractions to

Bullock's Museum in Piccadilly was enormously popular during the Regency and people flocked there to see its most famous exhibit of Napoleon's travelling carriage.

tempt visitors of all ages. One of the most popular of these was Bullock's Museum located in Piccadilly and often referred to as the Egyptian Hall because of its striking architecture. William Bullock opened his museum in the spring of 1812, attracting large crowds to view the exhibits which included preserved elephants, rhinos and giraffes as well as other exotic animals, birds and fish, weapons, costumes, artefacts, shells and fossils. Kitty Charing in *Cotillion* visited the Egyptian Hall when Napoleon's specially designed bulletproof travelling carriage (seized after the Battle of Waterloo) was put on display there, although neither she nor her distracted fiancé, Freddy Standen, were especially interested in the famous exhibit. In deference to Kitty's fervent desire to see some of London's most famous monuments, Freddy had already escorted her to several historic sites, of which only the Tower of London had really engaged his attention. Originally built by William the Conqueror in 1078 as part of the defence of the city, by the time of the Regency the Tower was a much larger edifice and offered visitors the chance to see Traitors' Gate and the Bloody Tower, the crown jewels, the Horse Armoury and the record office with its vast collection of documents dating from the reign of King John. Kitty and Freddy particularly enjoyed the menagerie in the Lion Tower originally built by Edward IV. Visitors paid a shilling to enter the yard and were shown round by the keeper who could tell them about the caged beasts housed there. In 1805 these included several lions and lionesses, tigers, leopards, a panther, a wolf, raccoons and a hyena, many of which lived well into the Regency.

One of London's most popular attractions during the Regency was Astley's Amphitheatre, founded in 1767 by Philip Astley, a former sergeant-major of dragoons. Astley was a superb equestrian, with a flair for the dramatic and exciting, and his horsemanship and acrobatic riding led him to establish one of the early modern circuses. Spectacular shows such as *Make Way for Liberty*

People of all ages enjoyed an evening at Astley's Royal Amphitheatre.

or the *Flight of the Saracens* drew large crowds to the amphitheatre near Westminster Bridge in Lambeth, and members of the upper class often took their children there. Sir Gareth Ludlow's young nieces and nephews in *Sprig Muslin* thought him the best of uncles for taking them to Astley's to see the troops of horses re-enacting scenes of war, the daring equestriennes performing extraordinary acrobatic feats on horseback and the famous equestrian ballet.

An equally popular though somewhat more refined attraction enjoyed by the upper class was the annual exhibition of paintings at Somerset House. Completed in 1801, Somerset House was a magnificent building on the Strand with its front facing the river Thames. It was home to the Royal Academy of Arts, and each year in May the *ton* flocked to Somerset House for the Academy's annual art exhibition in which nearly a thousand paintings were hung from floor to ceiling in the grand exhibition room. It was here that in *Arabella*, Lady Bridlington deliberately left Arabella alone with Mr Beaumaris on the pretext of finding and admiring Sir Thomas Lawrence's latest painting.

*It was considered de rigueur by many in the upper class to attend the
Royal Academy's Annual Exhibition at Somerset House.*

A less genteel pastime favoured by many in Regency society—
and young men in particular—were the travelling peep-shows.
These usually consisted of a perspective box in which were
placed painted and artistically arranged figures set against a painted
background. Using mirrors and artificial lighting they offered the
viewer the novelty of peering through a small peep-hole in one
corner of the box to see images of people in exotic locations or
pastoral scenes. Wandering showmen carried them from town
to town, setting up the boxes at local fairs or on a busy street
and charging a penny per view. In *Arabella*, the heroine's brother
Bertram was delighted by the peep-show he had seen in Coventry
Street. Peep-shows were also a popular attraction at Bartholomew
Fair, the centuries-old carnival famous for its theatricals, sideshows,
booths, gin stalls and fairings. Founded in 1133 during the reign
of Henry I, the fair opened on St Bartholomew's Day (24 August)
and was held at Smithfield on the site of what eventually became
the famous Smithfield meat market. It ran for three days and by
the time of the Regency was enormously popular with the masses,
although generally avoided by the well-bred and aristocratic who

were well aware of the seamier side of what was sometimes referred to as the 'British Saturnalia'.

In *Friday's Child*, Sherry was horrified to discover that his innocent young wife, Hero, had gone off to Bartholomew Fair with several of the more notorious members of the upper class. Well aware of the social stigma attached to being seen in such surroundings he rushed off to rescue her but then decided that it would be quite acceptable for *him* to escort Hero around the fair. Bartholomew Fair offered visitors a wide range of attractions including puppets, musicians, wire walkers, theatricals, prizefights, acrobats, wild animals, swings, roundabouts and even an early form of Ferris wheel. One of the most famous characters at the fair

In Friday's Child, *Hero was thrilled by the astonishing feats of Madame Giradelli, the famous Fireproof Lady at Bartholomew Fair.*

was the great theatrical showman, Richardson, whose fairground theatre was known as 'Richardson's Great Booth'. Sherry and Hero attended his production of the hair-raising melodrama *The Hall of Death* or *Who's the Murderer*, with the renowned Mrs Carey in the lead role of Ducheza Rosanna Vinsenza. Besides theatricals, some of the most thrilling attractions at the fair were the side-shows which advertised all manner of strange and unusual exhibits and displays. Sherry and Hero, along with many other Regency visitors, were fascinated by the extraordinary Fireproof Lady, also known as Madame Giradelli, who could dip her limbs in boiling oil, boiling lead and nitric acid, bite on melted lead and touch red-hot iron to various parts of her body, all without any apparent ill effect. Patrons also flocked to see the Living Skeleton, Simon Paap the famous Dutch Dwarf (only 28 inches tall) and Toby, the learned pig who could count, tell time and answer questions put to him by members of the audience. Such was Bartholomew Fair's reputation, however, that Sherry forbade his wife from telling anyone of their visit.

The Peerless Pond was another destination generally disdained by the upper class although it was often favoured by adventurous young men such as Jessamy and Felix Merriville in *Frederica*. Originally known as the 'Perilous Pond' because of the large number of drownings, the pool was a natural swimming hole which had been converted into England's first open-air swimming pool in 1743. It was located on Old Street in Moorfields, and visitors could enjoy the spacious pool and its shady, sylvan setting, with all the amenities of dressing boxes, bowling green and library. Although it was not considered a genteel location, the pool was extremely popular with young men of all classes and casual swim-mers could use the facilities for a shilling a time.

7

The Fashionable Resorts

BRIGHTON

George, Prince of Wales, first visited the seaside town of Brighthelmstone in 1783 when he was just twenty-one. Originally a fishing village, Brighton, as it came to be called, had been transformed into a fashionable resort in the mid-eighteenth century as a result of the work of Dr Richard Russell who had developed the 'sea-water cure' and created a vogue for swimming in and drinking the brine. In the late eighteenth century Brighton offered the Prince plenty of opportunity for merrymaking and, as he told Judith Taverner in *Regency Buck,* the town caught his fancy and he began making annual visits there to enjoy rides on the downs, shooting, gambling, the theatre, races and the company of his rakish uncle, the Duke of Cumberland. With a pair of fast horses, a racing curricle or phaeton and rapid changes en route, an accomplished driver such as the Prince could make the fifty-mile journey in less than five hours.

The Prince leased a farmhouse some 600 yards from the sea and in 1787 he commissioned the architect Henry Holland to convert it into a pavilion suitable as a summer residence. Because the Prince was renowned for his love of pleasure and high living, society naturally followed him to Brighton and discovered for themselves the delights of sea air and sea bathing. From the early nineteenth century onwards the *haut ton* rented houses along the newly built streets and squares of the town and dedicated themselves to the continual round of balls, card parties, assemblies and soirées held there during the Brighton season.

From its inception the Brighton Pavilion took up much of the Prince of Wales's (later the Prince Regent's) time and money, and what had begun as a simple transformation into a fairly modest domed house in 1787 had, by the end of Regency, turned into the fulfilment of John Nash's vision of a kind of oriental palace. The final Pavilion boasted several main rooms on its ground floor, each of them magnificently decorated with a strong oriental influence. The Prince's famous dinner parties and musical evenings brought the cream of society to his seaside palace and he entertained them lavishly in the five main rooms which ran along the eastern side of the building. The Music Room and the Yellow Drawing Room (now known as the Music Room Gallery) made up the northern wing, with the oval-shaped Saloon in the centre, and the Blue Drawing Room (originally the Green Drawing Room and now known as the Banqueting Room Gallery) and the Banqueting Room comprised the south wing, with the Great Kitchen built adjoining it, and a Pages' or Table Deckers' Room in between. It was to the Yellow Drawing Room that the Prince Regent invited Miss Taverner to give her a Petitot snuff-box in *Regency Buck* and it was there that he tried to kiss her.

Entry to the Pavilion was from the west side, through the Octagon Hall which led directly into the Entrance Hall—a square room decorated with serpents and dragons on pale green walls where Judith Taverner and her chaperone Mrs Scattergood left their shawls. From there guests could move into the Red Drawing Room on the south side of the Hall or straight ahead into the Long Gallery with its painted-glass ceiling and beautiful Chinese

In Regency Buck, *Judith Taverner was most impressed by the Brighton Pavilion, which the Regent described to her as his 'little summer palace'.*

fretwork and decorations. The Long Gallery led directly into the Music Room at the southern end of the house or to the Banqueting Room at the northern end. The Prince Regent entered his private apartments, in the northwest corner of the Pavilion, from either the Entrance Hall or from the Long Gallery.

THE BEST ADDRESS AND OTHER ACCOMMODATIONS

Brighton was not a large town—even after the Prince Regent made it fashionable. For those of the upper class who usually took a house for the summer season or, like Sir Bonamy Ripple in *False Colours*, maintained a permanent residence there, the best address was Marine Parade, a broad boulevard running parallel to the sea. There, elegant houses lined the northern side of the street and, being built on land high above the water, commanded unencumbered views of the sea and beach. It was not uncommon for the male members of the upper class to set up a telescope in a first-floor window of their hired house as Perry did in *Regency Buck* and spend part of their leisure time ogling the women on the beach going in and out of the bathing boxes lined up beside the water. At the eastern end of the Parade stood Royal Crescent with its row of bow-fronted town houses

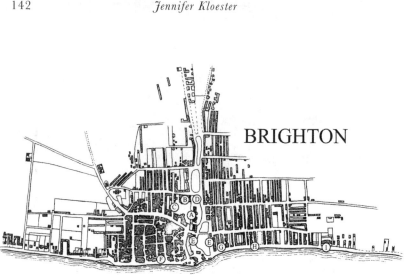

BRIGHTON

A: THE PAVILION B: ROYAL STABLES C: THEATRE D: CASTLE INN
E: THE STEINE INC.- RAGGETT'S CLUB, DONALDSON'S LIBRARY F: THE OLD SHIP
G: FISHER'S LIBRARY H: MARINE PARADE I: ROYAL CRESCENT.

built, in the early nineteenth century, by Mr Otto, an Indian nabob who had also seen fit to erect an oversize plaster statue of the Prince of Wales in the centre of the Crescent. For those who could not get a house on Marine Parade (or who preferred being at the centre of things like Evelyn Fancot in *False Colours*) the next best location was the Steine with its elegant promenade and close proximity to the shops and lending libraries. Although it could be noisy, the Steine was in the centre of town and had a view of the Pavilion. The most fashionable address in Brighton was of course the Pavilion, and the Regent often had friends to stay—although usually only for a few days and never for longer than a week.

Brighton's two leading hotels, the Old Ship and the Castle Inn, were well established by the middle of the eighteenth century, but the advent of Dr Russell with his 'miracle' cure of sea bathing served to make them even more popular. As the main Brighton coaching terminus, the Old Ship was the final stop for visitors arriving in the town and was within easy walking distance of the main street and the Pavilion. During the Regency it was customary for the Prince to be informed, on a daily basis, of new arrivals at the Old Ship so that those deemed suitable could be added to the list of guests to be invited to the Pavilion. In *Friday's Child*, Gil Ringwood suggested that Sherry and Hero take their honeymoon in Brighton because Hero would enjoy the balls at the Castle Inn and going to the Pavilion to meet the Regent. The Castle Inn was located on the north-east corner of Castle Square between the Pavilion and the Steine. As the Pavilion grew, so did the need for land, and both the Castle Inn's land and the building itself were eventually absorbed into the Pavilion site; the inn was torn down in 1823 and the old assembly room was converted into a private chapel for the King.

On the Promenade and Other Entertainments

By the early nineteenth century Brighton had become well known as the Prince's town. Each summer the generally quiet fishing village was transformed into a popular destination for the rich and fashionable. While the Pavilion stood at the centre of Brighton's social life there were also other entertainments and activities for the well-heeled and well-connected. By 1806, George Raggett, who owned the famous White's club in London, had established Raggett's club on the Steine and it was to Raggett's that the gentlemen of the *ton* would repair during the season to enjoy an excellent dinner or indulge in high play over a hand of cards or the roll of the dice. Hester Theale's father, Lord Brancaster, in *Sprig Muslin* was a member of the Prince Regent's set and spent most summers in Brighton playing whist at the Pavilion with the Prince and his brother the Duke of York, and engaging in every other hedonistic pastime put in his way. Across the road from Raggett's, also on the Steine, was Donaldson's Library, an elegant, spacious building where visitors could read the papers, exchange books, meet friends or attend one of the regular evening card parties or musical soirées. Evenings could also be spent promenading along the Steine just before sunset (at the fashionable hour of nine o'clock), exchanging nods and bows and perhaps receiving a gracious acknowledgement from the Prince Regent himself or, on one of her two visits to Brighton in 1814 and 1815, from his ageing mother, Queen Charlotte. It was while strolling along the Steine during the promenade hour that Captain Audley met Bernard Taverner in *Regency Buck* and the two men walked together to the Castle Inn where they shared a bottle of wine.

As the town grew, a second library, Fisher's, was opened on Marine Parade between Charles and Manchester Streets. With views across the sea, it was a comfortable venue for talking or reading, with all the major London newspapers delivered each evening by coach. The *Brighton Herald*, established in 1806 and with immediate access to the regular packet from Dieppe, often

Sea bathing became increasingly popular during the Regency as more people came to believe in the healthful effects of salt water.

scooped the London papers in reporting foreign events and in 1814 was the first English paper to report Napoleon's escape from Elba. As well as the libraries, Brighton had a good theatre in New Road, just west of the Pavilion, and an established programme of balls and card assemblies held at the Castle Inn and the Old Ship on alternate evenings. Race meetings were held at the course on the Downs just outside of town and were extremely popular with both male and female visitors. Brighton did not appeal to everyone, however: Lady Ombersley in *The Grand Sophy*, when asked where she would prefer to spend the summer months, declared that the town was not good for her constitution and her daughter Cecilia was adamant in judging the Regent's parties at the Pavilion as 'stupid'!

Sea bathing became increasingly popular during the Regency as visitors travelled to Brighton to bathe in the sea and drink its water. Sea bathing was often referred to as 'a cold medicated bath' with a strict ritual to be followed by anyone wishing to gain full benefit from the activity. In *Sprig Muslin*, Lady Hester's sister felt that a course of sea bathing might prove beneficial to her small, rather sickly son. Patients were required to prepare for bathing by regularly drinking sea water, and bathing was to be done in cold weather when the pores were 'safely' closed. It was considered dangerous to bathe after exercise, or in warmer weather, as this was thought to increase the risk of contracting a chill or worse. For some, however, sea bathing had become a pleasure and they would brave the waters even in the summer, undressing in the dressing machines and swimming naked or donning the more modest linen or flannel shift and stepping into the water from their horse-drawn wheeled box after it had been pulled into the sea. Ladies and gentlemen were usually separated, and for the uninitiated or less confident there were paid helpers (known as dippers) on hand to assist bathers.

BATH

The city of Bath in the Avon Valley in Somerset was well known for its famous mineral spas and many beautiful eighteenth-century buildings. Bath had been popular for its hot springs during Roman times but it was during the eighteenth century that it experienced its 'golden age' as a fashionable resort. The new, or upper, town was set apart from the old lower town by its classically designed houses and, in particular, by John Wood the Elder's magnificent Circus built between 1754 and 1758. Comprising thirty-three terraced houses set in a circle around a wide expanse of road, the Circus was inspired by the Coliseum in Rome and, in Bath, was rivalled only by the semicircular row of terraced houses west of the Circus known as Royal Crescent. The Crescent quickly became one of the iconic images of Bath and its building set a trend in the late eighteenth century for other spa towns, such as Buxton,

A: CAMDEN PLACE B: ROYAL CRESCENT C: THE CIRCUS D: UPPER ASSEMBLY ROOMS
E: EDGAR BUILDINGS F: YORK HOUSE G: MILSOM STREET H: GAY STREET I: THEATRE ROYAL
J: WESTGATE BUILDINGS K: GRAND PUMP ROOM L: STALL STREET M: BATH ABBEY
N: ORANGE GROVE O: LOWER ASSEMBLY ROOMS P: PULTENEY BRIDGE Q: LAURA PLACE
R: GREAT PULTENEY STREET S: SYDNEY GARDENS.

Leamington and Cheltenham, to build their own crescents. It was to Royal Crescent that Sherry escorted his mother, the Dowager Lady Sheringham, and Miss Milborne in *Friday's Child*, and it was while crossing the Circus in his curricle that he saw his wife, Hero, being escorted down Russell Street by another man. Other well-known Bath landmarks were the grand York House Hotel in George Street and the New or Upper Assembly Rooms in Bennett Street.

Bath reached the height of its popularity as a fashionable resort in the later eighteenth century and, although still well patronised by the time of the Regency, its hotels and lodging-houses were tenanted more by the elderly, the retired and the shabby genteel, than by the rich and fashionable. It was in Bath that Annis Wychwood in *Lady of Quality* chose to live without the protection of a male relative and in spite of strong family opposition to the idea of an unmarried woman setting up her own establishment. The various attractions of the town such as the Pump Room and the Upper and Lower Assembly Rooms continued to draw large numbers of people, however, and well-established social programmes offered a range of entertainments throughout the season. Visitors to Bath had a wide choice of inns, hotels and lodging-houses, but the most respectable and best-known hotels were the Christopher in High Street, the Pelican on Walcot Street, the less genteel White Hart in Stall Street and, best of all, the York House Hotel with its well-appointed rooms, fine food, excellent service and convenient location on George Street at the northern end of Milsom Street, just a short walk from the Upper Assembly Rooms. Ideally set up and situated to service travellers coming into Bath by coach from London, Bristol and the Midlands, with a large stable and plenty of rooms for tired travellers, it was also the most expensive hotel in Bath. Miles Calverleigh stayed at the York House in *Black Sheep* and his nephew Stacy shocked Abigail Wendover's prim sister Selina by questioning whether his devil-may-care uncle could really afford to stay there or whether he would leave town without paying his bill.

THE UPPER AND LOWER ASSEMBLY ROOMS

The Assembly Rooms were a vital part of Bath life. Here people met to dance, play cards, gamble, listen to music and talk, and here Richard 'Beau' Nash established himself as the first Master of Ceremonies and became the acknowledged leader of Bath society for much of the eighteenth century. A strict protocol was enforced in the Assembly Rooms and guests were required to sign the subscription book or risk incurring the displeasure of the Master of Ceremonies. In *Friday's Child*, Lord Sheringham made the fatal error of neglecting to sign the Master's book and as a result found himself being presented to the plainest female present when he attended a ball at the Lower Rooms. Balls began at seven o'clock and ended at eleven p.m. precisely. Full evening dress was *de rigueur* and, as Abigail Wendover obligingly explained to Miles Calverleigh in *Black Sheep*, while country-dances and cotillions were acceptable, waltzing was not permitted and those wishing to stand up for the minuet had to be in their places no later than eight o'clock. Tea was served part way through the evening and cost sixpence.

The Lower Rooms were the pre-eminent venue for assemblies until 1771 when the growth of the new, or upper town, saw the building of the magnificent new Upper Assembly Rooms in Bennett Street (also known as the New Assembly Rooms) comprising a grand Ballroom, Tea Room, Card Room and, linking all three, an Octagon Room. In *Black Sheep*, Abigail Wendover met several of her friends in the Octagon Room before attending a concert given by Neroli, and took tea afterwards with Mr Calverleigh who told her that the singer had put him in mind of a blancmange.

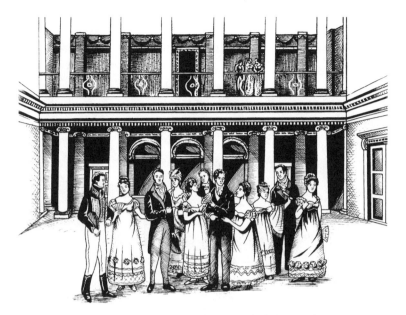

*Abigail Wendover was surrounded by a crowd of admirers when she
attended a concert at the Upper Assembly Rooms in* Black Sheep.

Although both the Upper and Lower Rooms offered subscribers a
range of entertainments, the Upper Rooms were generally considered superior and tended to dominate the weekly round of events
with a dress ball on Mondays, card assembly on Tuesdays, concert
on Wednesdays and fancy ball on Thursdays. As a result, the social
life in Bath was often marked by a rivalry between the two sets of
rooms and between the two reigning Masters of Ceremonies.

The role of Master of Ceremonies derived from a position
held at the royal courts, where a designated individual was held
responsible for supervising and, at times, deciding what constituted
acceptable public behaviour in the Pump Room, the Baths and the
Assembly Rooms, thus protecting visitors to Bath from uncouth
or unseemly conduct. The Master's presence, as demonstrated
by Nash in the eighteenth century, also implied a certain level of
decorum, manners and behaviour at social functions and reassured

those present that their fellow guests were of a particular social standing. It also gave an event a certain cachet, designating it as fashionable and, for those in his favour, it could mean an easy entrée into elite circles. It was customary for visitors to Bath to sign the Master's subscription book upon arrival, enabling him to make a formal call and effect necessary introductions at future social events. Neglecting to write one's name in the book was tantamount to an insult and inevitably resulted in some degree of social discomfort for the perpetrator. In *Bath Tangle*, Lady Serena advised her young mother-in-law of the wisdom of writing their names in the Masters' books despite the fact that both ladies were in mourning and unable to attend either balls or card assemblies. Once apprised of the ladies' arrival in Bath, both Mr King of the Upper Rooms and his rival Mr Guynette of the Lower were assiduous in their attentions and did all they could to make the Dowager Countess's stay agreeable.

In Bath Tangle, *Fanny, Lady Spenborough, visited the Pump Room regularly to meet friends and take the waters.*

The Pump Room

Taking the waters at Bath meant either bathing in one of the hot pools or, the preferred option, drinking the water in the Pump Room. This was the social hub of daily life in Bath during the Regency, for here residents and visitors would gather throughout the day to take the waters, stroll about the room, meet friends, exchange news, listen to the small orchestra and survey the scene for any newcomers who might be worthy of introduction to one's social circle—although Lady Serena in *Bath Tangle* caused her mama-in-law considerable consternation when she struck up a friendship with the outspoken, flamboyant and decidedly middle-class Mrs Floore. The Great Pump Room was opened in 1799 and visitors entering through the grand Ionic colonnade adorning the exterior found themselves in a large, spacious room, elegantly appointed with Corinthian pillars, tall multi-paned windows and furnished with benches, chairs and Chippendale seats. A pumper dispensed glasses of the famous mineral water to those regular visitors to the Pump Room who had paid their season's subscription and to occasional drinkers on payment of a small sum. On most days (when she had nothing better to do) Selina Wendover in *Black Sheep* made a point of drinking a glass of the famous water although she did not really enjoy it. Many claims were made for the wholesomeness of drinking Bath water but for some, such as Fanny in *Bath Tangle*, the benefits of attending the Great Pump Room were to be found more in the pleasant setting and social interaction than in the waters themselves. For those visitors wishing to bathe in the waters rather than drink them, there was a choice of several baths, such as the King's Bath, the Cross Bath, the Queen's Bath and the Hot Bath. During the Regency, mixed bathing was permitted in all the baths except for the Queen's Bath which was for women only. Bath attendants assisted both men (suitably clad in shirts and drawers) and women (in a linen shift) to enter the baths and supervised the bathers as they wallowed up to their necks in the warm, steamy waters. Bath's hot springs were famous for their curative powers and it was for this reason that in *Sylvester* the Duke of Salford went to such extraordinary lengths to get his invalid mother there.

Taking the Cure

Good health was highly prized during the Regency when the vast array of illness and disease meant that the chance of avoiding the physician's risky diagnosis, the surgeon's knife or the apothecary's brews was minimal. Neither wealth nor title was a guarantee of health and even the best physicians were still limited in their understanding of disease. Many people proved remarkably resilient, however, undergoing surgery without anaesthetic and enduring the purges, emetics, leeches, hot plasters, induced blisters, opiates and other 'curatives' in the doctor's arsenal without a murmur. Treatment was generally a response to symptoms, rather than a preventative measure, and it was not uncommon for the 'cure' to be as bad as, or, in some cases, worse than the illness itself. In *Friday's Child*, the Dowager Lady Sheringham was convinced that while in Bath she should avail herself of the newest treatments, including the four different waters at Dr Wilkinson's rooms and the Russian Vapour Baths.

Responses to illness and injury took various forms, and patients had a wide choice of advisers, healers, medications, cures, traditional wisdom and folklore. Many people self-medicated and women such as Mrs Dauntry in *Frederica*, believing herself to suffer from a weak constitution, took a wide range of medications including goat's whey for a non-existent consumption, paregoric draughts, restoratives and other remedies. Those wishing for medical advice could avail themselves of the services of the local apothecary, surgeon, wise woman, herbalist or village quack, while for those who could afford it a visit from a physician was considered desirable. For some patients the attentions of an understanding, well-spoken medical practitioner could be so comforting that they would call on him at the first sign of a symptom. Faced with the often dull life of a well-bred, older single lady, Selina Wendover in *Black Sheep* frequently developed nervous disorders or other 'interesting conditions' that required the attention of the best doctors in Bath.

Among the best-known Regency doctors were Matthew Baillie, Sir Henry Halford, Sir Richard Croft and Sir William Knighton. Each of these men built large and successful practices during the period and were in great demand among members of the upper class. Dr Baillie was a famous physician and lecturer in anatomy who also served as Princess Charlotte's principal physician until her pregnancy and confinement, when Sir Richard Croft was brought

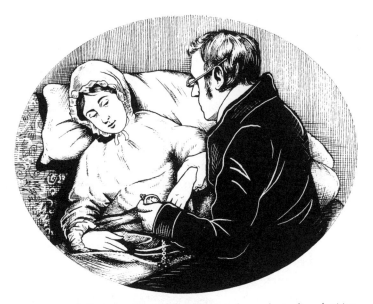

Some Regency ladies enjoyed the regular attentions of an understanding physician.

in as a specialist. A small, plain man, Baillie impressed patients and colleagues alike with his clarity of mind, good sense, and ability to communicate even the most complex medical conditions simply and effectively, and it was he who attended young Amabel in *The Grand Sophy*. A colleague of Baillie's, Sir Richard Croft was a tall, elegantly dressed man, with an aristocratic clientele and a strong sense of his own skill and importance. A leading *accoucheur* (man-midwife), Croft was in great demand in fashionable circles although there were those who thought little of his particular methods of dealing with pregnant ladies. In *A Civil Contract*, neither Adam Deveril nor his formidable Aunt Nassington agreed with Croft's 'reducing diets' (consisting mainly of liquids) for expectant mothers or with his practice of bleeding them. Adam became so concerned about his wife's poor health that he called in one of the Regent's personal physicians, Sir William Knighton to replace Croft. Hard-working, conscientious and empathetic, Knighton had successfully established himself as an *accoucheur* and was well known for his superb manners and keen intellect. Sir Henry Halford was another eminent medical specialist who found favour with the nobility and aristocracy during the Regency. A sound and reliable doctor, and a satisfactory rather than brilliant diagnostician, he had been physician extraordinary to George III, and established a thriving practice in Curzon Street in the heart of fashionable London. Known for his courtly manners (and referred to by some as the 'eel-backed baronet') Halford was physician to four British monarchs and his reputation alone was enough to convince concerned aristocratic mothers like Lady Legerwood in *Cotillion* that he should be brought in to assist the unimpressed family doctor.

The practice of medicine was still largely unregulated when the Regency began, and anyone could try his or her hand in almost any area except midwifery which was more strictly controlled. Remedies for illness and disease varied widely during the period but blood-letting or bleeding was one of the most popular. Used as a cure in almost every kind of illness, it was especially favoured by the Prince Regent who, like many others, believed that blood-letting would release the 'bad blood' from the patient's body and with it the cause of the disease. In certain cases bleeding did appear to relieve pain and many among the upper class also believed in bleeding as a means of alleviating the consequences of overindulgence in food and drink. In *The Reluctant Widow*, Lord Bedlington, overcome by the tragic news of his nephew's death, felt obliged to have half a pint of blood taken to help calm his nerves and swore by the efficacy of the 'cure'.

In its simplest form, bleeding was achieved by opening a vein with a small knife called a lancet and letting the blood run until the practitioner felt enough had been released. The amount of blood taken varied enormously and depended mainly on the whim of the surgeon (or apothecary, blacksmith or barber) and the constitution of the patient. Leeches (sixpence each) were also used and were applied to the skin to suck the blood until enough was thought to have been taken, before they were sprinkled with salt to make them let go. Another popular method of drawing blood was cupping, whereby the practitioner placed heated cups made of glass (occasionally metal) on the patient's body to create a vacuum which drew the skin up into the cup and brought the blood to the surface. Both dry cupping and wet cupping were common during the Regency although wet cupping—where the skin was scratched or cut to allow the blood to flow freely from the body—was more popular. In dry cupping the skin remained uncut and the benefit to the patient was felt to be derived purely from the increased circulation of the blood.

Blisters, plasters and poultices were also popular during the period as many people believed that the body could house only one illness at a time and introducing a second illness could force out the first. Burning or blistering the skin was felt to be an effective way of achieving this and a hot plaster was applied to the skin to produce a blister which could then be drained and thus remove the original illness from the body. Plasters and poultices were commonly used to treat inflammations, chest infections, abscesses, bruising and muscular soreness. In *Arabella*, Mr Beaumaris sent his groom off to buy a gum plaster and when questioned by Arabella as to why he might want such a thing defiantly told her it was for his rheumatism. Plasters usually consisted of some kind of 'curative' mixture spread on a bandage or dressing and placed over a wound or on the affected part of the body. Poultices such as the one made by Phoebe Marlow in *Sylvester* were often made from readily available ingredients such as bread and milk, onions, butter and flowers which could be mixed into a heated mass and wrapped in muslin before being applied to the affected area. They were mostly used for inflammation and swelling.

Gout was another intensely painful condition common during the Regency and was generally thought to be caused by too much rich food or drink. In *Charity Girl*, Lord Desford's father the Earl of Wroxton suffered horribly from an attack of gout which was thought to have been brought on by a lavish helping of curried crab and two bottles of port. Gout was actually caused by too much uric acid in the bloodstream and although alcohol did not cause it directly, its dehydrating effect could exacerbate the condition: it accelerated the process of crystallisation which turned the uric acid into needle-like crystals in the joints and caused the extreme pain so well known to sufferers such as the autocratic Dowager Lady Stavely in *False Colours,* who had gout in her finger joints.

One of the most commonly used remedies during the Regency was laudanum. Also known as 'tincture of opium', it was made by mixing opium, alcohol and distilled water and was taken by men and women as a medication during illness, to calm their nerves or to help them sleep, as Lady Barbara found in *An Infamous Army*. Freely available in the form of pills, lozenges, liniments, plasters, wines, vinegars and mixtures with reassuring names like 'Godfrey's Cordial' and 'Mrs Winslow's Soothing Syrup', for many Regency women and men laudanum was a source of comfort and a release from the afflictions of nerves, boredom or unhappiness. It was also addictive, as Drusilla Morville in *The Quiet Gentleman* inferred from the letter written by her mama which told her of 'poor Mr Coleridge' and his addiction to laudanum (he was taking up to two quarts a week). As well as having a bottle of laudanum at hand, sensitive ladies often carried smelling-salts (usually in a vinaigrette), hartshorn and Hungary water in case they should faint or suffer from an attack of nerves. Also known as sal volatile, smelling-salts were an aromatic infusion made from ammonium carbonate and alcohol and scented with lemon or lavender oil. Sufferers breathed the vapours which caused them to inhale sharply and then breathe more rapidly. They often carried their salts in a vinaigrette, a small decorative box or bottle with a perforated top which held smelling-salts or a piece of gauze soaked with lavender water or vinegar. Lady Castlereagh kindly lent her vinaigrette to Jenny, Lady Lynton, in *A Civil Contract* after Julia fainted at a party at Nassington House. Ladies (and some gentlemen) sniffed the contents whenever there was an unpleasant odour or if they felt faint. Hartshorn was another popular restorative and, although originally made from carbonate of ammonia distilled from shaved or powdered hart's (male deer) horns, by the time of the Regency spirit of hartshorn (aqueous ammonia) was simply ammonia infused with water and was another form of smelling-salts. Francis Cheviot in *The Reluctant Widow* demanded that both his hartshorn and his smelling-salts be brought to him immediately on the discovery of Mrs Cheviot's inert form. Both hartshorn and sal volatile could also be mixed with water and drunk as a restorative. Hungary water was named after Elizabeth, Queen of Hungary, and was a sweet-smelling distilled water made from rosemary and other herbs and flowers, and used as a perfumed restorative which could be dabbed on the temples or applied to the hands and face of a person suffering from headache or an excess of nerves.

OTHER DIVERSIONS

By the time of the Regency, Bath was no longer the highly fashionable resort it had been during the eighteenth century—fewer
of the aristocracy graced the Pump Room, baths and Assembly
Rooms—yet the town still attracted the well-to-do and genteel
to its elegant hotels and lodgings. There was a certain ritual to
life in Bath that suited many of its inhabitants, beginning with the
visit to the Pump Room each morning to drink the waters. Some
people went there several times a day in order to meet friends,
listen to music or take a second, or even third, glass of mineral
water. In between times, as young Lucilla Carleton in *Lady of
Quality* discovered while staying in the town, Bath offered other
diversions such as the excellent shops on Milsom, Bond and Stall
Streets, several circulating libraries, a number of coffee-shops, the
Theatre Royal in Orchard Street and numerous opportunities for
scenic walks, carriage rides, picnics and promenades.

Built in 1762, Milsom Street in the centre of Bath was a
bustling corridor of activity with modistes' and milliners' shops,
Duffield's bookstore and circulating library (where in *Bath Tangle*
Lady Serena unexpectedly met the handsome Major Kirkby),
and carriages and sedan chairs carrying passengers up and down
and various tradesmen's establishments offering a range of goods
and services. Duffield's and Meyler's, in the Orange Grove (an
area originally surrounded by trees and named after a visit by the
Prince of Orange), were two of Bath's main libraries in which,
for an annual fee of 15 shillings or 5 shillings a quarter, subscribers
could read the local and London newspapers, borrow the latest
novels, and peruse various French and English periodicals. Lady
Serena was a regular visitor to Duffield's as were the Wendover
sisters and their niece Fanny in *Black Sheep*. A famous Bath resident, Fanny Burney (Madame D'Arblay) once wrote that Bath
was a city in which no carriage was needed and, despite the hilly

topography and steep streets, many visitors and residents enjoyed walking about the town and surrounding countryside. For those unable—or unwilling—to summon the energy to climb the slopes, however, a sedan chair was usually the preferred mode of travel, carried by a pair of licensed chairmen at a cost of sixpence for 500 yards in the lower town, 300 yards on hilly terrain, a shilling for distances between 500 and 1,173 yards and 1s.6d. above that—but not exceeding a mile (1,760 yards). Mrs Floore in *Bath Tangle* was one Bath resident who refused to take a chair, however, having declared herself too stout and confessing to Lady Serena that she was afraid the chairmen might drop dead between the poles. For those content to walk, the fields below Royal Crescent were a delightful rendezvous for friends and lovers and were also popular with picnickers, while those wanting a view of the city generally found the longer walk to Beechen Cliff very rewarding. A ride up to Lansdown with its view of the Bristol Channel was an agreeable outing and one which Fanny Wendover in *Black Sheep* enjoyed in the company of her aunt and several friends. The town of Wells, with its beautiful cathedral, was another favoured destination within easy reach of Bath and made an agreeable day's outing in a carriage or on horseback. On Sundays it was considered *de rigueur* for the well-bred and fashionable to attend services at Bath Abbey, the lovely medieval church adjacent to the Great Pump Room.

Intended as the 'Vauxhall of Bath', Sydney Gardens opened in 1795 and were an immediate success, with their inviting alcoves and arbours, groves of trees, formal flower-beds, gravel walks and gently sloping lawns which offered enticing views across the town and the surrounding countryside. A subscription of 10s. entitled the subscriber, not only to all the pleasures of the season's programme of promenades, musical entertainments, alfresco breakfasts and illuminations, but also to the particular attractions of this 'Vauxhall' of Bath. In *The Foundling*, it was to Sydney Gardens that the Duke of Sale sent his young friend, Tom Mamble, to while away several hours enjoying all the famous attractions such as Merlin's Grotto, the Hermit's Cot, the 'Ruined Castle', waterfalls, the echo reverberating from the distant cliffs of Beacon Hill and—most famous of all—the Labyrinth, touted in a Bath guidebook as being 'nearly twice as large as that in the gardens of Hampton Court'. For those who found their way to the centre of the hedge-lined maze (maps could be purchased showing the path), there was the added attraction of Merlin's Swing, a ride which apparently operated on 'Archimedian principles'. As the handsome and charming Mr Kilbride so obligingly informed Lucilla Carleton when he accompanied her and a friend to the gardens in *Lady of Quality*, fêtes and gala nights were also held during the season and crowds of 3,000 or 4,000 people would gather into the gardens to dance under the lights and watch the fireworks.

8

Getting About

The Regency was the golden age of the horse with enormous status attached to the ownership of horses as well as to the level of expertise in riding or driving them. Many among the aristocracy were involved in breeding and training horses for the increasingly popular sports of horse racing, hunting and carriage driving. The kudos to be gained from being judged a 'neck or nothing rider' in the hunting field, a 'top-sawyer' in the saddle, or a 'capital whip' or 'Nonesuch' in the driving seat was such that enormous prices were frequently paid for a first-class horse or 'prime bit of blood'. Teams or pairs of matched carriage horses were also popular with driving enthusiasts and a well-proportioned pair known for their stamina, speed and high-stepping action could cost several hundred pounds.

ALL KINDS OF CARRIAGES

Carriages and coaches were the main form of transport during the Regency and ranged from the cumbersome public stage to the elegant town coach or barouche, the head-turning sporting curricle and the dashing high-perch phaeton. Carriages varied enormously in size, style and design but they all had two things in common: a body in which the passengers rode and a carriage or support section suspended on wheels on which the body rested. Some carriages were elegant, luxuriously appointed vehicles with velvet upholstery, silk lining and leather trim while others were purely practical, no-frills modes of transport. The basic coach was a four-wheeled vehicle, with a large, closed body hung over the centre of the suspension. It had a driving seat at the front for the coachman and a rumble seat at the back for one or two footmen with two seats inside, facing each other, which generally held two or three people each. Coaches built for the aristocracy were often built to be narrow, leaving room for only four people inside. The town coach or chariot was very similar to the coach and was often a showpiece for the aristocracy who would have their coat of arms emblazoned on the door panel and a sumptuous hammer cloth made to throw over the box or driving seat, with the footmen's liveries to match. Kit Fancot, making a visit of ceremony in the place of his twin brother Evelyn in *False Colours*, was driven to Lord Stavely's Mount Street house in the Denville town carriage which had the family arms on each door. A much-used form of transport was the post-chaise which was similar in design to the chariot but without the driving seat. It held two or three persons and did not have a coachman or driver but was driven or steered by one or more postilions mounted on the horses. A post-chaise was lighter than the town chariot and did not hold the road as well and this, along with the propensity to paint them yellow, led to their being nicknamed 'Yellow Bounders'.

One of the most elegant town carriages was the barouche. An open carriage drawn by two, four or six horses, it was designed mainly for town use in the warmer months and had a cup-shaped body and a high driving seat at the front with room for both the coachman and footman to sit together. It also had a folding hood covering one half of the carriage which could be lifted from the rear during inclement weather. In *Friday's Child*, Lord Sheringham bought his new bride a smart, yellow-bodied barouche for town use and a stylish travelling chariot for longer journeys. Another elegant town carriage, the landau maintained its popularity throughout the Regency although some among the younger set, including Lady Buckhaven in *Cotillion*, thought it dowdy and more suitable for the older generation. Although similar to the barouche in shape, the landau had a double folding hood which met in the middle and offered passengers greater protection from the weather. The phaeton, on the other hand, was one of the most popular vehicles of the Regency. Named for the son of Helios, the Greek god who allowed Phaeton to draw the chariot of the sun across the heavens for a single day until he almost set the world on fire, Phaeton meant 'the shining one'. Considered by many to be the height of elegance, the phaeton was a light, four-wheeled vehicle with seating for two which came in a wide range of designs from the stylish high-perch model, such as the one bought by Sophy Stanton-Lacy in *The Grand Sophy* with its seat high above the front wheels, to the famous and elegant Highflyer with its seat evenly suspended between its large rear wheels and smaller front ones. Usually drawn by two horses, the body could be hung forward or back, depending on the design, and was owner-driven by both men and women, often with a groom in attendance on the box. The Prince Regent was himself a notable whip and in his younger years was famous for driving not only a phaeton and four, but also a high-perch phaeton and six, a feat which appears to have been considered a royal prerogative and was not generally imitated.

The term 'gig' could be used to describe any two-wheeled carriage with a fixed seat. Designed to carry the driver and one passenger, and usually drawn by one horse—although two could be harnessed to the shaft in tandem—it was a popular form of conveyance throughout the nineteenth century. Its open design and cane or wooden railing around the seat made the gig a fair-weather carriage ideal for day trips, shopping or a summer tour. Jenny, Lady Lynton, in *A Civil Contract*, found a gig the ideal conveyance when driving herself about the estate and visiting the tenantry at Fontley Priory. Similar to the caned whisky and the chair-back gig, the tilbury was named after its maker, the famous designer and builder of coaches John Tilbury, and was a common sight on Regency roads. A lightweight two-wheeled vehicle with seating for only two persons, no boot and no roof of any kind, it was drawn by a single horse and used mainly for shorter distances rather than over-night travel. It was particularly popular among the gentry. Among two-wheeled carriages, the curricle was considered the epitome of style during the Regency and was much favoured by those sporting men with a penchant for speed. In *The Quiet Gentleman*, Lord Ulverston arrived at Stanyon Castle driving a curricle and four which, as the Earl of St Erth told his cousin Theo, marked his friend as a veritable Nonesuch. Named for the 'curriculum' or Roman racing chariot, the curricle had a fixed forward seat and was drawn by two horses harnessed side by side to the carriage using a curricle bar, which made it essential for them to be of equal height and gait. The presence of a groom on the rear rumble seat meant there was no weight on the horses' backs which gave them an easy forward movement. Racing curricles were frequently pulled by a perfectly matched pair of high-stepping steeds with the ability to reach speeds of up to sixteen miles an hour when driven by a skilled driver on a good road.

A town coach.

A barouche.

A post-chaise.

The four-in-hand, also known as a drag, usually referred to a closed carriage pulled by four horses such as the Mail and the public stagecoach. Similar in design to each other, these carriages were built to accommodate both people and freight, with a solid central body suspended over a wooden perch undercarriage with springs, a large boot at the rear with a seat for outside passengers and another space for luggage under the driver's box. The roof was also built to hold passengers as well as luggage and the total weight of a four-in-hand could sometimes exceed three tons. A sizeable coach had room for six people inside and eight to twelve persons could find room on the back, on the roof and on the coveted seat next to the driver.

A phaeton.

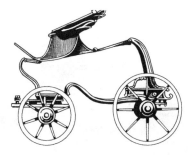

A high-perch phaeton.

A curricle.

Although not a coach, the pedestrian curricle or 'hobby horse' was a popular recreational vehicle in the last years of the Regency. An early form of bicycle, the curricle tempted many a daring and intrepid rider to experience the thrill of propelling himself along London's streets and reaching speeds of up to ten miles an hour. The pedestrian curricle had no pedals or brakes but was pushed along with the feet as the rider leaned forward to grip the handlebars while resting his elbows on a small padded block. Jessamy Merriville in *Frederica* became extremely skilled on his hired machine and enjoyed the heady excitement of lifting his feet from the ground and coasting down Piccadilly before coming to grief with a man mending chairs.

Jessamy Merriville in Frederica *mastered the art of riding a pedestrian curricle but came to grief in Piccadilly.*

On Drivers and Driving

Coach driving required great skill and many men, and some women, aspired to the appellation of 'Nonesuch' or 'first-rate fiddler'. 'Driving to the inch' was how the best driving was described and was an indication of a driver's prowess in being able to judge distance and guide his or her horses through a narrow gateway, pass or give the 'go-by' to another coach on a narrow stretch of road, 'feather-edge a corner' or hold close to a sharp bend, or turn an equipage in a confined space without damaging it. Judith Taverner in *Regency Buck* had been taught to drive by her father and on arriving in London quickly established herself as a notable whip, having first earned the approval of 'Curricle Worth' and his tiger, Henry. The best drivers had the ability to feel their horses' mouths through the reins, to read a team's mood and control their gait. A first-rate whip could drive a pair harnessed side by side or in the more difficult configuration of tandem, which was how Sophy Stanton-Lacy's horses were harnessed when she drove down St James's Street in *The Grand Sophy*. A driver who was 'at home to a peg' could also manage unfamiliar, headstrong or difficult horses and drive a team of four, or even six, holding them together and making them run in time. In *The Nonesuch*, Sir Waldo Hawkridge demonstrated the skill that earned him that sobriquet by effortlessly halting (at a moment's notice) the team of four high-spirited horses harnessed to his sporting curricle and minutes later just as easily turning them in a confined space. A great deal of driving was done at a trot, with the canter used intermittently and the gallop only rarely. Galloping, or 'springing' a team, was sometimes done on the downward slope of a hill in order to give the horses enough speed to get up the other side, or on those rare stretches of ground wide enough and flat enough to be considered safe, or in the event of an emergency.

For a coach to run smoothly, the horses needed to be well matched and able to work together. In a team where horses were harnessed one in front of the other, the rear horse or one closest to the carriage was the wheeler and the horse in front the leader. The number and configuration of horses harnessed to a carriage varied according to the type of vehicle, the kind of horses available and the skill of the driver. A single-horse carriage was fairly straightforward to drive, as was a pair harnessed side by side. Putting a pair of horses one in front of the other, or driving tandem, was considered a serious test of skill, as was driving pickaxe, where five horses were harnessed to a coach with three across at the front and a pair of wheelers behind them. Driving unicorn or random-tandem—as Vincent Darracott did so well in *The Unknown Ajax*—with a lead horse harnessed in front of a pair, was a serious test of a driver's skill but was seen much less often than the carriage drawn by a team of four. The Prince Regent had once driven his phaeton to Brighton with his horses in unicorn but when Peregrine Taverner in *Regency Buck* told his sister Judith, herself an accomplished driver, that he would not drive that way she made it clear that he could not even if he wanted to. Driving a four-in-hand was a popular pastime and many Regency men drove their own coach or drag or paid the coachman on the public stage for the privilege of taking the reins for a time. Very skilled drivers drove a curricle and four, but the height of achievement for the real coaching devotee was membership in the exclusive Four-Horse Club.

The Four-Horse Club was originally called the Whip Club and was established in 1808 by a group of aristocratic coaching enthusiasts recognised as experts in the art of driving. Only those who had proven their skill driving a team of four horses harnessed to a four-wheeled coach were eligible to join the club and the group wore a distinctive uniform for their regular outings that year from Park Lane to Harrow-on-the-Hill. Members met four times a year between April and June to drive the twenty miles to Salt Hill, partake of a sumptuous lunch and return to London. The coaches were driven single file, at a strict trot, with their drivers resplendent in the club uniform of a long white driving coat with fifteen capes and two tiers of pockets, over a single-breasted blue coat with brass buttons, a Kerseymere waistcoat with inch-wide blue and yellow stripes, white corduroy breeches, short boots with long tops and a white muslin cravat with black spots. Only men were eligible to join the club, although some members acknowledged the prowess of those female drivers able to drive 'to the inch'. Charles Rivenhall in *The Grand Sophy* was a member of the FHC as was his friend Cyprian Wychbold who, after being driven round Hyde Park by Sophy in her high-perch phaeton, told her that he would gladly support her candidature if the club ever decided to allow women to become members.

In many coaches—and sporting vehicles in particular—it was usual for a groom to sit or stand up beside or behind the driver. These men or boys usually had a particular affinity for horses, and grooms such as John Keighley in *Sylvester* and Lady Serena's groom, Fobbing, in *Bath Tangle*, often became the trusted attendants of a horse-loving master or mistress. When carriage driving, it was the groom's job to jump down and run to the horse's head in the event of an accident or upset and to hold the horses while his master or mistress paid a social call, engaged in business or visited the shops. In the stable, the groom was responsible for feeding, exercising and grooming those horses assigned to his care as well as cleaning their tack and overseeing the stable boys. During the Regency it became fashionable for some among the top-sawyers to employ a tiger—a small groom peculiar to London and usually seen only on a curricle or standing up on the footboard at the back of a cabriolet. Tigers ranged in age from fifteen to twenty-five, were always small in build, and had an absolute mastery of horses. Lord Sheringham's tiger Jason in *Friday's Child*, having shown himself to have an extraordinary affinity with horses, found that instead of being sent to the Roundhouse for picking the Viscount's pocket he was employed as his tiger instead. While most grooms wore some kind of livery, a tiger was always immaculately turned out with a close-fitting coat, white buckskin breeches, spotless top-boots and a well-brushed hat trimmed with gold or silver cord which he often set at a rakish angle on his head.

Carriage driving was one of the few physical activities, other than walking and horse riding, available to women. One- or two-horse vehicles such as a gig, tilbury, or one of the many types of phaeton, were considered most suitable for ladies to drive and they could often be seen tooling their coach around Hyde Park at the fashionable hour. Only the most accomplished drivers (of either sex) drove a high-perch phaeton or racing curricle, as these required considerable skill and the high-perch phaeton, in partic-ular, was easily overturned. An upper-class woman rarely drove alone and then usually only in the environs of the family estate. Judith Taverner's decision in *Regency Buck* to engage in a curricle race against her brother Perry would have been unremarkable if it had been run in the country on a private estate, but to travel down the busiest turnpike road in England in an open carriage with just her groom in attendance was to commit a grave social solecism and thereby lay herself open to public censure and ridicule. When in London, a woman driving a carriage would be always accom-panied by her groom although she could take up a passenger or run errands as long as the proprieties were met, including never driving her carriage down St James's Street—an activity forbidden to well-bred females.

PUBLIC TRANSPORT

The hackney coach or hack was an early form of taxi-cab and during the Regency more than a thousand of these horse-drawn vehicles plied their trade around the streets of London and other major towns and cities of England. They were mostly closed, four-wheeled carriages, pulled by a pair of horses of no less than fourteen hands in height. They generally took up to four passengers, although more could be carried at the coachman's discretion and at a cost of a shilling per additional passenger. Hackneys could be hailed at will and offered a degree of anonymity at times when the men and women of the wealthier classes (who usually travelled in their own carriages with their coachman, groom and footmen) wished to keep their personal affairs private. In *Cotillion*, Olivia Broughty, desperate to see her friend Kitty and solicit her help in an affair of the heart, took a hack to the house in Berkeley Square only to discover that she had insufficient funds to pay the driver.

The post-chaise was another popular means of public conveyance during the Regency, especially among those who could not afford to maintain their own carriage, but were disinclined to use public coaches such as the Mail or the stage. Stagecoaches were first run in the early 1600s and a general service, with London as its main hub, was operating by 1750. As Sir Richard Wyndham in *The Corinthian* knew only too well when compelled to travel on the public stage, the terrible state of the roads, the expense, the uncomfortable coaches and the slow rates of travel (eighty hours from London to Manchester in 1750) were a disincentive for many people to undertake long-distance travel unless they had to. By 1820, however, over forty major mail routes had been established between London and most major cities in England, Scotland and Wales, with a host of cross-routes connecting provincial towns and cities. Once the Mail was established it became a uniform service run by private contractors with twenty-five magnificent maroon-and-black coaches bearing the royal coat of arms on the door, with the name of the coach proprietor and the two terminals painted above it in fine gold lettering. A painted star adorned each of the four upper panels and a number on the boot identified the coach to passers-by. The guard was the only person directly employed by the Post Office and his priorities were the safe delivery of the mail and adherence to the timetable. It was a serious offence to delay or obstruct a Mail coach as the Duke of Sale discovered to his cost in *The Foundling* after his young charge, Tom Mamble, had almost caused the Mail to overturn while engaged in organising a backwards race between several farm animals. In its early days the Mail was allowed to carry only four inside passengers, but by 1814 the Post Office had introduced four classes of travel which allowed two, four or more passengers to travel outside depending on the route. The Mail ran mainly at night when the roads were clearer and each evening, except Sundays, at eight o'clock sharp, twenty-five coaches set off from the main London post office in Lombard Street on their various journeys around the country.

Stagecoaches were run by private companies who competed with the Mails for passengers. Although they were slower, stagecoaches had several advantages over the Mail, including cheaper fares, daytime travel, greater passenger capacity and routes that enabled travellers to get on or off at places the Mail did not allow. As road conditions and coach construction slowly improved, many people chose to travel by stage as Kate Malvern did when returning to London in *Cousin Kate*. A series of predetermined stops at various roadside coaching-inns made up the route. At the end of each stage the inn provided a new team of horses and passengers could partake of refreshments, or disembark the coach, while new passengers could be taken up. In *The Corinthian*, Pen Creed thoroughly enjoyed travelling on the stage where she whiled away the time conversing with the other passengers and even made room for a traveller not on the waybill. Provided they were properly loaded, most stagecoaches could hold up to six inside and eight to ten outside passengers, plus freight and baggage. An outside seat on the stage cost two to three pence per mile and an inside seat was between four and five pence, whereas an inside seat on the Mail cost between six and ten pence per mile and an outside seat was four to five pence. For those prepared

The stage was the most common form of public transport although many people,
such as the Duke of Sale in The Foundling, *found it an extremely*
uncomfortable way to travel.

to pay extra it was possible to buy the coveted seat next to the
driver and a generous tip could secure a turn with the reins for
a male enthusiast. In *The Foundling*, this privilege was offered to
the Duke of Sale on his first trip on the public stage and politely
refused; the Duke had discovered that travelling on the roof did
not agree with him and was glad to leave the stage at Baldock. As
the demand for shorter travel times increased, the stage eventually
followed the Mail and gave up their traditional overnight stops on
longer journeys and also reduced the time allotted for meal stops.

On the Road

Travelling by coach, whether public or private, could be dangerous.
Although highwaymen were becoming scarce there were plenty of
other hazards to impede a journey or play havoc with life and limb.
On the public stage and the Mail, as one of the passengers reminded
the coachman in *The Corinthian*, there were strict rules governing
the behaviour of coachman, guard and passengers. A waybill listing

the names, pick-up points and destinations of the passengers who had booked a seat was given to the guard at the commencement of each journey and it was his job to see that the coach made the correct stops and kept to its timetable. Although it was possible to gain a place on the stage or Mail without having booked or paid in advance, those travellers already on board and uncomfortably crowded sometimes objected vociferously to additional passengers being allowed into the coach.

Overloading of coaches, with either people or baggage, was prohibited by the coach companies, as was furious driving and allowing passengers to take the reins. Drinking was also forbidden but was difficult to control and coachmen, such as the one in *The Reluctant Widow* who transported Elinor Rochdale to the village of Billingshurst, were rarely averse to downing a quick glass in the taproom of a posting-house while the horses were changed. After setting off again it was not uncommon for the coachman to let eager young bloods (themselves sometimes under the influence) drive the coach for a spell—an unfortunate occurrence which frequently ended (as it did in *The Corinthian*) in the coach being overturned and horses and passengers injured. Most coaches, and particularly those that travelled at speed, carried a three-foot-long coaching horn, also known as a 'yard of tin'. A vital part of the guard's equipment on the public stage or mail coach, it was the coaching horn that enabled the guard to keep to the timetable for he blew a call to summon the passengers before departing from one posting-house and again on approaching the next. The sound of a coaching horn told the ostlers to have fresh horses ready for the change and alerted the innkeeper to the need for food and drink. Ostlers were the grooms or horse-keepers who worked at the coaching-inns and posting-houses situated along the great network of post roads that criss-crossed England during the Regency. In addition to caring for the horses owned by the inn, ostlers were also responsible for the horses left there after a change of teams was

Blowing up for the change on the Royal Mail.

completed at the end of a stage. Trained to replace carriage horses in under two minutes, the best ostlers could change a team in fifty seconds. They were expected to be ready with fresh animals at the first sound of the coaching horn and could only expect a tip if they were quick about their work. Arabella, on her slow journey to London in her uncle's ponderous travelling coach, watched enviously as the ostlers ran to change the horses of any smart chaise or sporting curricle which halted at the posting-house where she had stopped to eat a meal. And when the Royal Mail swept by with the guard sounding his horn 250 yards before the toll-gate to alert the keeper to open the gate (the Mail was exempt from tolls) Arabella could only wish that her coachman had been supplied with a yard of tin to blow up for the pike. Although it was mainly used to facilitate greater speed and efficiency, the horn was also sounded for safety and was blown continuously in a fog or to alert shepherds or drovers to move their flocks and herds off the roads.

LONG-DISTANCE TRAVEL

Long-distance coaches were those which went beyond a ten-mile radius from the centre of London, and long-distance travel for the upper class was generally undertaken in a post or travelling chaise. Posting-houses were a type of inn set up by enterprising individuals along the main roads out of London at which travellers could stop for refreshment while their horses were stabled and fresh ones poled up for the next stage of the journey. Some wealthy men such as Jasper Damerel in *Venetia* had post-horses stabled along well-frequented routes all over England to save the trouble of hiring unknown teams, but most travellers hired horses and post-boys. Originally, post-boys were men who travelled the postal routes carrying the mail on horseback or in a mail cart but from 1784 they were gradually replaced by the new mail coaches and the term 'post-boy' eventually became interchangeable with the word 'postilion' which denoted an entirely different occupation. Postilions were men or boys employed to ride a horse or horses harnessed to a carriage. Well-to-do families and individuals such as Jonathan Chawleigh in *A Civil Contract* often had their own private postilions but anyone who travelled by post-chaise had to use them as they were needed to steer this driverless carriage. This was done by a postilion mounted on the nearside (left-hand) lead horse with one postilion required for each pair of horses harnessed to a coach. Every postilion wore a specially designed iron guard on his right leg to protect his foot and leg from the centre pole. A change of horses could be booked ahead and at the end of each stage of a journey new postilions or post-boys were employed to replace the old ones whose responsibility it was to ride or drive the horses back to the post-house or inn from which they were hired. As Mr Tarleton was blithely informed by the post-boy on arriving at the village of Emborrow in *Friday's Child*, at a rate of one and six per mile, it cost eighteen shillings to travel the twelve miles of the first stage of a journey from Bath to Wells. Hiring a post-chaise and horses from one inn was a disadvantage because it meant that at the next a new vehicle and horse had to be hired. This also meant that passengers were forced to suffer the inconvenience of having to transfer their baggage at each change.

The distance which could be travelled by a single team varied according to the pace set, the number of changes made (if any), the condition and contour of the roads and the type of carriage they were pulling. For a traveller such as the young heroine in *Arabella*, opting to use her own carriage drawn by a single pair of horses without changes and which had to be rested at frequent intervals, it was a long journey of several days' duration from Yorkshire to London. By contrast, the heroine in *Venetia* discovered after an exhausting journey of some two hundred miles that a seat on the Mail could take a traveller from the General Post Office in London to Yorkshire in about eighteen hours. The benefit of the stage or post-chaise over the Mail was the longer stops at the posting-inns which enabled passengers to eat, drink and rest for a while. Overnight stops were not as common during the Regency as the stagecoach companies increasingly competed with the speedier mail coaches for customers. For those who did choose to sleep at a posting-house there was always the risk of damp sheets and poor food, although most of the well-established posting-houses servicing the main coaching routes prided themselves on their cosy parlour, well-supplied taproom, comfortable bedrooms, hot coffee and satisfying meals. Most inns had a private parlour which could be hired by wealthier guests wanting privacy and in which they could enjoy the comforts of a fire and refreshments while their horses were put to. During the Regency hundreds of posting-houses dotted the countryside as a single stage of a journey rarely exceeded twelve or thirteen miles. As a result most coaching proprietors ran small-scale operations, stabling fewer than twenty horses and horsing between ten and twenty miles of road, and many inns worked in loose partnership with others further up the road. Even the big London contractors, responsible for the majority of passenger bookings, only ran their horses on the first

Captain John Staple took up residence in a toll-house and acted as gatekeeper for a time in The Toll-Gate.

stages out of the city before relying on a string of partners to horse the remainder of a route.

TURNPIKES, TOLL-GATES AND TICKETS

Turnpikes were first established on the Great North Road in 1663 during the reign of Charles II as a means of charging road users a toll to supplement the cost of building and maintaining the highway. By the time of the Regency the poles or pikes originally used to bar the road had been replaced with wide wooden toll-gates, with small toll-houses built on the adjacent roadside as permanent residences for the toll-keepers or pikemen. It was in one of these toll-houses that Captain John Staple resided after he found himself unable to resist the promise of adventure and took over the role of gatekeeper in *The Toll-Gate*. The two main tasks of the trusts were to ensure the maintenance of the roads and the

```
┌─────────────────────────────────────────┐
│                                         │
│         KEARD TURNPIKE                  │
│         ─────────────                   │
│                                         │
│         Sheviock Gate                   │
│                                         │
│    22 day of August 1812                │
│                          ┌──────┬───────┤
│                          │ No. of│   d   │
│                          │ Horses│       │
│   Horses, Etc. drawing   │       │       │
│   Carriage - - - - - - - │       │       │
│   Chaise - - - - - - - - │       │       │
│   Phaeton - - - - - - -  │       │       │
│   Gig - - - - - - - - -  │       │       │
│   Waggon - - - - - - -   │   1   │   6   │
│   Cart - - - - - - - - - │       │       │
│   Van - - - - - - - - -  │       │       │
│   Dray - - - - - - - -   │       │       │
│                          └──────┴───────┤
│                                         │
│    This Ticket frees Crafthole and      │
│    Cremik Gates.                        │
│                                         │
└─────────────────────────────────────────┘
```

A turnpike ticket could be used to open several gates along a highway.

collection of the tolls, a long and often complex set of charges which depended on such things as who was travelling and whether they were on horseback, in a coach, driving a wagon or herd of animals, or transporting particular kinds of goods. Mail coaches travelled all toll-roads free of charge but in 1815 it cost a single-horse carriage sixpence, a coach and four a shilling and a wagon and six two shillings to pass the toll-gate and, as Captain Staple soon learned, it was not uncommon for travellers to tell any tale which might see them exempted from paying the toll. Once the toll was paid a ticket was issued which usually opened several more toll-gates along the highway.

9

What to Wear

MEN'S FASHION FROM HEAD TO TOE

A man of fashion was meticulous in both the choice and wearing of his clothes. From his elegant beaver hat and elaborately tied neck-cloth to his gleaming hessian or top-boots, the cut of his clothes, the polish on his boots, the fit of his pantaloons all combined to designate him a Tulip of the *ton*. As one of the great leaders of London society, Mr Beaumaris in *Arabella* was known as the Nonpareil—the Arbiter of Fashion who had taken Beau Brummell's place and whose taste and style in dress was copied everywhere by younger men. Not all gentlemen aspired to inclusion among the dandy set or even to turn out in fine trim but it would be a rare upper-class man who did not adhere to the established dress code of hat (when outdoors), shirt and collar, neckcloth, waistcoat, well-cut tail-coat, breeches and top-boots, or pantaloons and hessians—ensuring that his coat was dark-coloured and his trousers light. Gloves were essential outdoors or for formal occasions and a gentleman might also carry accessories such as a cane, quizzing glass or, in inclement weather, one of the new umbrellas. To guard against the cold, or while travelling, he could wear a top-coat or a driving-coat with any number of capes.

What a gentleman wore was dictated by the day's or evening's activities: whether he was in the town or the country; whether he was on the strut, visiting or driving; whether he was travelling, hunting or shooting; whether he was going to a ball, or to his club, or out for a night among the fleshpots, each activity had the appropriate dress. His choice of costume was also determined by his self-designated role as either a dandy, a Corinthian, a top-sawyer or a quiet man about town. But every gentleman wore black for mourning, buckskins and top-boots for riding, full dress on formal occasions, and a nightshirt—or nothing—to bed.

Hats were *de rigueur* for the Regency man and the most popular was the beaver hat. Made from felted beaver fur, it was similar to the modern top hat in shape with tall vertical sides (sometimes widening towards the top), a flat or slightly curved crown, and a slender brim which gently turned up at the sides. Men's shirts were mostly home-made with replaceable cuffs (and even fronts) to extend the life of the garment. They were designed to go over the head with an opening halfway down the chest which could be tied at the neck or buttoned. Made of cotton, linen or the finest cambric, shirts were white and generally plain-fronted for day wear and ruffled for the evening. Collars were attached separately and were raised to accommodate the cravat. During the Regency it became fashionable to leave the collar standing with the points touching the cheeks and some men, such as the aspiring young dandy Matthew Ware in *The Foundling*, wore their collars so high and the points so stiff that they could not turn their heads. Worn over the shirt, waistcoats were either single- or double-breasted and were often a testament to the wearer's taste and the tailor's art. While coats were of plain, usually dark-coloured cloth, waistcoats could be of a wide variety of colours and fabrics. White or black were the essential colours for evening dress but during the day spotted, striped, patterned—even flowered—waistcoats in colour combinations of green, yellow, blue, grey, black, cream and lilac could be seen. Striking designs such as the blue and yellow striped kerseymere waistcoat of the Four-Horse Club could set the wearer apart as a sportsman or leader of fashion, while the wearer of a waistcoat that was too florid or ornate (such as those worn by Nathaniel Coate in *The Toll-Gate*) would be censured. Waistcoats were longer in the front than the coat, with the lower edge—either cut straight or to one or two points—emerging from beneath the coat. The fronts were made with fine fabrics, such as satin, kersey-mere, marcella or Valencia, while the backs were of either cotton or silk; the waistcoat was pulled in from the back with tapes.

Until 1816, when the frock-coat was introduced, the skirt of a gentleman's coat was cut at the back into two long tails reaching to the back of the knee—and sometimes longer for those aspiring

Men of fashion often wore breeches, top-boots and a well-cut coat during the day.

to join the dandy set. Coats were either single- or double-breasted with a turn-over collar that was high at the back and lapels with a single or M-shaped notch at the point where they joined the collar. The coat waist was short and cut square with double-breasted coat fronts always shorter than single-breasted. Padding was sometimes added to the shoulders or breast of the coat and well-built gentlemen often had them made so close-fitting they needed assistance to get them on or off. Preferred fabrics were superfine and kerseymere, which both sat well and had an elegant finish, and colours were generally dark. Claret, bottle green, olive green, brown, corbeau, black and blue were the most popular colours for day wear, with blue the first choice for evening attire. The cut of a coat could indicate a man's social status and in *Cotillion* Freddy's concerns about the Chevalier d'Evron were somewhat allayed by the fellow's appearance in a bottle-green, long-tailed coat that had clearly come from the hands of a master tailor.

Below their coats men wore either breeches, pantaloons or trousers. Breeches were made of soft leather, wool or nankeen, or of satin or velvet for formal occasions. They had a high waist, were full at the hips and ended just below the knee where they were buttoned, tied or buckled and had a front opening or narrow flap, known as a 'fall', which buttoned at the waist and could be dropped down. They had a deep waistband which gave extra support with a fob pocket in the right-hand side. For riding or day wear, breeches were worn with top-boots, but for evening wear or attendance at Court they were worn with plain or clocked stockings and shoes. Buckskins were men's suede leather breeches made from the skin of the male deer which were naturally greyish yellow in colour. Soft and comfortable, each leg was made from a single piece of leather to avoid having an inner seam, making them especially comfortable for riding. Although they were worn as riding breeches they were perfectly acceptable for ordinary day wear. Pantaloons were an alternative to breeches and were, as

Mr Beaumaris told his grandmother in *Arabella*, knitted. A close-fitting trouser, also known as 'inexpressibles', they were shaped to the leg and eventually replaced knee-breeches for day wear. The fashion was for light-coloured trousers, and pantaloons were often yellow, cream, biscuit, buff or fawn; they were worn with hessian boots or half-boots—never with top-boots. Trousers were long like pantaloons but cut wide at the ankle and could be worn with shoes, half-boots or boots. They were generally light-coloured and made of nankeen or jean.

Regency men usually wore short or knee-length cotton or linen drawers under their breeches which were tied at the waist with ribbon. Drawers had a small vent in the front and could be drawn

A fashionable male always wore gleaming hessians with his skintight pantaloons.

in from behind with tapes. Ankle-length drawers were worn under pantaloons or trousers and these either had feet attached or were kept in place with a strap under the instep. Stockings were mostly worn with knee-breeches and came in a range of colours for day wear, with white or natural-coloured hose generally worn with evening dress. Knitted worsted, cotton and silk stockings were the most common, held up with garters, and stockings for evening wear were often decorated with the intricate embroidery at the ankle known as clocks.

The top-coat, also known as a Benjamin, was a loose-fitting overcoat, originally worn by the working classes. Its style was appropriated by upper-class gentlemen who wore it over their clothes in cooler weather or while travelling. Top-coats were usually ankle length and often drab-coloured—either light olive brown or grey. Also known as a box coat (from being worn by coachmen who sat on the box seat of a carriage), the driving-coat was a type of overcoat worn by gentlemen in cooler weather while driving, walking or travelling. Designed for a loose fit, they were usually light in colour, calf or ankle length, with several of the broad collars, known as capes, hung across the shoulders in layers. In *Regency Buck*, the Earl of Worth wore a driving-coat made of drab with fifteen shoulder-capes and a double row of silver buttons.

Shoes, gloves and a cane completed the gentleman's wardrobe and the well-dressed man always wore the correct footwear. Leather knee-high boots worn with breeches, top-boots had turn-over tops of a different colour from the uppers. Tops were generally either brown or black but some of the dandies wore boots with white tops for hunting or short boots with very long tops. Both top-boots and hessians were expected to be polished to a high gloss and some valets, such as Vincent Darracott's man Crimplesham in *The Unknown Ajax* (who considered the care of boots to be an Art), had their own jealously guarded recipes for boot blacking. Hessians were men's calf-length, low-heeled boots which curved up in front to a point just below the knee (sometimes with a V-shaped cut-out) and were cut at the back into a curving V-shape to allow the leg to bend. Generally black in colour, they were worn with pantaloons and were usually decorated with a small tassel at the point below the knee. Shoes were usually worn with knee-breeches and later with trousers. They were made of leather (and shaped to the foot), low-heeled with rounded toes and were tied across a tongue above the instep. Shoes worn to Court were known as pumps and were made of soft leather with thin soles and low sides; they usually had buckles or were tied with ribbon.

Gentlemen wore short cotton or leather gloves both during the day and in the evening; the colour, fabric and style were dependent on the occasion. A fashionable man had his gloves made to measure and generally owned several pairs. In *Friday's Child*, the Honourable Ferdy Fakenham wore elegant lavender gloves and carried a cane to his friend Sherry's wedding. Made of polished wood, canes often had ornamental heads of semi-precious stones such as amethyst, or of carved ivory, polished glass or porcelain. Black was the colour for funerals and for mourning, during which period a gentleman wore all black clothes and sometimes a black muslin band tied around his hat. Court mourning precluded the wearing of gilt buttons or buckles and the usual swords were replaced with black ones. Francis Cheviot in *The Reluctant Widow* wore silver tassels on his hessian boots instead of the usual gold to mark the sombre occasion of his cousin's funeral.

A gentleman of fashion was required, on certain occasions, to dress formally. Evenings at Almack's or formal balls demanded that he appear in the exquisite attire of full evening dress. This consisted of a freshly laundered shirt and carefully tied neckcloth, white waistcoat, long-tailed coat (coats of blue superfine were popular), black satin or light-coloured knee-breeches, white stockings (either striped or with clocks), black shoes with ribbon ties, and a chapeau-bras. The 'chapeau-bras', also known as an opera hat, was a black, crescent-shaped hat which could be flattened, and was mainly designed to be held under the arm although it was worn on occasion. In *Cotillion*, Freddy Standen was 'beautiful to behold' when he appeared in full evening dress at Almack's with his neckcloth the epitome of the wearer's art.

Attendance at Court demanded a full dress suit more in keeping with the glamour of the previous century than the more austere male costume of the Regency period. A single-breasted cutaway coat of embroidered velvet was worn over a matching velvet or white satin waistcoat and silk or velvet knee-breeches. The coat was generally a rich colour: either blue, purple, green or brown, with the cuffs and front edges sewn with silver lace. White silk

Freddy Standen in Cotillion *wore a perfectly cut coat and satin knee-breeches when he visited Almack's.*

stockings with clocks and black slippers with buckles were *de rigueur* and a dress sword and chapeau-bras completed the outfit.

THE INTRICACIES OF THE NECKCLOTH

For the man of fashion, the neckcloth or starched cravat was a crucial part of his daily dress. The great dandy and leader of fashion, Beau Brummell, had set the standard and was reputed to spend hours perfecting the set of his neckcloth before leaving the house. The neckcloth was a large square of fabric—usually muslin, lawn or silk—which was folded into either a triangle or a wide band and then wound around the neck and tied at the front. Several of the most fashionable styles required that the neckcloth be well starched so that it would stand stiffly about the wearer's neck and remain so throughout the day. A perfectly tied neckcloth required both patience and considerable skill, particularly if the wearer aspired to its being recognised as one of the several named styles in fashion during the Regency. In *The Corinthian*, Sir Richard Wyndham had developed the Wyndham Fall and, in *Frederica*, James the footman (whose secret ambition was to become a gentleman's gentleman) was pleased to have the chance to watch the Marquis of Alverstoke put the final touches to his exquisitely tied neckcloth.

The Oriental tie was required to be perfectly smooth, without the hint of a crease, and snowy white; another austere tie, the *Trône d'Amour*, was similar to the Oriental but with a single horizontal indentation made above the knot; the Mathematical, with its three precise creases (one horizontal indent above the knot, two diagonal creases from the ears to the knot), was demanding but its height was at the discretion of the wearer; while the American was similar to the Mathematical but without the horizontal crease. It was the Mathematical which young Christian Emborough in *Charity Girl* admired on his cousin Viscount Desford and which the Viscount kindly promised to teach him. Both the Osbaldeston and the Napoleon ties were more suited for summer, being of a narrower band and encircling the neck only once. The Osbaldeston employed a large knot at least four inches wide while the Napoleon was simply crossed at the neck. With the taller neckcloths it was important that the edge beneath the ears always remained higher than the edge beneath the chin, as a straight line was considered very poor taste.

Hats came in a wide variety of shapes and sizes and were often adorned with flowers, ribbons and feathers.

Many women enjoyed trimming a bonnet to match a new dress or pelisse.

One of the most popular ties was the Mail Coach or Waterfall, which required minimal starch, but a considerable degree of skill to achieve a perfect fall over its single knot. Favoured by Corinthians and the bloods of the fancy, it was wound about the neck and tied at the front with the ends pulled over the knot to hang; it presented a softer, fuller look than most other styles of neckcloth. Although coloured neckcloths had been fashionable in earlier times, and were re-introduced in about 1818, for much of the Regency it was expected that neckcloths would be white; the exception being the black-spotted, white muslin cravat of the Four-Horse Club which Lord Ulverston wore in *The Quiet Gentleman*. An alternative to the hand-tied neckcloth was the stock: a ready-made, high-standing neckcloth made of cambric or linen and stiffened with pasteboard. It was fitted around the neck and tied or buckled at the back; it was customary for clergymen to wear stocks rather than neckcloths.

WOMEN'S FASHION FROM HATS TO HOSE

The hat was an essential accessory for the Regency woman. From the bonnet which shaded her face from the sun to the lace cap worn indoors and which indicated her age or marital status; the evening hat or turban that completed an elegant ensemble and the straw, chip, or leghorn hat—the decoration of which could fill her leisure hours—some kind of hat or headdress was worn for a good part of each day and often in the evening. Hats were always worn outside and bonnets with brims large enough to protect the complexion were fashionable, as were veils which could be added or removed as desired. Nell Cardross wore a bonnet with a heavy veil when she went to visit a moneylender in *April Lady*. Military-style hats came into vogue during the Napoleonic wars and Shako-style hats, cylinder-shaped, with a high crown, ostrich plumes and neat peak, were a popular accessory to the military-style riding-habit then in

vogue. Caps were mainly worn indoors by matrons, widows and
women considered to be past their prime and were usually made of
lace and trimmed with ribbon. Sir Gareth Ludlow in *Sprig Muslin*
was displeased to find Lady Hester Theale wearing a cap but could
not persuade her to remove it. He had never thought of Hester as
being of an age when she ought to wear a cap but Hester felt it
essential to do so in order to emphasise her position as a mature
and respectable female. Hat design tended to vary according to
the wearer's hairstyle and throughout the period bonnets came in
a wide range of sizes, styles and fabrics; ladies regularly had them
made up in muslin, sarsnet, velvet, satin or silk to match a particular
pelisse or dress. Trimming hats was a popular pastime and even
those straw or fabric hats bought from the milliner were often
re-trimmed by their owners. Artificial flowers, feathers, ribbon,
and even fruit were all used to add colour and style to a new or
old bonnet. In *Arabella*, on finding herself complimented on her
pink-feathered hat by the Duke of Clarence, Arabella wrote to tell
the news to her mama who had made it for her. Turbans were an
elegant form of headdress for the evening and were often made of
silk or satin and adorned with ostrich feathers or jewels.

Lace caps were worn indoors and often by older women.

Turbans were especially popular with older women and in
The Foundling *the Dowager Lady Ampleforth wore a*
magnificent turban of 'rich violet silk, shot with orange'.

The dramatic shifts in fashion between the eighteenth and nineteenth centuries also extended to women's underwear. Before the introduction of the more revealing lawn and muslin dresses, underwear had consisted mainly of the chemise, corset and the all-important full-length petticoat and, although most English women continued to wear these essential items, by 1811 drawers had also begun to be worn. A knee-length linen or cotton shift of plain design, with or without sleeves, the chemise was the undergarment worn next to the skin. It was wide and straight-edged and could be nearly oblong in shape; generally the only concession to fashion was a square neck with a lace or muslin edging. Introduced as early as 1804, drawers were originally thought to be immodest but they gradually increased in popularity and, by 1811, the Prince Regent's daughter, Princess Charlotte, was known to wear them and the Duchess of Bedford had the bottoms of hers edged with Brussels lace. Drawers could be made of cotton, silk or muslin and consisted of two knee-length legs attached separately to a waistband. There was no gusset (which made access to the chamber-pot easy) and they could be buttoned or tied below the knee. Long drawers with feet attached for cold-weather wear were introduced during the Regency and several enterprising manufacturers offered 'ladies hunting and Opera drawers in elastic India cotton' or 'patent elastic woollen drawers of stockinette' to those wishing to ride in greater comfort. Soon referred to as 'pantalettes', to distinguish them from the close-fitting male trouser, women's pantaloons were another form of ladies' underwear. Longer than the knee-length drawers, they reached to just below the calf. Pantalettes were finished with a deep decorative border of lace and several rows of tucks which were meant to be seen. As a result they were mainly worn by the more daring in society and, in 1817, Lady Charlotte Lindsay shocked the sensibilities of her hostess, Lady Stanley, by wearing 'a green silk spencer, green silk boots, and trowsers to the ankle much below the petticoats'.

Also known as stays, corsets were worn over the chemise and under the petticoat. Corsets underwent several changes in design during the early nineteenth century. The decade before the Regency was the era of the long corset which pushed up the bosom and extended over the hips to flatten the stomach and create the long straight line needed for the light, clinging lawn and muslin dresses of the period. Made of buckram and jean, it was stiffened with whalebone and steel and laced at the back. In 1811, the short corset returned to favour—stiffer than ever and with shoulder straps and back lacing. It too was made of strong cotton such as jean but its shape was more curved and the aim was to emphasise the waist and bosom. The fashion for small hips encouraged tight lacing and was extremely uncomfortable for many female aspirants to fashion; when Miss Morville was knocked unconscious in *The Quiet Gentleman* Mr Leek was put in a quandary as to whether or not he should cut her laces. The petticoat was put on over the chemise and corset and worn directly under the dress. Mostly made of linen, cotton, cambric, or flannel for the winter, petticoats had a bodice (often high-cut at the back) which fastened at the front and was attached to the skirt, which the wearer secured around the waist with tapes. Petticoats were generally made to match the length of the dress under which they were worn and old or worn-out dresses were sometimes converted into petticoats. During the Regency decorative or ornamental petticoats or underskirts were worn under open dresses designed to show off a portion of the undergarment. Full-length under-dresses worn under ball gowns of gauze or lace were also known as petticoats.

Stockings were worn to the knee and held up with knitted or ribbon garters. They were usually white or pink, although prior to the Regency black and coloured stockings had been popular. Those who could afford them wore silk stockings with cotton feet attached for which, in 1811, they paid about 12s. a pair. Tiffany Wield bought several pairs of silk stockings when shopping in Leeds in *The Nonesuch* and inspired her friend Patience Chartley to put aside enough money to buy just one pair to wear to the Colebatches' ball. Stockings for evening wear were sometimes embroidered at the ankles (in order to cover the seams) with decorative patterns known as clocks. Cotton stockings were also fashionable and cost around 4s. a pair, while the cheapest and least liked were woollen or worsted stockings which were often made at home. Although warm and functional, worsted stockings were not thought to be modish and it was not uncommon to give them to the needy.

The most important garment in a woman's wardrobe, the dress had begun to change from the classical, semi-transparent gown of the previous decade as styles gradually turned towards a 'pseudo-classical' mode which allowed for shorter skirt lengths and the introduction of gores (triangular pieces of fabric) into the bodice and the skirt. Trains mostly disappeared after 1812 as the slightly wider skirt allowed for increased decoration and, as the period progressed, more and more elaborate trim, in the form of ruffs, tucks, frills, flounces, flowers and beads, was applied to the sleeves, bodices and hems of ladies' dresses. Dress designs also became more elaborate, with both the cut and trim frequently styled to match a spencer or pelisse, while decorative underskirts, worn under partially open dresses, also began to appear. In *Friday's Child*, Hero wore an elegant dress of worked French muslin with flounces and tucks which won the envious admiration of her aunt and cousins. Towards the end of the Regency, dresses with separate skirts and bodices began to be seen and, while waists remained high for much of the period, in the later years they began slowly to move lower until, by 1821, they were near their natural level. Dresses were made of a wide variety of fabrics, depending on the season, style and intended use, including muslin, cambric, lawn, jaconet, sarsnet, silk, merino, satin, crepe, gauze, kerseymere and velvet.

The social life of an upper-class Regency woman demanded a large and versatile wardrobe with a dress for every occasion. Between rising and retiring, a fashionable lady with a busy round of social engagements might change her dress three or four times in a day. Even on the quietest day it was expected that all members of an upper-class household would change for dinner—or at least make some alteration to their appearance—something Lady Legerwood in *Cotillion* felt to be obligatory. Ladies' magazines such as *La Belle Assemblée* or the *Ladies' Monthly Museum* depicted a wide range of dresses, cloaks, hats and accessories for different activities and times of the day; the differences between a walking dress, promenade dress, afternoon dress or carriage dress were not always obvious, however, as the various lines of demarcation shifted with changing fashions. Certainly the amount of exposed flesh was regulated according to the time of day and custom dictated that a lady cover her arms, neck and bosom in the morning and unveil them only for afternoon or evening wear. There were also subtle distinctions between an evening dress and a ball dress, or between a walking dress and a day dress, and it is likely that knowing the differences was one of the marks of a well-bred woman.

Mostly worn indoors, morning dresses were often as richly trimmed and elegant as those worn outside.

Put on after rising, the morning dress was made to cover the chest, arms and neck, with a close-fitting bodice and flowing skirt short enough for walking but not to reveal the ankle. It was often worn with a close-fitting lace cap. Later in the period morning dresses became less casual and took on the appearance of a day dress which could be worn outside. Nell Cardross in *April Lady* bought a very elegant and expensive morning dress of twilled

French silk which could have been worn both indoors and out. For general day wear a round dress or gown was worn, which had no train but consisted of a joined skirt and bodice with the hem sewn all the way around (hence a 'round' gown) so as not to reveal any kind of underskirt or petticoat. Either as an informal evening dress or ordinary day dress, a half-dress could be worn consisting of a thigh-length, short-sleeved tunic worn over a round gown and tied across the waist of the dress. A walking dress was one of the most commonly worn costumes and could be either long- or short-sleeved depending on the season, with a slightly shorter hemline for ease of walking. They were often high-necked, or worn with a tucker or fichu, and in the second half of the period were regularly advertised with the model depicted wearing a matching pelisse, spencer or mantle. Patience Chartley in *The Nonesuch* wore her best walking dress of figured muslin (with a double flounce and long sleeves) on an ill-fated shopping trip to Leeds. Similar to the walking dress in style, though often made of richer fabrics and more elegantly trimmed, the carriage or promenade dress was worn to impress while taking the air in an open carriage or going 'on the promenade' in Hyde Park or some other fashionable spot. Miss Abigail Wendover in *Black Sheep* wore the latest thing in carriage dresses on her return from London to Bath, and the gown's rucked sleeves and little winged ruff won instant approval from her sister Selina. The pelisse robe could provide an alternative to the carriage dress and was a style of robe which appeared from 1817, having evolved from the pelisse or close-fitting coat. It was fastened down the front from neck to ankle with concealed hooks and eyes or ribbons.

An afternoon dress was put on in place of the morning dress and worn for making formal calls, shopping, or while engaged in activities at home. An elegant gown with a low-cut bodice and, after 1812, no train, an evening dress could have either short or long sleeves and was trimmed around the hemline, on the sleeves

*A carriage dress was ideal for taking the air in Hyde Park or on an outing to
Richmond in the company of a gentleman of the* ton.

and often across the bodice. In *The Grand Sophy*, the evening
gown of pale green crepe which Sophy wore on her first evening
at the Rivenhalls' was richly trimmed with festoons of silk and
tied at the waist with a tasselled cord. Usually worn with elbow-
length gloves, evening dresses were sometimes draped with an
over-tunic or a piece of elegantly ruched fabric and accessorised
with a stylish headdress.

*An evening dress was an elegant garment often richly trimmed
and made of the finest fabrics.*

The most beautiful of all gowns, the ball dress was made of the
finest fabrics and often consisted of a satin slip worn under a delicate over-dress of crepe, net, spider-gauze, or sarsnet. White was
popular for debutantes in both the under- and over-dress, but soft
colours were also acceptable for either, with pastel shades of pink,
lavender or blue much worn, while more striking colours such as
jonquil, Pomona green and cerulean blue were mostly worn over
white. In *Frederica*, Charis Merriville drew every eye in an exquisite
ball gown of ivory satin worn under a three-quarter dress of white
sarsnet and adorned with pearl rosettes, while in *The Grand Sophy*,
Cecilia Rivenhall was the loveliest damsel at the ball in a dress of
white spider-gauze delicately embroidered with silver acorns. Ball

dresses could also be delicately embroidered or lavishly trimmed
with lace, ruffles, artificial flowers or beads and were nearly always
worn with some kind of ornamental headdress.

Although the wide skirts and hoops of the eighteenth century
had been banished from everyday life by the French Revolution,
the grand fashion of the earlier era persisted in the English Court.
Hoops, silk or satin, lace and ostrich feathers continued to be
compulsory attire for women at the Court of St James's until 1820
when the Regent ascended the throne and brought the tradition
of eighteenth-century costume to an abrupt halt. The *grande toilette*
that was Court dress consisted of a huge hoop under an embroidered petticoat over which could be worn a skirt of satin, lace

A ball dress was the most beautiful of all the dresses in a lady's wardrobe.

or net drapery. Dresses were often white and sewn with pearls or beads but colours were also worn. In *A Civil Contract*, Jenny, Lady Lynton, wore violet satin with an amethyst-encrusted crape petticoat to her presentation and was persuaded to dispense with most of her jewels and wear just a delicate diamond necklace, a pair of diamond drop earrings and only two bracelets instead. Ostrich feathers were an important part of Court etiquette and attendance at a Drawing-room required the debutante or newly married woman to wear anywhere from three to eight large upright feathers as a headdress. They were often attached to a tiara or jewelled aigrette and although imposing, coupled with her wide hoop, could make getting in and out of a closed carriage a perilous undertaking.

The riding-habit was specifically designed for horse riding and, in particular, for the side-saddle which was used by all female riders. Based on a man's eighteenth-century coat, the Regency habit consisted of a close-fitting jacket with long tight-fitting sleeves over the wrist and a very full skirt, sometimes with a train. The overall look of the riding costume was often that of a coat and some were cut with lapels and a high collar, or favoured the more military style, with frogs, epaulettes and braided sleeves. Lady Barbara Childe in *An Infamous Army* wore a severely cut habit of cerulean blue which was, apart from two rows of silver buttons, quite plain. Habits were made of linen, drab broadcloth or other woollen materials. *Tonnish* women often employed a tailor rather than a modiste to make their habits in order to ensure the quality of the cut and fit of what was a more 'mannish' costume than was usual for women at the time. The riding-habit was worn with a hat, gloves and boots and a lady usually carried a riding crop as well.

Mourning clothes were worn to mark the death of a relative or member of the royal family. The period varied according to the nature of one's relationship with the deceased or, in the case of Court mourning, the individual's social standing. Women were expected to wear black for the entire period of full mourning and grey, lilac, or black with white relief for half mourning, and they usually continued to wear black gloves when out socially. Mourning clothes were often specially made using black cotton, calico or bombazine, while traditional black crape was used for veils or to trim hats. Court mourning was ordered by the Lord Chamberlain on the death of a member of the royal family and was observed over three stages, with each stage marked by an alteration in dress style and fabrics. When Queen Charlotte died, Mrs Hendred in *Venetia* advised her niece to wear a high-necked gown rather than one cut low across the bosom, as well as the requisite black ribbons and gloves. Although colours and accessories were gradually introduced, at all times mourning clothes were expected to be quiet and unobtrusive with nothing shining or gleaming on them to draw the eye.

*A pelisse was an elegant coat often trimmed with fur
and matched with a magnificent fur muff.*

Because Regency dresses were often lightweight with short sleeves, keeping warm required an array of fashionable coats, cloaks and accessories. An essential item of clothing, the pelisse was a coat which followed the dress style of the period (eventually evolving into a dress in its own right). Originally knee-length, by the time of the Regency the pelisse had lengthened to the ankle with the waist below the bosom. Pelisses were close-fitting, with front fastenings across the bosom or extending all the way from neck to ankle, and they were elegant, ornamental garments often with trimmings that matched those of the dress. In *Cotillion* Meg, Lady Buckhaven, wore an elegant new pelisse of Sardinian blue velvet when visiting her mother but was advised by that fashionable lady to wear it with chinchilla or ermine rather than the dark sables her daughter was wearing. Sleeves were long and generally extended over the hand and could be puffed, gathered or trimmed with fur at the shoulders; collars varied but were often high or flat and wide. Sometimes two or more shoulder capes were added. Worn in both summer and winter, pelisses were made of almost every type of fabric, although those of wool, kerseymere, velvet, brocade or other heavy cloth were favoured in the cooler months. An extremely fashionable garment during the Regency was the spencer, a very short jacket resembling the bodice of the pelisse, with long sleeves extending over the hands. Designed to cover the chest, they were made of a variety of materials including silk, velvet, kerseymere, wool and satin, and could be collarless—although many women favoured those with high frilled collars. Both elegant and utilitarian, shawls were a versatile accessory which could be worn, artistically draped across the arms or shoulder, over an evening dress or could be, when not out socially, used to cover the shoulders and upper body in cooler weather. Either square or rectangular, shawls came in a wide variety of sizes with some as much as six feet long. Cashmere shawls made of fine goat's hair and imported from Kashmir in the Himalayas were both warm and beautiful and proved popular as did English Norwich silk shawls, despite costing as much as £60 and being only a yard square in size. Lady Bridlington in *Arabella* was tempted to buy her young protégée a handsome Norwich shawl before she remembered that she had a superior one at home to lend to Arabella. A mantle was similar to a cloak but of variable length; it fastened at the neck and was made of fur, velvet or other warm fabrics; and occasionally had a cape or sleeves.

Shoes were also known as slippers and were quite dainty and often unsuited to the demands of daily life or the exigencies of walking and dancing. Either flat or low-heeled, they had a slim leather sole and were fastened with ribbons or laces tied around the ankle or instep. For everyday use shoes tended to be made of kid leather or jean although, despite their impracticality for outdoor wear, velvet, silk and satin were also popular and even recommended in the ladies' magazines, especially for evening

A reticule was an indispensable item in a lady's wardrobe and was carried everywhere.

wear. Half-boots, worn for walking or riding, were low-heeled, short in length (they reached to the bottom of the calf), and were either buttoned at the side or laced at the side, front or back. They were made of either kid leather, jean, or nankeen, and occasionally of silk. Frederica wore half-boots of orange jean when visiting Lady Buxted and, on her long journey to London, Arabella found that her half-boots of crimson jean did not keep out the cold.

Accessories were an essential part of a well-dressed lady's wardrobe and generally included a variety of bags, gloves, fans and muffs. A reticule was the Regency woman's handbag and also known as a 'ridicule'. It usually had a draw-string opening and came in a range of shapes, styles and fabrics. The style of dress during the period precluded pockets, making the reticule an indispensable accessory for any lady wishing to carry her money, handkerchief, scent or smelling-salts. Women often fashioned their own reticules and decorated them with embroidery or beads. In *The Unknown Ajax*, Anthea Darracott, following the advice in *The Mirror of Fashion*, attempted to make a reticule in the shape of an Etruscan vase which her mother assured her would look very elegant once it was painted. An alternative to the reticule for carrying money, the stocking purse was a long narrow tube with a single opening at the centre enabling the user to drop coins into each end. Usually knitted, crocheted or netted, they were closed by means of two metal rings encircling the central opening which could be pushed in either direction to secure the contents. Lady Bridlington kindly bought one for Arabella while shopping in London but ladies often made stocking purses to their own design and ornamented the ends.

No well-dressed woman went out of doors without her gloves which, although useful for keeping the hands warm, were considered an elegant and essential accessory for both day and evening wear. During the Regency they were mostly worn short during the day and elbow length in the evenings. Short kid leather or York tan gloves were mostly worn for riding, driving or other outdoor activities; coloured silk gloves were reserved for more genteel pastimes; long white kid gloves were exclusively for evening wear and knitted woollen gloves or mittens, though utilitarian and less attractive, were useful in the winter months. In *Lady of Quality*, Lucilla Carleton was thrilled when Ancilla granted her permission to buy her first pair of evening gloves to wear to a rout party.

Muffs, large hollow cylinders usually made of fur, swansdown, fabric or sealskin, were used by both men and women, although favoured by the latter, to keep their hands warm. They varied greatly in size, with the heavier winter muffs as much as two feet in length, and were often made of sable or ermine while summer muffs were lighter and made of feathers or swansdown. An elegant

A stocking purse was particularly convenient for carrying money, and Patience Chartley in The Nonesuch *held tightly to hers while on a shopping trip to Leeds.*

accessory, muffs were often designed to match a woman's tippet or the edging on her pelisse and could be used to conceal or carry small objects such as billets-doux or money. Sophy carried a large swansdown muff when she visited the moneylender, Mr Goldhanger, in *The Grand Sophy* and found it extremely useful for carrying her money, several important papers and her pistol.

Introduced to fashionable English society from China, the early parasols were made of silk and often shaped like a pagoda. Primarily used to shade a lady's complexion from the sun, they were also considered an elegant accessory and were often chosen to match a particular gown or pelisse. Bamboo, cane and the new telescopic steel sticks were used for the frame, and hinged parasols, which could be used like a fan, were popular for a time. Unlike their male counterparts who carried their furled umbrellas held firmly in the middle, ladies carried their furled parasols by the handle.

And finally, every lady of fashion carried a fan in her reticule or slipped over her wrist at a ball or evening party. In previous decades the fan had been an instrument of dalliance and ladies were well-versed in the language of the furled or open fan, twirling, tapping, opening or closing it to convey messages of love and rejection. By the time of the Regency, however, the fan was used less for flirtation and more as an elegant accessory which could also provide some relief from the often oppressive heat of a crowded ballroom. Folding fans with multiple elaborately decorated sticks, known as brisé fans, were among the most popular and were often articles of great beauty. Those created by the celebrated eighteenth-century artist Angela Kauffmann, or which used the French *vernis* technique developed by the four Martin brothers, were highly prized. *Vernis Martin* fans were so-called because of their varnished (*vernis* in French) decoration; they were hand-painted, often with oriental scenes. In *A Civil Contract* Jonathan Chawleigh had already bestowed a *Vernis Martin* fan on his daughter Jenny when her husband Adam gave her an elegant painted fan with mother-of-pearl sticks. Fans could be made with sticks of delicately carved ivory, tortoiseshell, mother-of-pearl, bone, metal or lacquered wood, with leaves of silk, crape, lace or chicken skin. These delicate works of art had become smaller by the early nineteenth century and during the Regency were usually between six and ten inches long with a span of approximately 120 degrees. French fans and those made by oriental craftsmen were among the most popular fans for ladies during the period.

A fan was an elegant accessory which every lady carried with her to a ball or party.

HAIRSTYLES

The penchant for the Grecian style which influenced fashion in the early nineteenth century also extended to men's and women's hairstyles. For much of the Regency, men wore their hair short with just enough length to have it curled or waved. Partings were rare and many men wore their hair as it fell naturally while followers of fashion frequently affected one of the well-known styles of the day. Sir Richard Wyndham in *The Corinthian* favoured the Windswept which was one of the most difficult hairstyles to realise: the aim being to look as natural as possible without any indication of the time required to achieve it. The dishevelled style known as the Brutus was first made popular by Beau Brummell and was fashionable until the later years of the Regency although it took both time and patience to create the desired tousled look.

Some men still adopted a version of an earlier Grecian style called the Titus in imitation of the Roman emperor; it had short side-whiskers and was carefully cut and styled to sit up at the front and to follow the contours of the face at the temples. Other popular pre-Regency styles were the *Coup au Vent*, which was short at the back and worn long over the eyes at the front, and the *Chérubin*, which was all over short curls. Although a few members of the older generation still wore wigs, the 1795 tax on hair powder had seen them worn less and less and by the time of the Regency they were mostly worn only at Court. By 1813 many men had begun to cultivate side-whiskers and by 1818 both short and long side-whiskers had become fashionable.

During the Regency the fashionable 'natural' look of men's hairstyles often took a great deal of time and patience to achieve.

Women, too, styled their hair along Grecian lines with soft curls around the face and the rest of the hair pulled back into a chignon or braided. The antique Roman style also became popular after 1810 with the hair lifted to the back of the head and styled into two soft knots or ringlets which hung lightly to the neck. A plain or jewelled bandeau was often worn around the hair in imitation of the ancient modes. By the middle of the period long hair had become the vogue and it was fashionable to wear one's hair in bunches of ringlets on either side of the head or, less commonly, in a braided coronet on the crown of the head as Jenny Chawleigh was persuaded to do in *A Civil Contract*. The 'natural' look which was so popular often took much time and patience to achieve and

In A Civil Contract *Lydia Deveril persuaded her sister-in-law Jenny to adopt an elegant new hairstyle and exchange her ringlets for smooth braids.*

for those who did not have natural curls, it was necessary to produce them with metal curling tongs heated in the fire or by using curl papers. Styles such as *à la Méduse* (like Medusa) consisted of long curls or ringlets carefully dressed to create a 'natural' look. Upper-class and wealthier middle-class ladies often had a personal maid or dresser to attend to their hair or they could call upon the services of a professional hairdresser who would attend them in their home and charge between 2s.6d. and 5s. for cutting and styling. For formal occasions such as a ball it was fashionable to wear a tiara or even a wreath of flowers in one's hair but for presentations at Court ostrich feathers were *de rigueur*.

SEALS, FOBS, SNUFF-BOXES AND QUIZZING GLASSES

Seals were small, decorative stamps used to impress one's insignia on the wax seal of a letter. They were often finely crafted and could be made of ivory, silver, gold or other metal. Fashionable men often hung them from their fob-watch ribbon. Most gentlemen carried a fob or pocket watch in a specially designed pocket in the waistband of their breeches or pantaloons. Attached to the watch was a fob

ribbon which hung outside the waistband and was weighted down
with an ornamental fob. This not only advertised the fact that the
gentleman could afford so expensive an item as a pocket watch but
also made it easier to draw the watch from the pocket. As well as
a fob, fashionable men often attached their watch key and a seal to
the fob ribbon, while aspiring dandies and fops often hung several
fobs and seals from their watch. Fobs were handcrafted, highly
decorative pieces, usually made of gold or silver.

Snuff taking did not become widespread in England until the
early 1700s and in the first half of the century it was taken from

*Most gentlemen carried at least one seal
on their fob ribbon while fashionable
fops were known to carry several.*

bottles and jars as well as boxes.
Ladies took snuff from a small bag
hung from their dress, while some
men purportedly carried it loose in
their pocket. From mid-century,
however, snuff was mainly taken
from boxes and, by the time of the
Regency (when snuff taking was
in the last decade of its enormous
popularity),   snuff-boxes   had
become objects of fashion and
status and, in upper-class circles,
formed part of a complex social ritual with its own precise rules
and etiquette. It was Kit Fancot's lack of dexterity with his brother's
pretty Bernier snuff-box in *False Colours* that caught Sir Bonamy
Ripple's attention and earned Kit a piece of salient advice about
how to handle it. Snuff-boxes varied greatly in size and shape as
well as design: they could be almost any shape, including octagonal,
heart-shaped, oblong, circular, oval, shell, sarcophagus and scroll,
but they were also made in the form of people, animals, birds, fruit,
flowers, books, shoes, sedan chairs and boats, and their inner and
outer surfaces were often decorated with imaginative and beautiful
designs. They could be made from almost any material but during

the great period of manufacture, from about 1730 to the Regency, many of the most popular boxes were made of gold (almost always in alloy form as pure gold was too soft), silver, porcelain or hard-stones such as quartz, agate, onyx and jasper. But boxes made from ivory, bone, tortoiseshell, papier mâché, lacquer, wood, pewter, copper, brass, steel, leather and *Vernis Martin* were also an option. They could be plain or decorative, with any amount of jewellery or carving, and many boxes had etched, painted or engraved surfaces. They sometimes had cameos mounted into the lids, or the sides were painted or enamelled with pastoral scenes or family portraits. Many snuff-boxes were ingeniously designed with hidden openings, double lids or false bottoms for hiding love notes or portraits of a lover or mistress. Some collectors had a snuff-box to match every outfit, or one for every day of the year as Lord Petersham had in *Regency Buck*, with heavier snuff-boxes for winter and lighter ones for summer. Men and women often had boxes specifically designed for their gender and made distinguishable by shape, design or decoration. During the Regency there were many avid collectors and connoisseurs of snuff-boxes—both male and female—among the upper class.

Eyeglasses that could be held on the face with side arms were not invented until 1727 and prior to that date lenses used for reading or vision were hand-held or made to pinch the nose (hence pince-nez) which was uncomfortable. 'Glasses' often consisted of one lens set into a frame or heavy metal casing. During the eighteenth century these elegant magnifying lenses became known as quizzing glasses—possibly because the aristocracy used them as

Snuff-boxes were often miniature works of art and connoisseurs such as the Earl of St Erth in The Quiet Gentleman *were extremely knowledgeable about design and origin.*

a weapon against pretension—whereby the person looked at was 'quizzed' or made to feel inferior. In *The Corinthian*, Sir Richard Wyndham used his quizzing glass to such good effect that it was considered one of society's deadliest weapons against any form of pretension. Quizzing glasses were used by all classes, however, with those used by the less affluent being made of brass with crudely ground lenses compared with the often finely wrought, elegant gold and silver glasses of the upper class. Gentlemen generally wore them around their necks on a piece of ribbon attached to the handle.

A finely crafted quizzing glass was often used by members of the upper class as a weapon against pretension.

JEWELLERY

Although perennially popular, during the Regency most jewellery was worn in the evening. The simpler styles of dress worn earlier in the period lent themselves to embellishment, and necklaces, bracelets, brooches, aigrettes and jewelled combs or hair bandeaus were favourite adornments for the soft silks and satins of a lady's ball gown. Some elaborate heirlooms such as the Cardross necklace which caused Nell such distress and worry in *April Lady* were considered quite antiquated and unfashionable. As the period progressed and dresses gradually evolved into more elaborate costumes, jewellery was often reset to match the new mode. Precious and semi-precious stones were both highly sought-after and diamonds, rubies, emeralds and pearls were popular along with garnets, topazes, turquoises and aquamarines. Ornaments for the hair were also favoured during the Regency and jewelled combs, pearl bandeaus, tiaras, aigrettes and circlets of silver filigree were much worn. Earrings were often worn during the day and at night and ladies sometimes had their ears pierced with a needle and silken thread so that they could wear a pair of diamond drops or fine pearl earrings. Jewellery for men was confined mainly to a handsome pocket watch worn with fob and seal attached, a plain or jewelled tiepin for his cravat and possibly a signet, such as the one worn by the Duke of Sale in *The Foundling*, or other kind of ring. Both men and women wore rings as a token of affection, loyalty or marriage.

AGEING GRACEFULLY

For many among the older generation, the rituals and traditions of the previous century in relation to dress were not easily put aside and there was considerable disdain—particularly among older men—for those of the younger generation whom they considered to have adopted a negligent, slovenly approach to their attire. It was not uncommon for some older men, such as Lord Lionel in *The Foundling*, to cling to the fashions of their youth, preferring knee-breeches for both day and evening wear and refusing to entertain even the thought of trousers or pantaloons. Wigs were also still to be seen, although powder had largely disappeared thanks to Mr Pitt's 1795 tax. Manners were everything and most older men would have considered it an appalling breach of etiquette not to have changed their attire before sitting down to dinner with friends or family. Regency fashions were not always kind to older women, particularly those with a fuller figure. As a result some ladies, such as the wealthy Mrs Floore in *Bath Tangle*, clung to the more flattering, supporting attire of the previous century and continued to wear the wide skirts and panniers of the pre-Revolutionary period. Wigs also continued to be worn by those older women who felt that the soft curls and tousled ringlets of the classical style could only make them look ridiculous.

General Fashion Glossary

Aigrette: A tall plume of feathers—especially egret or ostrich feathers—worn as a headdress or attached to a hat; it could also be a piece of jewellery in the shape of a plume of feathers. Often worn at Court.

Angoulême bonnet: A high-crowned straw bonnet with a broad front brim, usually tied at the side of the neck.

Bandbox: A wide cylindrical box, deep enough to hold a hat; lightweight with a lid and handle.

Belcher handkerchief: A blue handkerchief with large white spots, each with a dark blue centre. Usually worn tied around the neck, it was named for the famous boxer, Jem Belcher, who used to wear one.

Blacks: Mourning clothes for both men and women.

Blond lace: Made by twisting two threads of silk into 'hexagonal meshes'.

Bombazine: Black fabric used for mourning clothes. It was made of wool and silk and had a matt surface considered more suitable for mourning than silk, satin or velvet.

Broadcloth: Fine merino cloth, twilled and woven on a wide loom and in such a way as to make one side of the fabric shiny.

Bugles: Glass beads sewn on to ladies' clothes as decorative trimming, tubular in shape and most commonly black in colour, although they also came in blue and white.

Cambric: Very fine linen cloth.

Chicken-skin gloves: Despite the name they were often made of other types of thin durable leather dressed with spermaceti oil.

Chip: A narrow piece of straw which could be woven into a hat.

Crape: Available from the seventeenth century, crape was transparent black silk gauze which had been crimped to give it a dull finish. It was commonly used for mourning clothes.

Crepe: Available from the nineteenth century, crepe was a crimped transparent-coloured gauze used mainly for dresses.

Clocks: Originally the term for the gore or triangular piece inserted into a stocking to widen it at the ankle and which came to be embroidered along the seam lines. Eventually stockings were embroidered with or without the gore and this embroidery became known as clocks.

Cossacks: A baggy-legged trouser with tight waist and ankles drawn in by a ribbon. They first appeared in 1814 after the visit of the Tsar of Russia for the Peace celebrations and were inspired by the uniforms of the Cossack soldiers who accompanied him.

Cumberland corset: A man's corset stiffened with whalebone and laced at the back. Along with the Brummell bodice and the Apollo corset, it was often worn by overweight dandies.

Domino: A traditional hooded Venetian cloak worn by both men and women over their costumes at masquerades. Originally black, by the Regency they could be tailor-made in almost any colour. Men tended to prefer darker colours such as black, purple or midnight blue while women often chose dominoes in pink, lilac or green or to match their costume.

Drab: A thick, durable cloth, dull in colour and twilled; it was used to make men's coats.

Ermine: The white winter fur of the weasel or stoat (the summer fur was brown).

Fichu: A triangular-shaped neckerchief made of lawn, muslin or other light material, worn around the shoulders and often crossed over the breast.

Figured: A term used to describe fabric on to which designs had been woven using coloured threads.

Fillet: A decorative satin band twisted through the hair for evening wear and often ornamented with pearls or other jewels.

Flounce: A hand-pleated or gathered frill or ruffle, often quite deep, attached by its top edge to the hem or lower part of a lady's dress.

Frog: An ornamental fastening using loops of gold braid or cord which were passed over a braided button, used on military uniforms. Fashionable ladies frequently had them on their riding-habits in imitation of the military style of dress.

Furbelow: Showy ornamental trim for clothes—often in the form of ruffles or flounces.

Fustian: Durable fabric made of cotton and flax or cotton and wool. It was twilled and had a nap which looked similar to velvet; it was also known as 'mock velvet'.

Gauze: Transparent fabric, originally made of silk but later of linen or cotton.

Hoop: The term refers to the hooped petticoat which was made hugely circular using hoops made of wire, cane or whalebone and worn under an over-dress. During the Regency they were only worn at Court.

Hose: Women's stockings.

Hussar boots: Inspired by those worn by the military, Hussar boots were calf-length with a slightly pointed front upper. They were worn with pantaloons and sometimes had turn-over tops.

Inexpressibles: Another name for men's trousers or breeches, especially those of the close-fitting variety.

Jaconet: Fine cotton cloth similar to muslin and cambric.

Jean: A heavy, durable twilled cotton cloth.

Kerseymere: A soft, finely woven woollen cloth of unusual texture owing to the method of weaving.

Lappets: A small piece of plain or lace-trimmed fabric used to ornament the back or sides of an indoor headdress.

Lawn: Linen cloth so fine as to be semi-transparent; believed to have originated in the French town of Laon.

Leading strings: Long thin pieces of fabric attached to children's clothes at the point where the sleeve joined the back of the dress or shirt. Used to restrain or assist the child while walking, when not in use they looked like 'hanging sleeves'.

Leghorn: Used to make hats, leghorn was a kind of Italian wheat straw which could be plaited or woven. Probably named for the Italian town of Livorno (in English Leghorn).

Loo mask: A mask made to cover only the upper half of the face. They were usually worn at masquerades.

Mourning gloves: Made of black kid, they were worn by both men and women to funerals and by women for the period of full mourning. For half mourning, grey gloves could be worn.

Muslin: Light, thin, finely woven opaque cotton fabric.

Nankeen: Durable yellow-coloured cotton originating in Nanking, China.

Open robe: A woman's dress with the skirt styled open at the front to reveal a decorative underskirt.

Pelisse robe: Derived from the outdoor coat known as a pelisse, the pelisse robe was a dress for day wear which looked similar to the pelisse but which was fastened all the way down the front.

Plumpers: Usually worn by older ladies and gentlemen, these were artificial cheeks in the form of a thin round cork ball which was placed inside the mouth to restore the smooth contours of the face. (A 'plumper' was also the slang term for a lie.)

Poke bonnet: Any bonnet with a forward-poking brim—the size of which varied enormously.

Redingote: A kind of overcoat which began to become popular towards the end of the Regency. Similar to the pelisse, it was very fitted and fastened across the chest; it could be differentiated from the pelisse style of coat by its wide, flat collar.

Riband: Ribbon.

Sable: The highly prized glossy black or dark brown fur of the marten.

Sarcenet: Also known as sarsnet; a soft silk fabric of fine weave and texture, with a slight lustre.

Small clothes: Another word for breeches.

Spangles: Originally made in France of gold and silver and similar to today's sequin, these were small thin round pieces of metal with a hole in the middle, generally used to decorate ladies' dresses.

Stockinette: Machine-made woollen material with a closely woven mesh similar to that of knitted fabric; used for making pantaloons, stockings and underwear.

Stuff: Woollen fabric without a nap or pile.

Superfine: A high-quality English broadcloth made from merino yarn which was felted and carefully finished by raising and cropping the pile; although heavy, it had a soft lustrous finish.

Tippet: Often made of swansdown, but also of fur or lace, the tippet was a short cape or stole for the shoulders. Worn by women, they were often made to match a muff.

Tucker: A piece of fabric or lace tucked into the bodice of a lady's dress to raise the line of the neck and reduce the amount of décolletage or visible cleavage.

Twill: A method of weaving which produced a ribbing effect in the fabric of parallel diagonal lines.

Wellington boots: Made in the same manner as a top-boot but without the turn-over top. Wellington boots became fashionable after 1817.

Whalebone: Actually cartilage, not bone, taken from the upper jaw of the whale. It was prized for its flexibility.

Worsted: Yarn or fabric made from long-staple wool which has been combed straight and then spun. Material made from worsted yarn was close-textured and smooth and had no nap.

York tan gloves: Soft leather or suede gloves, usually buff or fawn-coloured, they could be either wrist or elbow length.

Zephyr: A very fine, light cotton or gingham which was thin and silky.

10

Shopping

SHOPPING IN LONDON

Shopping was a centuries-old tradition in London, with jewellers, printers, linen drapers, haberdashers and furniture makers, among others, making their wares available to those with the money to buy. As both the Regency and industrialisation progressed, and more and more manufactured and imported goods became available, shopkeepers increasingly capitalised on the growing wealth of the new middle class and the desire within all classes to 'ape their betters'. The knowledge that others in the upper class and those of the middle and merchant class, keen to rise up the social ladder, would follow where the elite led, compelled many shopkeepers to survive largely on credit. Aristocratic clients would often purchase food and goods knowing full well that they might not pay the bill for years. In *Friday's Child,* Lord Sheringham's usual response, prior to his marriage, to tradesmen's bills was to throw them into the fire. The promise of inheritance or title could be as good as cash in the hand for some members of the *ton* as shopkeepers would supply them with merchandise in the hope that they would be paid eventually. It was also hoped that if it was known that a shop enjoyed the regular custom of such notable (but debt-ridden) personages as the Prince Regent, Beau Brummell, the Duchess of Devonshire or Lord Alvanley, the cost of supplying them with goods would be outweighed by the number of paying customers who would follow them. In *Frederica,* Miss Starke, milliner in Conduit Street, recognised at once the commercial advantages of having the beautiful Miss Charis Merriville wear her hats (rather than those from Clarimonde's in New Bond Street) and reduced the prices accordingly. To shop where the *ton* shopped, to buy a coat made by Weston or a pair of boots from the hand of Hoby, to bump elbows with a lady at Grafton House or buy an ounce of snuff known as Lord Petersham's 'sort' at Fribourg & Treyer's, gave those outside the inner circle the sense of being one step closer to acceptance by the *beau monde.*

LONDON SHOPS

Traditionally, many shops had been set up in the City—the business section of London near St Paul's—but towards the end of the eighteenth century more and more shops opened along Piccadilly, Bond Street and Oxford Street and whole new precincts, such as Nash's Regent Street, were designed and built specifically for the retail trade, encouraging a shift by retailers away from the City. Bond Street stood at the centre of the move by shopkeepers seeking to establish quality businesses in the expanding, wealthy neighbourhood of Mayfair. Bond Street had long been home to gentlemen's tailors, boot makers, hatters and hairdressers and for some time was considered a male precinct into which no lady would dare venture unaccompanied—if at all—and rarely in the afternoon when the Bond Street beaus were on the strut and ready to ogle any woman who came into view. By the time of the Regency, however, women could and did shop there although when the eponymous heroine Venetia expressed her intention of doing a little shopping on Bond Street after paying a morning call, the benevolent Sir Lambert Steeple insisted on escorting her as a protection against the attentions of the Bond Street beaus.

West of Bond Street was Berkeley Square where Gunter's, the famous confectioner's shop, had been established in the late eighteenth century. Famed for their sweetmeats, pastries and fruit ices, by the nineteenth century Gunter's was the upper-class host or hostess's first choice for catering when arranging a ball or formal party. Further south on Piccadilly stood Fortnum & Mason, the high-class grocer, and in St James's Street, Berry Brothers, the wine merchant and grocer. These shops were well established by the time of the Regency and hugely popular with the aristocracy, and many a noted citizen, including royalty and Beau Brummell, was weighed on the great scales at Berry Brothers (generally kept for weighing tea and sugar). John Hatchard began his famous bookshop, Hatchard's, in Piccadilly in 1797 with £5 and just a few second-hand books, while Fribourg & Treyer's, the famous snuff merchants, carried on a thriving trade in their shop at number 34 the Haymarket, just off Piccadilly.

Outside the West End the more traditional shopping precincts, such as Soho and the Strand, attracted all classes of people. Ackermann's Repository of Arts, the famous print shop and gallery, opened in the Strand in 1771 and was enormously popular. During the Regency Ackermann's opened its doors one evening a week to the *ton*, and members of fashionable society would meet there to view prints, discuss and buy items from the latest collection. Ludgate Hill, north of the Strand, was home to the fashionable jeweller, Rundell and Bridge, who not only sold jewellery, snuffboxes and all kinds of trinkets—such as the seal bought by Bertram in *Arabella*—but also came to the aid of debt-stricken aristocrats with jewels to sell or to leave as surety against a short-term loan. Across London more and more shops were opening and for those with money there were all the delights of returning to favourite establishments or discovering new emporiums in which to spend it.

Daily Needs

Although London continued to expand throughout the Regency, the countryside remained close enough to maintain a connection between the provision of food and its sources. Fifteen thousand acres of market gardens lay within a mere ten miles of the city while just beyond that were the farms which raised the livestock and produced the eggs and cheese which were transported to the urban centre on a daily basis. Every night hundreds of farmers and their wives loaded carts, drays and wagons and brought their produce to London to sell at the market. Herds of cattle and flocks of sheep and goats were sent in on the hoof from outlying farms, fish was brought up from the river ports and game and poultry made available from nearby farms and estates.

The great London markets were Billingsgate, Leadenhall, Farringdon, Newgate, Smithfield and Covent Garden. Meat on the hoof was taken straight to Smithfield, there to be slaughtered or sold to local butchers for slaughter in the yards behind their shops. Farringdon and Newgate sold dead meat, and Leadenhall traded in hides and live poultry. Billingsgate was the main city fish market while Covent Garden was renowned for its vast supply of fruit, vegetables and dairy produce, as well as the ready-made pies, gingerbread, sausages and pasties which individual hawkers sold from trays hung around their necks. Middle- and upper-class householders did not go to the markets themselves but preferred to send their servants instead. Unlike recreational shopping, which was considered a pleasure, daily food shopping, or marketing, was considered tedious and a chore to be avoided if possible. The difference was in the nature of the shopping experience as much as in the items purchased. In a shop a customer could sit down and be shown a range of enticing goods by a deferential shop assistant, whereas markets were bustling, crowded, noisy, dirty places—the cattle market at Smithfield reeked with piles of offal and carcasses, and literally ran with blood—making the daily purchase of food-stuffs an unpleasant task best given to a servant.

Milk was not sold at the market but was produced in London itself from herds of cows kept in backstreet yards or in several of the city's parks. It was in Green Park with its dairy cows and attendant milkmaids that the heroine in *Frederica* got into such trouble after failing to control her dog Lufra. Milk was also supplied from suburban farms and carted in daily over distances of up to twenty miles. Mainly used for cooking rather than drinking, milk was sold door to door by milkmaids or milkmen carrying traditional wooden shoulder yokes with a five-gallon pail hanging from each end. Coal was the other important household staple and was generally bought direct from the coal merchant. Wealthier households often had a set arrangement for weekly or monthly delivery of supplies which were delivered straight into the coal hole.

Lock's for Hats

Hat makers, or hatters, made hats for men, while milliners made hats for women. The only exception to this was the lady's riding hat which was usually ordered from a gentleman's hat shop. Hat making was a long and complex process which included making, shaping, dyeing, stiffening, moistening, brushing, ironing and lining. The entire process was usually carried out on the hat maker's premises by a team of men, each of whom was skilled in one part of the procedure. Although beaver hats were usual for town wear, in *The Unknown Ajax* Claud Darracott was emboldened to try one of Baxter's daring new creations when visiting the town of Rye in Sussex. One of the best-known London hatters was James Lock at number 6 St. James's Street. Lock made hats for some of the most eminent gentlemen of the day and in his earlier years had made hats for Lord Nelson, several of which included a specially designed eye shade to cover the eye Nelson had lost in battle at Corsica in 1794. Lock supplied the finest beaver hats to the first gentlemen of the day, military helmets to officers in the Hussars and the Royal Dragoon Guards, and elegant, folding chapeau-bras to be worn by gentlemen at Court or at Almack's. In 1815 Lock supplied the Duke of Wellington with the plumed hat which he wore at Waterloo. Like other fashionable London hatters such as Baxter, Yeow, James Swallow and hatter and hosier Mr Dolman, Lock gave substantial credit to his aristocratic customers, often waiting years for payment, but he also gave a discount of a shilling per pound to customers who chose to pay on receipt of their goods. Lock enjoyed patronage from clients across the country and would dispatch hats by coach in response to orders sent by mail. With its quaint multi-paned windows on either side of the small centre door, Lock's remains one of the few Regency shops still in existence today.

MILLINERS, TAILORS, MODISTES AND MANTUA MAKERS

Although they had originally been sellers of all kinds of Milanese fancy ware, by the time of the Regency, milliners had begun to specialise in the making of hats, caps and bonnets and their trimmings. Muffs, tippets and cloaks could also be purchased at a milliner's shop, and upper-class ladies could visit fashionable establishments in Bruton, Conduit or New Bond Street to try on the latest style in bonnets, take in a hat for refurbishment, or order accessories for a new gown. Although during the eighteenth century, men had served in milliner's shops and male corset or stay makers had attended ladies in their homes, by the time of the Regency, millinery, along with corsetry, was generally considered to be an exclusively female domain. Millinery was one of the few professions available to gently born women lacking independent means or a family to support them. Hats and accessories were usually made on the premises by the milliner herself assisted by as many employees as the demands of the business required. Feathers, artificial flowers, ribbons, spangles and lace were all common trimmings for a wide range of headwear made, most often, from silk, satin or straw, but also from velvet or crepe. Fashions changed quickly during the Regency and a good milliner could always offer her customers the very latest in styles from the Court, the Continent or from the coloured plates of the newest fashion magazine. In *April Lady*, Nell Cardross was horrified to discover that she had somehow managed to buy nine hats in less than three months—one of which had cost forty guineas.

During the Regency, every article of a gentleman's wardrobe, except for his stockings, was made by hand, usually in the home by his mother, sister, wife or daughter, or other female relative. Gentlemen of means, however, whose clothing needs or aspirations were beyond the skill of their womenfolk, usually paid for a tailor to measure, cut and fit individual garments. London tailors were considered the best in Europe, having gained an unshakeable ascendancy over the French after the Revolution and there were many who would have agreed with Lady Steeple in *Venetia* when she declared, 'No Frenchman can make a riding habit.' London tailors set the standard, and the best and most exclusive of them were master cutters with a precise eye for line and a passion for detail and a perfect fit. The best-known were Beau Brummell's tailors Schweitzer and Davidson at 12 Cork Street and John Weston at 27 Old Bond Street, both of whom also made clothes for the Prince Regent, and Stultz and Scott who were favoured by military gentlemen. So superbly cut was the Earl of St Erth's evening dress in *The Quiet Gentleman* that his cousin Martin found himself wishing that he too had had his made by Weston. A perfectly fitting coat was a great tailor's trademark and his reputation could be made by his ability to enhance or highlight nature's art. Men who were less well-endowed by nature in terms of well-shaped legs or broad shoulders could be helped by the tailor's skill—along with a little sawdust stuffing or buckram padding.

A small tailor did all his own measuring, pattern making, cutting and sewing, but a larger business, with a good clientele and a reputation to maintain, employed a staff of tailors overseen by a foreman. It was the foreman's job to measure customers and cut out the pieces which were then handed to the working tailors for sewing. The master tailor would personally measure and cut only for his most important customers as they were the best advertisement for his business. When visiting Weston's in *Regency Buck*, Peregrine Taverner found himself attended by the tailor and advised by him to follow either the Prince Regent's or Mr Brummell's taste in coats. To gain the favour of royalty or one of the leading dandies of the day was a guarantee for increased custom from other members of the *ton*.

A Regency female's wardrobe consisted almost entirely of items made by hand—either by herself or by someone skilled in the art. Although industrialisation was making rapid inroads into machine-made fabrics, during the Regency only stockings were made entirely by machine (aside from hand-knitted stockings, of course) and ready-made clothes were still some years away. In the years following the French Revolution in 1789, many French *émigrés* fled to England—some of whom were dress-makers, milliners, lace makers and embroideresses. A number of these women set up establishments in fashionable streets, such as Bruton or Conduit Streets in London or Milsom Street or South Parade in Bath, and advertised themselves as modistes with elegant French names designed to attract the cream of society ladies to their salons (although in *Black Sheep*, Madame Lisette was actually Eliza Mudford, formerly in service to the Princess Elizabeth). On visiting a modiste, ladies would be shown delicious examples of the dressmaker's art from which they could order to suit their needs. In some cases, as when Abigail Wendover returned from a visit to London in *Black Sheep*, pre-purchased fabrics could be taken to a dressmaker and made into an agreed style of dress or other garment. The modiste, or mantua maker as they were also known, would discuss in detail with a customer the best choice of fabric, style and trimming for a dress before measuring her and taking a pattern. Patterns were generally made of paper or cloth, with cloth patterns sometimes used as the final lining of the dress. An exclusive dressmaker such as Madame Fanchon in *Cotillion* was expected to have exceptional taste, an eye for colour and line and a talent for designing and creating a garment ideally suited to the shape and complexion of her client. Dressmaking was a demanding occupation with long hours and close, careful work often done in poor light. During the Season when the aristocracy was at its busiest and many gowns were needed for a single debutante or society belle, or when a member of the royal family died and mourning dress became *de rigueur*, a dressmaker's life—or that of her workers—could become one of unending toil. For a modiste with a well-established shop and a good name, however, dressmaking could be extremely profitable.

HOBY'S FOR BOOTS

The most fashionable bootmaker of the period was George Hoby, whose shop on the corner of Piccadilly and St James's Street was patronised by all the best-dressed men of the *ton*. Renowned for a superb fit and the finest leather, Hoby made boots for royalty, officers in the military—including the Duke of Wellington—and for the most notable bucks and dandies of the *beau monde*. A boot by Hoby was instantly recognisable, as the valet Crimplesham explained to Hugo in *The Unknown Ajax*. Gentlemen could buy every kind of boot from Hoby's, including Hussar boots, Wellington boots, military long boots and halfboots. The most popular were the highly polished hessians with their high V-shaped fronts and tassels, or the top-boots used for everyday wear or for hunting. For Court wear, evening wear, formal occasions or for dancing a man could also buy low-cut shoes or pumps. Hoby employed up to 300 workers and the success of his business made him extremely wealthy as well as rather arrogant (despite being a Methodist preacher as well a bootmaker). From his youth, the Duke of Wellington always had his boots made by him and after Wellington's victory at Vittoria, Hoby was reputed to have attributed the General's success to the combination of Hoby's boots and prayers. Neither his arrogance nor his insolence to even his wealthiest customers appears to have affected sales of his magnificent footwear. It was to Hoby's that Sir Nugent Fotherby in *Sylvester* went to have his hessian boots with their specially designed tassels made and it was to Hoby's that the boots went back five times before Sir Nugent was satisfied.

The best top-boots were made by Hoby.

A pair of highly polished hessians was the mark of a gentleman.

Ladies often had their evening shoes and slippers made to match a particular dress.

As with most Regency trades, the shoemaker was also the shoe seller. In the towns and villages shoemakers often worked from home without a shopfront or display of wares, but in London many shoemakers had shops with goods exhibited in the window. Larger shops catered to both women and men, offering a range of made-to-measure shoes, boots and accessories such as leather gaiters or the cloth leggings known as spatterdashes which were worn to protect one's stockings from mud splashes. Footwear was rarely bought ready-made by the upper classes, although in *The Toll-Gate* Captain Staple was forced to find himself a pair of brogues in a warehouse in Tideswell, Derbyshire. For most

shoes, however, the shoemaker had to measure his customers'
feet and cut out the leather or fabric for their shoes himself. In
a large and successful business the master shoemaker employed a
foreman for this task while he waited on customers and oversaw
the dressing, cutting and sewing of the leather or other material
by his staff. It took a great deal of skill to make an elegant, well-
formed shoe, and a shoemaker, or his journeyman, was usually
adept at making either women's or men's shoes but not both.
The material for ladies' shoes was generally finer than that needed
for men's footwear and so neater seams were essential in order
for the finished product to look its best. In the shops catering
particularly to the upper class, the shoemaker would often make
and keep labelled 'shoe lasts' for individual customers. These
were wooden moulds, with a left and right last carefully made
to match the customer's feet, from which the shoemaker could
construct a pair of shoes to order.

*Half-boots were especially popular for outdoor wear and
could be made in a range of colours and fabrics.*

Fribourg & Treyer's famous shop in Piccadilly.

FRIBOURG & TREYER'S FOR SNUFF

One of the most famous tobacconists in Britain was Fribourg & Treyer's in Piccadilly. Many Regency men—and women—indulged in the fashionable habit of taking powdered tobacco or snuff in small pinches breathed up the nostrils, and over the years it became so popular that the famous Piccadilly tobacconists, Fribourg & Treyer, reported that in the hundred years to 1820 ninety per cent of their retail custom was in snuff. There were many different types with variations in texture, colour and smell. The best known was Havana snuff which was the base (Brazil snuff excepted) of all other types. Snuffs such as Spanish Bran, Brazil, Lisbon and Macouba could be carefully mixed to produce new varieties known as 'sorts' and connoisseurs such as Lord Petersham made up their own trademark mixtures which became well known

among tobacconists. Judith Taverner in *Regency Buck* had her own
jar labelled as 'Miss Taverner's sort' at Fribourg & Treyer's. In
addition to its own fragrance, snuff was frequently scented with
additives such as the Prince Regent's favourite, Otto or Attar of
Roses. Snuff taking reached the height of its popularity in England
between 1760 and the end of the Regency in 1820, becoming less
common as the century progressed and tobacco smoking became
increasingly preferred.

Linen Drapers

Linen drapers sold all kinds of fabrics, threads, trimmings and
a wide range of accessories, and the predominance of linen
drapers in the larger cities reflected the importance of fabric
choice for all classes of customers whose personal wardrobe
and household linen—including sheets, table linen, curtains
and bath cloths—were all hand-made. For country customers
without the means to visit London or order from drapers in
the larger towns and cities, itinerant haberdashers, travelling
lace men and travelling linen drapers (also known as talleymen
or Scotchmen) supplied most householders' needs. In London
many linen drapers established large shops both before and
during the Regency. Wholesale drapers were mainly located
in the City of London but the increasing popularity of shopping as a recreational activity and the establishment of shopping
streets in the fashionable areas west of the City saw many businesses open premises in Piccadilly, Oxford, Regent and New
Bond Streets. In 1817 there were thirty-three linen drapers in
Oxford Street alone, with five additional drapers specialising
in woollen fabric, twelve haberdashers, four furriers, a ribbon
warehouse and two drapers-and-tailors. Kate Malvern shopped
at Bedford House in *Cousin Kate* where she was able to purchase

a variety of goods including ribbon trimmings, a shawl and a handkerchief. Linen drapers also attracted other businesses to retail districts and shoemakers, glovers, hat and bonnet makers, perfumers, button, fringe and trimming sellers, plumassiers or feather workers, silk mercers and hosiers would often set up businesses in the same street in hope of attracting follow-on custom to their shops.

Layton and Shear's at Bedford House, Newton's in Leicester Square, and Grafton House at 164 New Bond Street, were all well-known London linen drapers and so popular with ladies of the *ton* that it was considered advisable to visit before 11.00 a.m. to avoid the crowds. Kitty and Meg visited Grafton House in *Cotillion* and were delighted by the range and variety of wares in that popular emporium. Customers were always served by men, as female shop assistants (other than in the exclusive precincts of the milliner's or modiste's shop) did not become a force in the retail industry until well after the Regency. Fabrics were often hung in the window or placed outside the front door where they could be shown to their best advantage and would entice customers into the shop.

Many women enjoyed shopping for fabrics and trimming at the linen draper's shop.

Jewellers

Although the Regency period witnessed a marked trend towards wearing simple or minimal jewellery during the day, the demands for truly elegant evening wear enabled many London jewellers and goldsmiths to create magnificent necklaces, brooches, jewelled tiaras, hair ornaments, aigrettes, rings and bracelets to set off the finest dresses and most fashionable hairstyles. Among the best-known Regency jewellers were Rundell and Bridge at 32 Ludgate Hill (est. 1788), Phillip's on Bond Street, Gray's in Sackville Street and Jeffrey's—jeweller to His Royal Highness the Prince Regent (and to whom at one point the Prince owed £89,000 in unpaid bills). Diamonds and pearls were especially popular during the period, although many kinds of precious and semi-precious stones such as rubies, sapphires, emeralds, topazes, garnets and amethysts were also favoured. Lady Denville in *False Colours* had a topaz necklace set in filigree made for her by her jeweller as well as a necklace of clear amber beads—although this she unfortunately discovered did not at all become her and would have to be given away.

Jewellers were often commissioned to create specially designed snuff-boxes, cameo brooches, lockets and picture rings into which could be incorporated a tiny miniature of the customer's spouse, lover or mistress. In *The Quiet Gentleman*, Gervase, Earl of St Erth, chose to wear a signet ring with a very fine emerald (cut to his order) instead of the ring left to him by his father. As well as jewellery, most jewellers also dealt in silver and gold *objets d'art*, ornamental pieces such as candelabra, epergnes (table centrepieces), bowls and vases, and household items such as wine goblets, ice buckets and plate. Entire dinner services in gold or silver were sometimes bespoken by a member of the aristocracy or wealthy middle class and could be engraved or designed with a family crest or other symbols meaningful to the family. Jonathan Chawleigh in *A Civil Contract* offered to lend his vast collection of silver plate to his son-in-law for the Lyntons' first rout party—an offer which Adam was resolute in refusing. A few years before his Regency, the Prince of Wales commissioned Rundell and Bridge to create a full dinner service in silver plate for grand State occasions. The silver-gilt service was so magnificent that in 1807 it was exhibited (by invitation only) in the jeweller's showroom for several weeks to the delight of many among the upper class.

Appointed as the royal jewellers from 1789, Rundell and Bridge enjoyed the benefits of considerable royal patronage throughout the Regency. In 1816 the Regent's daughter, Princess Charlotte, in company with her grandmother the Queen, visited Rundell and Bridge prior to the Princess's wedding to Prince Leopold. There the Queen helped Princess Charlotte to select several superb items of jewellery to wear during the marriage ceremony—including a stunning wreath of diamond roses, a diamond cestus (belt or girdle) and a magnificent set of pearls. Most jewellers both bought and sold jewellery and other items of gold and silver and during the Regency it was not uncommon for those with large gambling debts to try to offset them by selling personal or family heirlooms. Mrs Byron's jewels were sold after her death in 1811 to Rundell and Bridge for £1,130 and among the aristocracy there were many who availed themselves of the services of Philip Rundell's partner, John Bridge, who was well known for his discretion and pleasant demeanour and who would give valued clients a reasonable price for their treasures. In *The Grand Sophy*, it was Mr Bridge who handled the sale of Sophy's diamond earrings with such tactful insight and who kindly kept her in his private office until the shop was clear of customers.

COSMETICS

Throughout the eighteenth century upper-class men and women had delighted in painting their faces with (often poisonous) white paint or enamel, applying patches and wearing elaborate powdered wigs. By the time of the Regency, however, most of these beauty aids had vanished—although some among the older generation still clung to the traditions of their youth. The less complicated dress fashions of the Regency period encouraged a simpler look, with an emphasis for women on 'innocence', and a less obvious use of cosmetics. Although coloured lip salves, eyebrow stains and pencils, eyelash tints, paints and powders continued to be used, much of the beauty advice in magazines and books discouraged the use of cosmetics and nominated rouge as the only acceptable enhancement to beauty—and then only if absolutely necessary. Arabella, on being persuaded to add just a touch of rouge to her cheeks when dressing for Lady Bridlington's ball in *Arabella*, was so appalled by the result that she instantly washed it off. The best rouge was powdered carmine made from cochineal; a vibrant red, it needed subtle application and was sometimes mixed with hair powder to lighten the colour.

Ladies bought their rouge from a perfumer and, although there was less demand for actual cosmetics, there were many other beauty products to tempt the Regency debutante, society belle or fashionable lady. Beautifying creams, anti-wrinkle lotions, balsams, ointments, oils, salves, scented waters, perfumes, pastes, powders and pomades (perfumed hair oils) were all available in shops throughout London, and by 1817 there were five perfumers on Oxford Street alone. The beautiful Lady Denville in *False Colours* used Olympian Dew to protect her complexion during the day which was advertised, along with other aids to beauty such as Denmark Lotion and Bloom of Ninon, in the ladies' magazines and society journals so popular during the period. Men also used beauty products, including perfume, face cream, hair oil, soap, shaving lotion, mouthwash and, for some among the dandy set, rouge.

Many sellers of cosmetics claimed to have royal patents, or to be suppliers to the Prince Regent or other members of the royal family, and a handful displayed the British coat of arms as a means of reassuring potential customers of the authenticity of their products, for which they frequently made extravagant claims. Price and Gosnell (Perfumers and Soap Makers to his Royal Highness the Prince Regent) advertised their 'invaluable preparation for washing, softening and beautifying the skin: Johnstone's Royal Patent Windsor Soap' and their 'elegant treble distilled lavender water', while warning readers to beware of counterfeits. Ladies attending number 12 Three-King Court in London's Lombard Street could also improve and preserve their complexions by purchasing a bottle of Price and Gosnell's Patent Naples Cream and Milk of Almonds for only 5s. a bottle, while Gowland's Lotion promised to be 'the most pleasant and effective remedy for all complaints to which the Face and Skin are liable'.

Cures for freckles, sunburn, wrinkles, rough skin, dry skin, blotched skin and even facial hair were all offered with impressive assurances of their miraculous powers and efficacy. The first patent for a depilatory was taken out in 1804 and by the time of the Regency various treatments for the removal of unwanted or excess hair were being offered in newspapers and magazines—often at great expense to the unwary man or woman seduced by persuasive advertising. The manufacturers of Trent's Depilatory promised (at a cost of £1 sent by mail) 'efficacy and innocence' and beautifully smooth skin as a result of applying their product, confident that there was no way for dissatisfied customers to regain their money.

Home-made beauty aids were also popular during the period and hints and recipes were a common feature in the books and magazines of the time. Two books popular in the early nineteenth century were *The Toilet of Flora; or a collection of the most simple and approved methods of preparing baths, pomatums and sweet-scented waters; with receipts for cosmetics* (1775, translated from the French, with numerous editions) and *The Mirror of Graces* (1811). Both books offered readers recipes and suggestions for enhancing beauty such as pimpernel water as the 'sovereign beautifier of the complexion' or the juice of green pineapples for removing wrinkles and giving 'the complexion the air of youth'. In *The Grand Sophy*, Lady Ombersley and the Marquesa de Villacañas discussed the respective merits of the 'Lotion of Ladies of Denmark', distilled water of green pineapples, raw veal laid on the skin, and crushed strawberries and chervil water as aids to the complexion. Recipes often called for expensive ingredients such as spermaceti, rose oil and pure white wax (for chapped lips), brandy and white wine (for lavender water) or exotic items such as myrrh, alkanet root, benzoin or gum sandrach for making products to improve the complexion.

11

Eat, Drink and Be Merry

Food, Removes, Repasts and a Light Nuncheon

London during the Regency was still surrounded by market gardens and small farms with dairy farms in Islington and Belsize Park, fields of grain in Chelsea and Hammersmith, and cows grazing in the meadows along Kensington High Street all helping to feed the growing population. Meat was the centrepiece of the English diet—bacon for those of the poorer classes who could afford it, mutton and beef for the middle classes and the same for the upper classes with the addition of pork, poultry, game, fish and occasional delicacies such as turtle. Fruit had long been considered by many to be indigestible but the discovery in the eighteenth century that scurvy could be prevented by eating fresh fruit and vegetables led to an increase in their consumption in the nineteenth century.

Among the wealthy, three courses was considered the optimum number for dinner. The first course generally consisted of soup, a series of entrées, several meat dishes and fish, while the second course focused mainly on meat including game birds, poultry, beef, pork and mutton with a number of vegetable dishes, savouries and sauces served in addition. In *False Colours*, the portly gourmand, Sir Bonamy Ripple, felt that a second course of just a goose, cauliflower, French beans, peas, asparagus, lobster and a basket of pastries with side dishes of perhaps a braised ham and a haunch of venison would be the ideal thing for a 'small' dinner. The third course was the dessert or 'afters' course, usually consisting of an assortment of pastries, creams, jellies, ices, nuts and fruit. Each course was laid out according to a particular pattern, depending on the types of food included in the menu. A first course with soup and entrées, for example, saw the soups placed on the four corners of the table ready for serving and the entrées placed in lines along the sides of the table thus making them 'side' dishes. Once the soup was finished with, servants would remove the tureens and replace them with dishes of fish such as turbot, smelts, salmon or eel. Dishes to be taken away and replaced in this manner were known as 'removes'. Guests selected their food mainly from the dishes nearest to them as no one was expected to eat from every dish on the table. It was considered acceptable, although not always desirable, to ask one's nearest neighbour to pass a particular dish or to call on a servant to bring one's choice from the other side of the table. Kitty Charing was overwhelmed by the vast array of food when she was invited to dinner at the vulgar Mrs Scorton's in *Cotillion* and was unable to eat much more than a French olive. In some houses the table was cleared and completely relaid between courses while the dinner guests continued conversing around the servants' activities; the cloth was always removed before the dessert was laid out. For a formal dinner the best linen, crystal, china and silverware were used and the guests were seated around the table according to rank. Dinner guests were expected to gather in the drawing-room before the evening meal for at least a quarter of an hour of introductions and conversation before being summoned to the table. On the butler's announcement of 'Dinner is served' the men would offer their arms to the women and the host would escort the highest-ranking lady present to the dining room, followed by the rest of the guests in order of precedence. Despite a general preference for Sir Thomas Bolderwood's lovely daughter Marianne in *The Quiet*

Gentleman, etiquette demanded that several of her admirers escort other ladies in to dinner. The Earl of St Erth gave his arm to the Duchess of Rutland, his brother Martin took in a countess, Lord Ulverston escorted another high-born lady and to Mr Warboys was given the privilege of escorting the baronet's daughter.

Although an ever greater array of food became available during the Regency with imported dishes from foreign climes, a wider variety of fish due to faster transport and new recipes brought to England by foreign chefs—particularly after the French Revolution—traditional English fare remained popular and predominant. Hot and cold meat continued as the focus of every meal and it was not uncommon for men to eat cold beef or ham for breakfast, washed down with a tankard of ale. In *The Reluctant Widow*, Nicky Carlyon was glad to serve himself a large plate of cold roast beef before sitting down to join his brother and Mrs Cheviot for breakfast. Meals or repasts could be large or small depending on the occasion but as the gap between breakfast and dinner was gradually extended it became more common for the wealthier classes to indulge in a small repast between these two meals. To this end a refreshment known as a nuncheon was some-times served, particularly when guests were in the house, which often consisted of cold meats, cheese, bread and fruit. A repast could be a meal of any size but it was usually specified as either a 'light repast' or a 'grand repast'; the Prince Regent was particularly fond of the latter.

MEALS AND MENUS

For the wealthier classes meals were an important part of the daily routine with breakfast eaten at nine or ten in the morning and dinner at five or eight in the evening, depending on whether those dining were keeping country or town hours. Breakfast tended to be a more substantial meal than in the previous century and often included kippers, herring, eggs or slices of ham kept hot in chafing dishes laid out on a sideboard in the dining room from which guests could serve themselves. This was usually in addition to the traditional toast, tea, coffee, chocolate and fresh rolls with butter which was the preferred breakfast for many Regency ladies (and which was frequently served to them in bed by their maid).

The gradual shift to a later dinner hour than had been usual in the previous century also saw the introduction into some households of a midday meal in the form of luncheon (not to be confused with the light refreshment of a 'nuncheon' which could be eaten at any time of the day), a practice which had become increasingly common by the end of the Regency. Traditionally, dinner had always meant the midday meal, eaten at around noon, but by the early nineteenth century the country dinner hour was usually five, or sometimes six, o'clock, while in the city the fashionable hour, for what had by then become the main meal of the day, could be as late as eight or even nine o'clock in the evening. Upper-class visitors to the country often observed town hours while staying at a country estate or shooting-box although Arabella, used to dining at five, caused Mr Beaumaris's French chef, Alphonse, great distress by unwittingly forcing him to bring dinner forward by two hours instead of having it ready for the usual time of half past seven. While cold meats were deemed acceptable for daytime repasts, it was considered usual for a dinner menu to include two main courses with several different kinds of meat as well as fish and shellfish, several sauces, vegetable dishes, savouries such as an omelette or pie, and a selection of cakes, creams and sweetmeats for dessert. Supper was designated as a light meal to be eaten late at night. Not all country dwellers made the change, however, and for some provincial families a midday dinner remained the main meal of the day.

For those who could afford them, gargantuan dinners were the order of the day in many upper-class households and elaborate evening meals often consisted of an extraordinary number of dishes making up each of the courses served. Menus were devised by the chef or head cook with individual dishes personally made by them or by one of their assistants under their direction. After the Revolution in France, many French chefs, *pâtissiers* and confectioners emigrated to England to escape the Terror and were employed in the houses of the aristocracy. The Duke of Sale in *The Foundling* had a confectioner in his kitchen and Scholes, the French-trained chef in *A Civil Contract*, made himself indispensable in the Lynton household. A good French chef was a status symbol among the nobility and the Prince Regent himself paid an extortionate amount in late 1816 to acquire the services of the celebrated chef Marie-Antoine Carême for just a few months. The Regent was famous for his lavish celebratory dinners served at Carlton House or the Pavilion at Brighton and when he held a grand banquet at the latter on 17 January 1817 it was Carême who was responsible for the sumptuous menu, which listed over one hundred separate dishes in nine courses, including thirty-six different entrées. The menu also paid homage to the art of the pastry-cook with eight magnificent set pieces created in pastry and depicting historic entities such as 'the ruins of a Turkish mosque', 'a Syrian hermitage' and 'the ruins of Antioch'.

WHAT'S FOR DESSERT? GUNTER'S

Originally known as 'The Pot and Pineapple', Gunter's was founded in 1757 by an Italian pastry-cook, Domenico Negri, who set up a confectionery shop at number 7 Berkeley Square, in the centre of the increasingly upper-class West End of London. Negri specialised in a wide range of sweet and savoury foods and was one of the first confectioners in England to establish ice cream and water ices as a sought-after delicacy. His elegant trade card listed such tantalising treats as Cedrati and Bergamet Chips, Naples Divolini, sugar plums, biskits, marshmallow, English, French and Italian wet and dry sweetmeats and ices, fruits and creams made in the traditional Italian style. In the late eighteenth century James Gunter took over ownership of the Berkeley Square premises and renamed the business Gunter's. The name quickly became synonymous with the finest pastries, sweets and ice creams and every society host or hostess went first to Gunter's when catering for a large dinner, important ball or party. It was Gunter's who supplied much of the fare for Lady Ombersley's ball in *The Grand Sophy* and from whom Lady Bridlington's chef ordered additional refreshments for the elegant ball in *Arabella*. Confectioners were often remarkably inventive with an extraordinary range of ice and ice-cream flavours including jasmine, elderflower, orange and lemon, pistachio, burnt filbert and even Parmesan ice cream to tempt their customers. In *April Lady*, Felix Hethersett offered to take his cousin Nell to Gunter's for an ice after he met her in Clarges Street but found his lovely cousin was not in the mood for the treat. Gunter's had a vast ice house in the cellars under the shop and an advertisement which appeared in 1827, a few years after the Regency, alerted customers to the availability of their famous fruit ice cream thanks to the arrival of the ship *Platoff* with a cargo of ice brought from the sea off Greenland. Gunter's enjoyed royal patronage throughout the nineteenth century and remained in business until well into the twentieth century.

DRINKING BY DAY AND BY NIGHT

Alcohol was an inherent part of Regency life that cut across all classes and although excessive drinking was very much a male indulgence, both sexes considered it perfectly acceptable to drink alcohol during both day and night. Water was generally eschewed as a beverage, mainly because of uncertainty about its quality and the dangers associated with drinking dirty or contaminated water. In *The Foundling*, Mr Shifnal was shocked when the Duke of Sale asked for water in preference to alcohol. Milk was sometimes drunk in the morning or at bedtime but was more often used in cooking. Tea, coffee and chocolate were the preferred drinks at breakfast although many men liked to take ale with their morning meal. Wine was drunk at other meals and Madeira, burgundy, claret, sherry and brandy were the drinks of preference throughout the day and into the evening, while port was generally reserved as an after-dinner drink. The custom of separation between men and women—so prevalent during the Regency—was also manifested in the types of drinks deemed suitable for the two sexes. Carefully brought-up girls might decline to drink at all in certain circumstances or else choose to nurse a glass of punch or champagne at an important social event if unsure of the effect on their senses. The heroine of *Arabella* was greatly relieved when the butler removed her glass of wine and replaced it with a goblet of lemonade when she dined with Mr Beaumaris at his shooting-box. The exclusive Almack's club was well known for its 'insipid' liquid refreshments of claret-cup, orgeat, tea and lemonade, but these were considered the drinks most suitable for debutantes. Claret-cup was made by mixing claret with soda, fruit juices and sugar, sometimes with brandy added, and was generally served chilled. Orgeat was distilled from barley or almonds and orange flower water and was intended as a light, refreshing drink. Tea and lemonade were, of course, non-alcoholic drinks, with lemonade made from large quantities of lemon juice mixed with sugar and water. The other common ladies' drink was ratafia, a liqueur flavoured with either peach, apricot or cherry kernels or with the essence of bitter almonds. In *Friday's Child*, Lord Sheringham ordered ratafia for Hero (and burgundy for himself) to toast their wedding. Women also sometimes drank porter, a type of bitter-tasting beer, dark brown in colour and brewed from brown malt. It was considered by some to be a healthful drink and very strengthening.

In general, upper-class women did not get drunk, although the prevalence of alcohol in society sometimes made this difficult. The arrack-punch served at Vauxhall Gardens was drunk by both men and women, despite a reputation for potency. It was said to have been made from the grains of the Benjamin flower mixed with rum and was freely imbibed on gala nights. Some men preferred to mix their own punch as Freddy did in *Cotillion* and rum punch

In *Arabella, a debt of honour led Bertram Tallant into the back-slums of Tothill Fields where he drank too much rough liquor and was cared for by Leaky Peg.*

(rum, lemon, arrack and sugar), Regent's punch (various fruits, rum, brandy, hock, Curaçao, Madeira and champagne) and Negus (port, lemon, sugar and spices) were popular brews. Fortified wines such as Madeira and sherry were also popular with men and some women during the Regency but red wines such as claret, burgundy and port tended to be the more exclusive province of male drinkers. Brandy, gin and rum were drunk by upper-class men, although they often chose to drink the rougher forms of these spirits in the less salubrious surroundings of the inns and taverns of the poorer quarters of London.

Drunkenness was common, particularly among young men for whom it was deemed an acceptable condition. To engage in a revel-rout, wine party or a spread (where an undergraduate invited up to a hundred other students to a drinking party) was practically a requirement of an Oxbridge education. Among upper-class men, to be inebriated was not only acceptable but, in some circles, expected—although to be drunk in the middle of the day as Dysart frequently was in *April Lady* was not considered appropriate behaviour for a well-bred man. The propensity for men to drink heavily after the evening meal made it a well-established custom for the ladies to leave the table at the end of dinner and withdraw, at which point the doors were locked and the port brought to the table. Not everyone drank to excess but of those who did it was quite usual for two or three men to drink as many as eight bottles of wines such as claret, burgundy or champagne at a single sitting.

12

The Sporting Life

Sport was considered by many to be the natural pursuit of the true Englishman. Love of a contest, the test of courage, fair play and a readiness to step into the fray and defend his home or his country were often touted as the inborn characteristics of the English male. During the Regency sport was a major preoccupation for men of all classes and many men would go out of their way to attend a boxing match or horse race, or to watch two dogs or a couple of cocks fight to the death as Peregrine Taverner did in *Regency Buck*. Hunting, fishing, shooting, racing, fighting and cricket were the major sporting pastimes in which Regency men participated either as spectators, punters or players. Of the various physical activities and outdoor entertainments enjoyed by men, a limited number were also available to women and, for the upper class in particular, these generally centred on the equestrian sports—mainly riding, coaching and, for a few women, hunting. It was in horseman-ship that women found one of their few outlets for strenuous exercise and independent activity, as well as the opportunity to match men in both knowledge and expertise. In *Bath Tangle*, Lady Serena Carlow found a much-needed outlet for her pent-up energy and frustration in taking her horse for a gallop through the hills surrounding Bath. In general, women were not expected to be interested in sports but women of all classes could and did attend horse races, and some females of the lower orders enjoyed watching (and occasionally participating in) boxing matches and contests between animals.

Boxing at the Fives Court, Prizefights and Pets of the Fancy

Fist fights as a means of resolving disputes, attacking an enemy or defending oneself in a weaponless situation had long been a part of English life and, despite the fact that boxing matches were forbidden by law, a wide cross section of the population eagerly embraced the sport and would travel miles on foot, on horseback, in a carriage or any conveyance they could find, to attend a match. In *The Unknown Ajax*, Richmond Darracott was thrilled at the prospect of going to a prizefight at Sevenoaks with his cousin Vincent to watch Cribb's latest protégé battle it out with Tom Bugle for twenty guineas a side. Although the magistrates rarely put a stop to illegal bouts, fights were generally held outside the main cities and towns and their location kept a closely guarded secret until the night before a match. In London, however, sparring was a regular attraction at the Fives Court in St Martin's Lane, Leicester Fields. Up to a thousand spectators could be accommodated in the old, high-ceilinged, brick building where men had traditionally played at hand tennis or 'fives'. Sparring exhibitions and boxing matches were held at the Fives Court each afternoon at two o'clock and, for a three-shilling admission, enthusiasts could watch up-and-coming pugilists demonstrate their skill, and learn something of the science of boxing, although Jessamy Merriville in *Frederica* felt that he had led his younger brother into a 'haunt of vice' by taking him there. Combatants had to be approved by the great man of Regency boxing, 'Gentleman' John Jackson, and several of the most famous names of pugilism, including Jem

Belcher, Tom Cribb and Bill Richmond, made appearances there to the delight of the 'fancy'.

The 'fancy' was a collective term for those who followed boxing and 'pets of the fancy' were those pugilists who had made names for themselves as champions or fighters with 'bottom' or great courage. They had huge followings among the populace and, as the Taverners discovered in *Regency Buck* when they arrived at Grantham on the day before a major match, fighters like Cribb, Belcher or Molyneux could draw crowds of twenty or thirty thousand spectators whenever they fought. Whether they walked, rode or drove, men of all classes would often set out the day before a match to be sure of a good vantage point and the opportunity to place their bets.

Men of all classes attended sparring matches at the Fives Court.

In 1795, John Jackson had won the title of English Champion from the great Jewish boxer, Mendoza, and immediately afterwards set about establishing a boxing school for gentlemen. He took rooms at number 13 Bond Street and equipped the elegant saloon with a set of scales, boxing gloves, weights, fencing equipment, wooden staves for single stick and chairs for subscribers. The walls were decorated with pictures of famous bouts, well-known pugilists and diagrams explaining the art and science of boxing. Open three times a week throughout the Season,

Much admired as an arbiter of sport, 'Gentleman' John Jackson taught many gentlemen how to box.

Jackson's Saloon became a kind of boxing headquarters during the Regency and Jackson drew a huge following from among the aristocracy to the sport. He condemned fixed fights (known as crosses), never made a bet and his presence as either a referee or a spectator at a fight was a sign to onlookers that the bout would be fair. Entrée to Jackson's Saloon could only be obtained through introduction and many upper-class men aspired to boxing lessons from the great man. Some among the nobility, such as Sir Richard Wyndham in *The Corinthian*, were privileged enough to strip to the waist, don a pair of boxing gloves and engage in a sparring contest with 'Corinthian Jack', and many famous Regency men, including Lord Byron, learned the art of self-defence at his Bond Street rooms. Charles Rivenhall in *The Grand Sophy* sparred there regularly and Jackson was wont to say that he could have made him a champion if he had not been an aristocrat. Jackson's manners and well-bred demeanour earned him the sobriquet 'Gentleman' and he was respected by nobility and commoners alike.

After John Jackson, the most famous English Champion during the Regency was Tom Cribb, who fought his greatest matches between 1805 and 1811. Renowned for his courage and stamina, as well as for his ability to read an opponent and engage in the 'science' of boxing, Cribb was most famous for his hard-fought victories over the American Tom Molyneux and in particular the match fought in 1811 at Thistleton Gap in Leicestershire which Cribb won. Apart from an exhibition match given for the Allied Sovereigns during their visit to England in 1814, Cribb chose not to continue boxing after his victory over Molyneux. He bought the King's Arms tavern and established 'Cribb's Parlour', a neat little snuggery or separate room off the main taproom in which pugilists and the sporting men of the *ton* would gather to talk, smoke and admire the Champion's cup—a prize Bertram Tallant in *Arabella* was thrilled to be able to hold. The King's Arms was

*Cribb's Parlour was a popular pleasure haunt among
the Corinthians and Regency bucks.*

always crowded with men of all ranks and professions and it was
not uncommon for eager young men with visions of glory to try
and goad Cribb into fighting with them—only to find themselves
hauled directly to the watch house or magistrate by the unimpressed Champion.

COCKS AND DOGS

One of the oldest-known spectator sports, cock-fighting had a
large following during the Regency and men (and sometimes
women) would gather regularly at both indoor and outdoor
venues. Betting was as much a part of the sport as spectating
and sometimes entire estates were wagered on the outcome of a
'main' which consisted of an odd number of battles, sometimes
run over several days, between two rival teams with each cock
fighting once. The main was won by whichever team gained
the majority of victories with prize money paid for each battle

and a larger sum offered to the overall winner. In *Regency Buck*, the bet was a thousand guineas a side and forty guineas for each individual contest. Similarly, crowds would often gather in pubs, yards or purpose-built venues to watch dog-fighting where two or more dogs would fight to the death. Eager spectators would gather at local venues or the Westminster Pit in London to watch contests between different breeds. Battles between bulldogs and bull terriers were popular and dustmen, butchers, grooms and barristers would jostle with MPs, gentlemen and the nobility for a ringside view. As with all Regency sports, gambling was a vital part of the event and vast sums often changed hands during a contest at the Westminster Pit.

REVEL-ROUTS AND BOXING THE WATCH

The propensity for Regency men to drink heavily led many of them to take part in drunken revels late at night when few people were on the streets and the chances of being caught greatly reduced. Aristocratic young men up from the country, or sons of the nobility sent down from Oxford or Cambridge for outrageous behaviour, took great pleasure in getting drunk and engaging in the kind of 'larks' that such an uninhibited state allowed. A revel-rout was a gathering of usually young men for the specific purpose of drinking and engaging in revelry. In London the opportunities for mischief were many and a favourite sport for young bucks such as Dysart in *April Lady* was known as 'boxing the watch'. The 'watch' were the city's nightwatchmen, also known as 'Charleys', whose job it was to patrol the streets calling out the time and the weather on the hour, and ensuring that law and order were maintained. They were not very effectual as many of the watchmen were old and interested only in the small wage paid to them by the Parish.

Small wooden booths were set up at various points around the city in which the watchmen could sit and observe the passers-by. Each booth had a single door and inebriated young men considered it a great lark to overturn the booth (with the Charley inside) or to turn it door-side to the wall so he could not get out. This was known as 'boxing the watch'. It was not uncommon for young men, finding their favourite gambling hell closed to them in the early hours of the morning, to wander the streets looking for a fight, break windows, wake a shopkeeper with a false call of 'fire' or cut the traces of a hackney cab while the coachman slept inside and take his horses to some other part of the city. Many revellers' drunken antics ended with the unrepentant young men being locked up in the watch-house before appearing in the magistrates' court the following day while those who had managed to avoid arrest often chose to end the night at the Covent Garden coffee-house known as 'the Finish' where they fell asleep on a bench.

On the Strut to Tattersall's

In 1766 Richard Tattersall of Lancashire, horse master to the Duke of Kingston and equine aficionado, established a horse sale-yard off Grosvenor Place in London. The business prospered and he acquired a ninety-nine year lease on premises at Hyde Park Corner and in (about) 1773, opened an auction house there. Although Tattersall died in 1795 he had built such a reputation for integrity and knowledge of horseflesh that his name had become synonymous with bloodstock sales and Tattersall's had become an institution. In addition to its thoroughbred auctions, racehorses, coach horses, hunters, hacks, hounds and carriages could be bought and sold at the weekly sales, with stabling for over one hundred horses, kennels for the dogs and a coach-house for the carriages and harness available for inspection. Faced with a mountain of debt after the death of his father in a hunting accident, the new Viscount Lynton, Adam Deveril of *A Civil Contract*, felt compelled to sell his stable and sent sixteen hunters to Tattersall's to be put up at auction. During the winter (the hunting season) sales were held on Mondays and Thursdays but in the summer only on Mondays. It was considered fashionable during the Regency to 'take a look in' at Tattersall's, to stroll about the premises, examine the horses and discuss their respective merits or defects with other sporting men. Henry Stornaway in *The Toll-Gate* considered himself to be quite at home at Tattersall's and spent considerable time there despite being generally held to be a poor judge of horseflesh. For a guinea a year a man could gain admittance to the subscription room where he could lay bets on any forthcoming race or sporting event. Monday was settling day (known by the less fortunate as 'Black Monday') during which gamblers received their winnings or were required to pay their debts. Known also as the 'Repository', Tattersall's held its auctions outside in a courtyard enclosed on three sides by a wide veranda supported by pillars. Prospective buyers and onlookers would gather in the yard and the horses would be run around the perimeter before being offered for sale. Tattersall's took a small commission on each sale and charged both sellers and buyers for any necessary stabling of their animals.

Many gentlemen took a 'look in at Tattersall's' on the way to their club.

Hunting, Horse Racing, Curricle Racing and Wagers

Hunting was a winter sport and many people considered it a boon to have the hunt meet in their neighbourhood. The hunt drew the rich and fashionable to the countryside and especially to the famous village of Melton Mowbray and the hunting country of the 'Shires' (Leicestershire, Northamptonshire and Rutland) as well as to the three greatest hunting packs of the Quorn, the Belvoir and the Cottesmore. The position of Master of Foxhounds (or MFH) was a prestigious one and it was often held by the local squire or a member of the aristocracy with his own pack of hounds. During the actual hunt the hounds were controlled by one or more whippers-in who worked to keep the hounds together in a single pack by 'whipping-in' any animal that broke loose or strayed from the group. Hounds were vital to the hunt as it was the job of the pack to pick up the fox's scent, pursue it and eventually run the fox to ground while the men and women of the hunt rode in pursuit. For those addicted to the chase, like Phoebe Marlow's father in *Sylvester*, hunting was an expensive sport. A bruising rider like Lord Marlow needed a minimum of six horses to hunt the Shires for several days a week and in lesser country he required at least three hunters to manage four days a week during the hunting season. But for intrepid riders, the thrill of a cross-country gallop with hedges, stone walls, ditches, gates and water courses to jump made hunting the only sport.

By the early nineteenth century Newmarket had become the effectual headquarters of the racing world and during the racing season men of leisure would organise their lives around the racing calendar. Racing was enormously popular with all classes and 'betting on the turf' a principal occupation for many gentlemen. Wagers could be laid on races at the course itself or at Tattersall's which was open to all classes (though not to women). Fortunes were won and lost on horse races and many men would go to the races with the intention of recovering from debt only to find themselves much worse off at the end of the day—although Simon Carrington proved himself the exception to this rule in *Charity Girl*.

Curricle racing was never a formal sport, but rather an activity engaged in by men of fashion with a competitive nature, an interest in horses, and a desire for ever greater speed. Curricles were two-wheeled carriages generally pulled by a pair of horses, although expert drivers sometimes harnessed four, or even six, horses to the vehicle. A race could be between two drivers and their teams, or against the clock over a specified distance. The drive from London to Brighton was a popular racing route because the much-used road tended to be well maintained and there were several excellent posting-houses along the way. Reliable posting-houses were essential in a race because of the need for lightning-fast changes of the team. It generally took a stage-coach and four six hours to travel the fifty-two miles to Brighton; in 1784 the Prince Regent—then Prince of Wales—accomplished it in four and a half hours driving a phaeton and three unicorn style (one horse in front and two behind the leader). During the Regency, however, a driver tooling one of the new, lighter racing curricles designed for speed and drawn by a pair of well-matched carriage horses, with good new teams for the changes along the way, could complete the journey in well under four hours.

The betting book at White's was started in the early years of the club by members who wanted a written record of bets made between them. Up to the middle of the eighteenth century bets were recorded by a club official but after that wagers were written in the leather-bound book by those making the bet. Many famous names were recorded in the betting book, with large sums wagered on a range of contests or questions ranging from racing to politics, matrimony to life expectancy. Some of those who bet were themselves the subject of wagers. Beau Brummell was a frequent entrant in the betting book, accepting wagers on issues as diverse as whether the Empress Maria Louisa would be in Paris by October

1815 (for 100 guineas), whether peace would be made between Napoleon and the Allies in 1814 (for 25 guineas) or whether Sir William Guise would beat Mr Dalton for the seat of Gloucester in February 1811 (30 to 25 guineas). Brummell was also the subject of a number of bets, such as the one in 1815 between Thomas Raikes and Charles Greville who each wagered 25 guineas that Brummell would beat a certain Mr Mosseux to the altar. Although, as Mr Liversedge pointed out to Captain Ware in *The Foundling*, some of the bets were improbable (and many were entirely frivolous), others were an interesting reflection of the club members' reactions to some of the important events and issues of the period. In terms of the number of bets made and the size of the sums wagered, the Regency was the high period of the White's betting book.

Gambling, Vowels and Debts of Honour

Betting and gaming were a major preoccupation during the Regency. Although both men and women gambled, upper-class

Card games such as whist, faro and macao were hugely popular during the Regency.

women mostly confined their gaming to card games such as loo, silver-loo, faro, macao, whist and rouge-et-noir. Men also gambled at cards (particularly whist and faro) and often heavily, wagering vast sums on a hand in the clubs and hells of Pall Mall and St James's, or risking their fortunes and estates on the roll of the dice when their luck at cards appeared to have deserted them. Almost any kind of bet was acceptable but once entered into was held to be binding: gambling debts were taken very seriously and, though legally unenforceable, were considered 'debts of honour'. It was implicitly understood and accepted among the upper class that a debt created between individuals at the gaming table, over a hand of cards or as the result of any kind of wager between them, took precedence over, and must be paid before, any other kind of debt—even if the repayment cost a man his entire fortune and his estate. Because of the propensity for gambling and the very large sums involved, where a debt of honour was concerned there could be no thought of asking that payment be delayed or the debt forgiven—even of one's closest friend. A man of honour would not dream of defaulting on a gambling debt, although he might easily make his tailor or other tradesmen wait months or even years before paying them. Money owed to tradespeople was perceived quite differently by the upper class and for those tradespeople who preferred not to wait the weeks, months or years it often took for many among the *ton* to pay their bills it sometimes became necessary to dun their aristocratic clients. This usually took the form, as Nell Cardross found to her great dismay in *April Lady*, of repeated invoices, courteous written reminders, forcibly expressed letters or a personal visit from the creditor to the debtor's home to demand payment.

A man caught up in reckless gambling and finding himself short of ready money to pay what he owed could write an IOU or vowel (so-called because of the vowels, i.e. the *I*, *O* and *U* it represented) and pay his creditor the next day or over an agreed period. As Bertram tried to explain to his sister in *Arabella*, such was the degree of seriousness attached to a debt of honour that borrowing from a woman, going to the moneylenders, taking the King's shilling (which meant enlisting in the army as an ordinary soldier instead of being commissioned as an officer—a dire fate for an upper-class man) or even death, were all more honourable outcomes than forfeiture of payment. Although women also gambled during the Regency—and some of them such as Lady Denville in *False Colours* to dangerous excess—few of them viewed gaming debts as men did, although they too were still obliged to pay. For those men and women with enormous gambling debts, often the only alternative left to them was to sell what they could, borrow from friends or the bank, or, as a very last resort, go to the moneylenders. It was not uncommon for a man to rise from the card table with losses of several thousand pounds and go straight to Clarges Street and the house of the moneylender and radical pamphleteer Jonathan 'Jew' King, there to mortgage his house or pledge the family silver in order to pay what he owed. Moneylenders were also known as 'cent per cents' because of the interest charged on the loans and, during the Regency, establishments such as Howard and Gibbs, King's, Hamlet's (the Cranbourn Alley jeweller) or less reputable practitioners, such as Mr Goldhanger in *The Grand Sophy*, enjoyed considerable patronage from among the desperate and debt-stricken social elite.

DUELLING

There were a number of fencing academies in London during the Regency but probably the most famous of these was the school which had been established in the previous century by the famous master of the sword, Dominico Angelo. Angelo was an elegant, athletic man, who had cultivated every physical attribute and been esteemed by his friends and pupils alike for his extraordinary skill and dedication to his work. During the Regency his famous Bond Street school (next door

Going to a moneylender was usually a last resort for those who found themselves deep in debt.

to Jackson's Boxing Saloon) was run by his son Henry who, like his father before him, was considered by the *ton* to be a master in the art of the fence. Well-bred gentlemen like Gervase Frant in *The Quiet Gentleman* became extremely skilled with a sword and sometimes attended the school to take lessons from the master, and Angelo's subscription list included some of the noblest names in England.

Although a small number of duels were still fought with swords during the Regency, the growing popularity of guns and game shooting, coupled with improvements in firearm design and manufacture, increasingly saw pistols as the weapon of choice in settling an argument. There were three main reasons for challenging a man to a duel: taking liberties with a female relative; accusations of cheating, defamation or dishonourable behaviour; and attacking someone physically. A set of strict rules known as the Code of Honour governed the behaviour of any man involved

Peregrine Taverner was forced into a duel in Regency Buck.

in a duel and it was always the injured party's prerogative to call out the offender and to choose the type of weapons to be used in an engagement. Once a challenge had been accepted the two parties—known as principals—would name their seconds, usually close and trusted friends, to act on their behalf. The Code of Honour decreed that a combatant place his honour in the hands of his seconds and it was their responsibility to see that protocols were adhered to and an equal contest was arranged. As both Ferdy Fakenham and Gil Ringwood in *Friday's Child* knew only too well, the first duty of the seconds was to try and prevent the duel taking place while maintaining the honour of the principals. There was no dishonour in offering an apology or admitting error unless a blow had been struck (in which case no apology could be received) and the seconds would always try for an amicable settlement before arranging an engagement—a task which proved extremely challenging for Mr Warboys in *The Quiet Gentleman.*

A duel had to be fought within forty-eight hours of a challenge and at a time and place mutually agreed upon by the parties. Early morning was considered the best time for an engagement and most duels were held at locations just outside of town. It was the seconds' duty to check the weapons, load each gun and mark out the firing distance—usually one of between ten and fourteen paces (a pace was about a yard). The distance selected by the seconds usually depended on the abilities of their principals, with a longer range for an expert marksman and a shorter distance for an indifferent shot. Lord George Wrotham held out for a distance of twenty-five yards in *Friday's Child* which his friends considered most unfair given that he was a crack shot. Combatants saluted each other before 'leeching' or stepping up to their marks, saluted again, turned sideways with their arm extended and the pistol cocked, and waited for the signal to fire. Once they were in position a handkerchief was raised by a third party and the seconds, servants and surgeons moved at least thirty yards away, with the surgeons turning their backs until they heard the shots. At the drop of the handkerchief both combatants fired at each other or into the air if they wished to admit fault by deloping as both Sherry and George did in *Friday's Child*. Each party was required to stay on his mark until both pistols had been fired and it was considered wise not to lower one's arm, even after firing, until the other shot had been taken. In the event of a combatant being wounded before he had fired he was still at liberty to shoot, provided he did so within two minutes of his opponent's shot. If a gun missed fire or failed for any reason no second shot was allowed. At the end of the duel both parties (if they were able) saluted, expressed their regret and left the field.

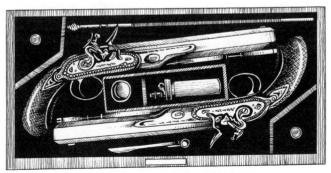

The Duke of Sale purchased a superb pair of Mantons duelling pistols in The Foundling.

A pocket pistol of the type used by Sophy on her visit to the moneylender,
Mr Goldhanger, in The Grand Sophy.

A duelling pistol was an elegant weapon, usually with a ten-inch
barrel and a finely worked flint- or percussion-lock above a curved
handle, and the guns were often finished in silver or decorated
with delicate filigree work. The finest duelling pistols had a hair-
trigger as part of the lock; this finely worked piece of craftsmanship,
although an advantage, could be dangerous. The hair-trigger had
to be treated with the utmost caution as, once set, it could go off at
any moment. Combatants were always advised to keep their pistol
pointed at the ground once it was made ready to fire. During the
Regency, the most sought-after guns were those made by Joseph
Manton, the most famous gun maker of the day. Named after
their maker, these superbly balanced pistols were considered to be
among the finest weapons then available, with an exquisite 'feel'
that gave the shooter the sense that the gun was part of his hand.
Although many men aspired to own a brace of Mantons, at fifty
to sixty guineas for a pair of duelling pistols, only the very wealthy
could afford them. In *The Foundling*, the Duke of Sale took delivery
of an elegant pair of Mantons before setting out on his adventures.
Joseph Manton also ran a shooting gallery in London's Davies
Street where sporting men could practise their marksmanship by

shooting at rows of paper wafers attached to three-foot-wide, circular cast-iron targets. A man who could hit or 'culp' more than twelve wafers over a distance of fifteen yards in under six minutes (and reload his guns between each shot) was considered proficient. A man who could better such an accomplishment, and did so in the presence of spectators at Manton's, would be termed a marksman and enjoyed the advantage of being unlikely ever to be called out for a duel. Although some women were competent with firearms, they were precluded from visiting Manton's, something Charles Rivenhall in *The Grand Sophy* regretted when he discovered that his cousin Sophy was proficient with a pistol.

13

Business and the Military

The Postal Service

Letter-writing was an important part of Regency life although the cost could be prohibitive. Postage was calculated according to the distance travelled to deliver it—with the charge borne by the recipient rather than the sender. It cost two pence for delivery within London, increasing to a shilling to send a letter 400 miles, and charges were doubled if the writer enclosed anything in the letter or used an additional sheet of paper. The need to restrict letters to a single page often caused letter writers such as Arabella to cross her lines by writing the letter in the usual way and then turning the page sideways and writing at right angles over the top of the existing words. This could make correspondence very hard to read as Nell Cardross discovered in *April Lady* when she tried to decipher a letter in which her mama had crossed and recrossed her lines—Lady Pevensey had written horizontally, vertically *and* diagonally across the page. There were no envelopes in the modern sense and so letters were folded in a particular way and sealed with either a blob of melted sealing wax or a wafer (a small thin disc made of gum and flour which, when dampened, could be affixed to the letter). Members of the peerage and of both Houses of Parliament were entitled to have their mail delivered free of

Arabella wrote a long letter to her family 'in a fine, small hand, and on very thin paper, crossing her lines'.

charge using a system known as 'franking', according to which an MP or peer had to sign his name and write his address on the outside of the letter to avoid the charge.

THE CITY

The financial heart of London was the ancient City of London, originally recognised by charter in 1070 when William the Conqueror, deciding it would be prudent to treat London as a separate city, guaranteed the citizens their property, privileges and protection from aggressors. Governed by the City Corporation, the City included the 'one square mile' inside the ancient Roman wall and several areas outside it known as 'liberties'. Throughout its long history the City remained separate, both physically and administratively, from the royal court, the parliament, halls of government and the courts of justice, preserving its own legal, political and administrative autonomy as a unique independent entity with the Corporation of the City of

London as the governing body administered by the Lord Mayor, two sheriffs, twenty-six aldermen, and two hundred common councillors (elected by the freemen ratepayers). In *A Civil Contract*, the wealthy merchant Jonathan Chawleigh set his sights on becoming an alderman of the City and might eventually have become Lord Mayor. The City was a panoply of company halls, exchanges, banks, insurers, shops, warehouses, trading companies, shipping offices, markets and wharves, all combining to make it the great commercial centre of the early nineteenth-century world. The commercial heart of the City, fittingly represented by the Bank of England, the Royal Exchange and the Mansion House (the Lord Mayor's official residence), lay at the intersection of Cheapside, Moorgate, and Threadneedle and Lombard Streets. Here the City men (known as 'Cits') would meet in coffee-houses and at the Exchange to gather the latest financial news, discuss their affairs and execute their business.

The Stock Exchange

Besides putting their money back into their land, many in the upper (and middle) classes invested in the Stock Exchange. The official London Stock Exchange was founded just prior to the Regency in 1802 although its origins lay in the seventeenth-century coffee-houses. Anyone with money to spare could invest in the stocks traded at the Stock Exchange which consisted mainly of public funds, bank stocks, Exchequer and Navy bills, India bonds and annuities. The Funds paid a generally reliable return on investment of between three and five per cent but among the best-known investments were the three per cents or consolidated annuities known as 'consols'. These were Government Bonds which paid a three per cent dividend twice a year and were considered extremely safe. For an investor such as Hugo Darracott in *The Unknown Ajax* with half a million pounds in the funds, this meant a return of a very healthy £15,000 a year. The price of consols could rise and fall but mostly within a reasonable range with few wild fluctuations. There were exceptions, however, as when, in June 1815, news came from Brussels that Wellington's army was in retreat and Napoleon on the verge of claiming victory. Many City men panicked, including such savvy investors as Jonathan Chawleigh in *A Civil Contract*. With visions of massive increases in government expenditure on a protracted war or even (unthinkably) a French invasion, the City men sold off their consols, causing the price to tumble. A few canny investors, including Chawleigh's son-in-law Adam Deveril, refused to believe in Wellington's defeat, however, and seized the opportunity to buy the stocks at a greatly reduced price. When the news arrived only a day later of the victory at Waterloo, they had the satisfaction of seeing the stock price rapidly rise and thereby made a large profit.

Fortunes could be made or lost on the Stock Exchange but many people lived on the proceeds of their investment in the Funds.

BANKING

During the Regency there were several banks favoured by the upper class, including one of the country's most notable institutions, the Bank of England, which had been founded in 1694 by a Scotsman, William Paterson. Child's Bank, where Lord Cardross did business in *April Lady,* was one of the oldest banks in London and had originally begun as a goldsmith's shop. Francis Child became a partner before the business was moved in 1673 to its present site of number 1 Fleet Street and eventually inherited the bank. Although Child's was a relatively small bank during the nineteenth century, the Child family amassed a large fortune which Francis Child's grandson Robert Child famously settled on his granddaughter Sarah Fane who later became Lady Jersey, one of the patronesses of Almack's. Drummond's Bank was founded in 1717 by Andrew Drummond who developed a banking business from his goldsmith's shop at the Sign of the Golden Eagle, east of Charing Cross. The bank had an impressive clientele and was favoured particularly by the Tories and the Scottish aristocracy. It was to Drummond's Bank that Adam Deveril went to borrow £50,000 to invest in the Funds in an attempt to restore his fortune in *A Civil Contract.* Hoare's Bank was established in the late seventeenth century by two goldsmiths, Richard and James Hoare, who, from as early as 1673, kept 'a running cash' (money lent on gold securities) at their shop at the 'Golden Bottle' in Cheapside. In 1690 they moved the business to a building on the site of the old Mitre Tavern at what were numbers 34–39 Fleet Street and hung a model of the family's golden leather bottle above the entrance of the bank. Successive generations of the Hoare family continued to run the bank and by the eighteenth century they had amassed a fortune, acquired a great estate and joined the landed gentry. Horace Stanton-Lacy banked with Hoare's and it was to the bank in Fleet Street that Charles Rivenhall took his cousin Sophy in *The*

Grand Sophy so that she could present her father's letter of authorisation. It was unusual for a woman to enter a bank or to engage in any form of business if she had a male relative—husband, father or brother—to do it for her but Sophy was an extremely independent woman who wished to set up her stable, buy a carriage and pay for any expenses she incurred while staying in London.

Lady Ombersley in The Grand Sophy *was shocked when her niece announced her intention of visiting Hoare's Bank.*

Money Talk

Slang term	Name	Value	Year of issue
A plum (it also meant a moderate fortune)		£100,000	
A monkey		£500	
A ton		£100	
A pony		£25	
A goblin	A sovereign	£1 (20s.)	1817
	Half sovereign	10s.	1817
A yellow boy, yellow George	A guinea	£1.1s. (21s.)	1663
A screen	A pound note	£1 (20s.)	1797
A coachwheel, bull, bull's-eye	A crown	5s.	1662
A hind coachwheel, a half bull, or two and a kick	Half crown	2s.6d.	1663
A borde, a hog	A shilling	12d.	1663
A half borde, a sow's baby, a tanner, a kick, half a hog, a fiddle	Sixpence	4d.	1674
	A groat	3d.	
Threps, thrums, half a fiddle	Threepence	2d.	
Tuppence	Twopence	1d.	1797
A copper	Penny	2 farthings	1797
A meg, a tonic, or a h'pence	Halfpenny	¼ penny	1672
A grig	Farthing	⅛ penny	1672
	Half-farthing		

The Military

In the nineteenth century the British army had four main arms: the infantry, the cavalry, the artillery and the engineers. The largest section of the army, the infantry were the soldiers whose main job in battle was to advance against the enemy on foot, usually in lines or columns, and to fight until they were killed or wounded or the battle was won. During the Regency the infantry were mainly armed with rifles and bayonets and were most effective in battle when acting in determined, cohesive companies. The cavalry were the soldiers on horseback and included dragoons, lancers and hussars armed with swords, pistols and carbines (the lancers also carried lances). During the Napoleonic era the British used heavy cavalry for sudden charges and 'shock action', and light cavalry for fighting, pursuit and scouting as well as for situations where mobility could be an advantage. Dragoons (named for the short musket or 'dragon' which they had originally carried) were actually mounted infantry who fought on horseback and on foot. Lancers were first introduced into the British light cavalry in 1816 and were equipped with nine foot long wooden lances tipped with steel which they could carry into battle. The Hussar regiments were used for scouting and communication as well as fighting, and would charge into battle where necessary.

The artillery was the weapons arm of the military and was responsible for moving and firing the big guns with their lethal round, grape- and case-shot. By the early nineteenth century lighter gun carriages, improved methods of transport, better ammunition and increased accuracy made the artillery a crucial part of any battle. The engineers (also known as 'sappers') met the army's practical needs in terms of building, surveying, mapping, demolition and design. Although they did not usually engage in fighting directly they were essential for a successful campaign. During the Regency the British army was made up of individual fighting regiments, each with their own uniforms, history and traditions. Famous regiments included the Black Watch or Royal Highland Regiment (42nd Regiment of Foot) who were renowned for their courage, kilts and bagpipes, the Cherry Pickers or 11th Hussars, the Blues or Royal Horse Guards, the Life Guards, the Seventh Hussars or Lilywhite Seventh—so-called because of the white facings on their pelisses—and the 95th Rifles in which Harry Smith of *The Spanish Bride* was a brigade-major.

By the early nineteenth century British sea power was legendary and the exploits of admirals such as Nelson and victories like the Battle of Trafalgar in 1805 merely served to consolidate Britain's naval supremacy. During the Napoleonic Wars the number of sailors employed by the navy reached 114,000 (in 1812) of which a large number had been 'pressed' including young Ben Breane's older brother in *The Toll-Gate*. In time of war the need for sailors above the number readily available was met by the press-gang which roamed the coastal districts looking for likely men, kidnapped them and delivered them to the nearest naval vessel. For those men or boys who elected to join the navy it could be an exciting, though arduous and dangerous, life.

THE PENINSULAR WAR

The Peninsular War lasted from 1808 until 1814 and was instigated by Napoleon Bonaparte's desire to bring Britain to her knees by crippling her economically. Having failed to defeat Britain's navy at Trafalgar in 1805, and abandoning his plans for an invasion, in 1806 the French Emperor imposed a blockade on all British ports (known as the 'Continental System'), effectively banning all trade between Britain and the Continent. Portugal's refusal to comply with the edict spurred Napoleon to march on Lisbon by way of Spain. With 100,000 troops in Spain to support the invasion he took the opportunity to seize the Spanish throne and install his brother Joseph as the country's new king. The Spaniards rebelled and, at the instigation of Sir Arthur Wellesley (who later became the Duke of Wellington), the British sent an expeditionary force to Lisbon to aid both the Portuguese and the Spanish in their fight to push Napoleon's forces out of the Iberian peninsula.

Wellesley returned to England in October 1808 after the debacle of the Convention of Cintra but in April 1809 returned to the peninsula to take command of the British–Portuguese forces. Napoleon had returned to Paris, leaving his army in the command of his marshals, including Soult, Ney and Kellerman. Over the next three years the combined British, Portuguese and Spanish armies fought the French back and forth across the peninsula, but all the while steadily pushing east through Portugal and into Spain as Wellesley's army won important victories at Talavera, Cuidad Rodrigo, Badajoz and Salamanca. In August 1812 the British entered Madrid and towards the end of the year the news of Napoleon's disastrous retreat from Moscow helped to turn the tide. By mid-1813 Wellesley had taken the offensive and in June his army won a major victory at the Battle of Vittoria. The French counterattacked with some success but their offensive could not be sustained and on 7 October Wellesley crossed into France. Fighting continued for some months as, at his command, Napoleon's army resisted the Allies' advance towards the capital but on 30 March the Allies entered Paris and on 11 April, six years after his invasion of Portugal, Napoleon abdicated and the Peninsular War ended.

THE PEACE

Napoleon's empire was in disarray after the catastrophe of the retreat from Moscow in 1812 and his disastrous losses at the Battle of Leipzig in October 1813. He was finally deposed in April 1814 after the Allies (Britain, Russia, Austria and Prussia) signed the Treaty of Chaumont and marched on Paris. On 11 April 1814 Napoleon abdicated and went into exile on the Island of Elba in the Mediterranean. In England the Peace was officially declared in June and was followed by two months of festivities, including the visit of the Allied Sovereigns, the procession to Guildhall and the official celebrations in Hyde Park.

THE HUNDRED DAYS

On 26 February 1815 Napoleon escaped from the island of Elba. The former emperor sailed for France landing at Antibes on 1 March and marched to Paris, gathering an army as he went. The period known as 'the Hundred Days' began with his arrival in the capital on 20 March where he received a tumultuous welcome and the news that the king, Louis XVIII, had fled. When the Allied forces of Britain, Prussia, Austria and Russia heard of Napoleon's return to power they prepared for war and on 5 April the Duke of Wellington took command of the Allied armies in Belgium. The army was not the force it had been during the Peninsular Campaign but instead was comprised of so many inexperienced British and foreign troops that Wellington described it as 'an infamous army, very weak and ill equipped'. As Napoleon marched his army north into Belgium Wellington did what he could to prepare for battle—demanding more troops and staff officers and undertaking regular reconnaissance expeditions to familiarise himself with the possible battlegrounds.

By 6 June news came that Napoleon was on the march but the Duke remained calm and even gave his blessing to the Duchess of Richmond's plans for a ball at her home in Brussels on 15 June. The ball went ahead, with Wellington and his staff in attendance, but during the evening word came that Napoleon had attacked and battle was joined. The Battles of Ligny and Quatre Bras took place on 16 June and led to a retreat by the British and Prussian troops the next day. The Prussian Field Marshal Blücher lost 16,000 men at Ligny and, although Wellington's men had held their ground at Quatre Bras, he had lost nearly 5,000 soldiers—a fact which, coupled with the news of Blücher's losses, impelled the Duke to withdraw and regroup. Although Blücher's army had not yet rejoined Wellington's forces, by the morning of 18 June in pouring rain the British and Dutch forces had established themselves on a ridge in front of Waterloo and prepared to meet Napoleon's army. With the British and Prussian armies still separated, Napoleon was confident of an easy victory and, according to Wellington, 'did not manoeuvre at all'. The battle lasted all day, with major attacks by the French on the farmhouses of Hougoumont and La Haye Sainte, and many times it looked as though the French had won. Wellington was everywhere throughout the battle, however, urging his men on, giving orders and at all times remaining unshakeably calm. At 6.30 p.m. the French had taken La Haye Sainte and it seemed a British defeat was inevitable, but for some reason Napoleon did not press home his advantage and, instead of a full force, sent only his Imperial Guard against the squares of British infantry. The British and Dutch rallied again and again, resisting every French attack. With the Prussian army beginning to come up at last, by evening the tide had turned and the French attack had turned into a rout. On the night of 18 June 1815, despite appalling losses, the Hundred Days ended in victory for the Allies. That same evening Wellington wrote a report of the battle with the heading 'Waterloo'.

MILITARY MEN

Marshall Beresford, William Carr Beresford, 1st Viscount Beresford (1768–1854): Beresford joined the army in 1785 and rose through the ranks before being given command of the Portuguese army during the Peninsular War of 1808–14. In 1811 he defeated the French marshal, Soult, at the Battle of Albuera and in 1812 took part in the capture of Badajoz but was badly wounded in the battle of Salamanca.

Gebhard Leberecht von Blücher, Fürst von Wahlstadt (1742–1819): A Prussian field marshal, throughout his long career Blücher saw active service in numerous battles and fought against the French several times. In 1813 he took command of the Prussian army and defeated Napoleon at Leipzig. Two years later on 16 June 1815 he suffered a crushing defeat at the hands of the French at Ligny just two days before the battle of Waterloo. Blücher regrouped and won great renown among the English for his arrival on the field of Waterloo just in time to enable the Allies to vanquish Napoleon's army.

Rowland Hill, 1st Viscount Hill (1772–1842): Hill was a career soldier and one of five brothers to join the army. He served in Portugal during the Peninsular Campaign and was knighted in 1812. He was one of Wellington's staff during the 1813–14 push into France and with him again at Waterloo and

The Emperor Napoleon.

was awarded a barony in 1814. Hill was made a viscount in the last years of his life.

Napoleon I, Emperor of France (1769–1821): Napoleon Bonaparte was born in Corsica but educated in France where he won a scholarship to the military academy at Brienne before attending, at age fourteen, the Ecole Militaire in Paris. He had a moderately successful military career before his marriage to Joséphine de Beauharnais in 1796 (whom he later divorced to marry the Emperor of Austria's daughter, Marie Louise) and her influence secured him the command of the army of Italy. By 1799 he had become First Consul of France and, supported by the army, he proceeded to expand his rule, until in 1804 he was proclaimed Emperor. By 1811 he had gained control of much of Europe and only Britain continued firmly to resist him. The tide turned against Napoleon when he invaded Russia in 1812. Unable to maintain his position on two fronts, he was forced to retreat and by 1814 his empire was lost. Napoleon abdicated and went into exile on the island of Elba in the Mediterranean but in 1815 he escaped and, gathering loyal forces around him, marched on Paris. The 'Hundred Days' witnessed Napoleon's attempt to regain his former power and culminated in the Battle of Waterloo in which the French army was decisively beaten. Exiled to the island of St Helena, a thousand miles off the west African coast, he died there in 1821.

Marshall Soult, Nicolas Jean de Dieu Soult (1769–1851): Soult was created a marshal of France by Napoleon in 1804. He spent six years leading the French armies in the Peninsular War and was finally defeated at Toulouse in 1814. He joined Napoleon for the Hundred Days and was appointed his chief-of-staff at Waterloo. After Wellington's victory and Napoleon's exile to St Helena, Soult was also exiled at the Second Restoration in 1815, but in 1819 he received full restoration of his honours and remained active in government until his death.

Arthur Wellesley, 1st Duke of Wellington (1769–1852): The third son of an Irish peer, Wellington attended Eton before being sent to a French military academy at Angers. In 1787 he entered the army as an ensign, was promoted to captain in 1791 and to lieutenant-colonel in 1793. His greatest victories were in the Napoleonic Wars during which he commanded the British forces throughout the Peninsular campaign—forcing the French out of Portugal and Spain, and eventually routing Marshall Soult's army at Toulouse in 1814. Already created a viscount in 1814, he was made 1st Duke of Wellington and it was under this title in 1815 that he led his 'infamous army' to triumph over Napoleon at Waterloo. Known to his men as 'Douro' or 'old Hookey' (due to his hooked nose), and to a grateful nation as 'the Iron Duke',

The Duke of Wellington.

Wellington was a man of few words, who cared more for the welfare of his men than any honour he might win—conservative, pragmatic and precise, he was impatient with those who looked for glory in war. On his return to England, Wellington resumed his political career, serving in Lord Liverpool's Tory ministry and eventually becoming prime minister himself in 1828.

Who's Who in the Regency

The Royal Family

George III, King of Great Britain and Ireland, and Elector of Hanover (1738–1820): The grandson of George II, George III came to the British throne in 1760. The first Hanoverian monarch to be born in Britain, he was a plain, rather stolid man with a keen interest in agriculture that earned him the nickname 'Farmer George'. He was a devoted yet repressive parent, a faithful husband and devout Christian, with a liking for plain living. His long reign was first interrupted in 1788 by the illness (thought now to be the rare blood disease, porphyria) that eventually drove him to complete madness and seclusion in 1810, at which time his eldest son, George (later George IV), was appointed to rule as Regent until his father's death.

Queen Charlotte, Charlotte of Mecklenburg-Strelitz (1744–1818): Married to King George III in 1761 when she was just seventeen, Queen Charlotte proved to be an uninspiring but devoted bride. The pair were well-matched with a mutual liking for domestic living, a regulated family life and children. Charlotte gave birth to fifteen royal offspring between 1762 and 1783, of whom thirteen children survived to adulthood. She was a dedicated mother but lacked empathy, and she and her husband were highly critical of their sons' dissolute behaviour.

George Augustus Frederick, Prince of Wales, Prince Regent, King George IV of Great Britain and Ireland, and King of Hanover (1762–1830): The eldest son of the British monarch, George was made Prince of Wales at birth. A handsome, intelligent and high-spirited child, he burst the bounds of his excessively strict upbringing at an early age, indulging his passions and alternating between wanting his parents' approval and outright rebellion. He had many affairs, but the great love of his life was a widow, Maria Anne Fitzherbert, whom he married clandestinely in 1785. The marriage was illegal as she was a Catholic and (according to the Royal Marriage Act) he was under age. The two lived for several years as husband and wife, however, until the Prince's debts and the need for an heir forced him to consider a lawful marriage. Princess Caroline of Brunswick was the bride selected and they were married in April 1795, but the union proved disastrous and although a daughter, Charlotte, was born in 1796 they soon separated. Intense mutual dislike dogged them both and the Prince sought refuge in a series of affairs, returning first to Maria Fitzherbert before moving on to a succession of high-born older women. George IV's hostility towards his wife was evident when he was told of Napoleon's death by a government minister who declared, 'Sire, I have the gratification to announce that your Majesty's greatest enemy is dead.' To which he reportedly replied, 'Is she, by God?' Although he was popular in his youth, and dearly loved by his sisters, the Prince's treatment of his wife and daughter, his numerous affairs, his profligacy and huge debt saw the people take an increasing dislike to him. Much of his debt was incurred in creating many of the (now iconic) architectural and cultural monuments to his Regency, such as the Brighton Pavilion and Regent Street, but at the time his love of art and beauty, coupled with his histrionic tendencies, made him seem irresponsible and a burden rather than a blessing to the nation. Although he had been tall and handsome in his youth the Prince grew corpulent (so much so that he eventually had to wear corsets) and his face and figure bore the marks of a dissipated life. Yet, as Jenny, Lady Lynton, found in *A Civil Contract*, throughout his life 'Prinny' retained a charm of manner and a graciousness that endeared him to many; he was intelligent, accomplished and, in public, always affable. An unremarkable ruler politically, George, Regent and King, gave his title to a period and left a priceless legacy of art and culture to his people.

Princess Caroline of Brunswick (1768–1821): In 1794 Princess Caroline was chosen as a suitable bride for the Prince of Wales who felt an urgent need to marry in order to provide an heir and to alleviate his debt. The two were first cousins and had never met prior to her arrival in England in 1795 for the wedding. The April marriage was a disaster from the outset. Although willing and eager to please, Caroline was also headstrong, boisterous, unkempt and altogether incompatible with the 'delicate' and fastidious Prince.

The couple were together long enough to conceive a daughter, but separated after her birth partly because of the Prince's continuing intimacy with Lady Frances Jersey whom Caroline hated. The Prince and Princess established separate lives but there was a great deal of vindictive feeling between them. In 1806 reports of Caroline's excessive and indiscreet behaviour prompted 'a delicate investigation' in which she was eventually cleared of charges of adultery. Husband

Princess Caroline of Brunswick.

and wife never achieved a reconciliation and Caroline spent much time in Europe surrounded by a disreputable entourage whose behaviour gave rise to intense gossip. In 1820, when George became King, Caroline returned to England in an attempt to become Queen but was faced instead with a Bill of Pains and Penalties. The case was heard in the House of Lords: the government's aim was to forfeit her right to be Queen and allow the King to divorce her. When told of the divorce proceedings against her Caroline reportedly said, 'Well, I can only say that I was never guilty of misconduct but once, and that was with Mrs Fitzherbert's husband!' The bill was eventually dropped but Caroline never officially became Queen. She was refused admission to the coronation in 1821 and died two weeks later.

Princess Charlotte, Charlotte Augusta, Princess of Wales (1796–1817): The only child of George, Prince of Wales, and his soon-to-be estranged wife, Caroline of Brunswick, Charlotte had a restricted childhood with little contact with the outside world. Her parents' intense dislike of each other was a continual source of conflict for her and chafed her as much as the repressive life she was forced to lead. In 1813 her father arranged a marriage between her and William, Prince of Orange, to which she reluctantly agreed before abruptly terminating the arrangement on discovering she would have to live in the Netherlands. In 1814 she met Prince Leopold of Saxe-Coburg and they became engaged. They were married in May 1816 and found great happiness in each other's company. On 5 November 1817 Charlotte gave birth to a stillborn boy and died some hours later. The entire nation was devastated and went into deep mourning for their beloved princess.

Frederick Augustus, Duke of York (1763–1827): The Duke of York spent much of his life involved in the army and was made Commander-in-Chief of the army in 1798. A pleasant, affable man, he was fond of gambling, women and the pleasures of the table. In 1809 he was forced to resign his leadership of the army after it was discovered that his mistress, Mary Anne Clarke, had used her position to sell commissions. He was reinstated in 1811, when his brother became Regent, and proved a better administrator than field officer. In 1791 he had married Frederica of Prussia, an intelligent, pleasant woman who lived in affable separation from her husband at Oatlands near Wimbledon where she kept a great many dogs. She happily played hostess to the Duke and his friends when he brought them down for gambling weekends.

William, Duke of Clarence, also William IV, King of Britain and Ireland (1765–1837): A midshipman in the navy at the age of thirteen, the Duke of Clarence eventually became in turn rear admiral, vice admiral, admiral and finally, in 1811, admiral of the fleet. Like many of his brothers he was terrible with money and his private life was not exemplary, although he was devoted to his mistress, the actress Mrs Jordan, with whom he had ten illegitimate children known as the FitzClarences. She died in 1816 and, after Princess Charlotte's death in 1817, the Duke joined the rush to provide a new heir to the throne, marrying Adelaide of Saxe-Meiningen in 1818 in a childless but happy union. Known as the 'Royal Tar' and 'old Tarry Breeks', the Duke was often vulgar, thought nothing of talking aloud during church and swore like a trooper, but he was also affable and unpretentious and generally well-liked. In 1830 he became King William IV, the 'sailor king', and in many respects proved to be a surprisingly able monarch.

Edward, Duke of Kent (1767–1820): Like his brother Frederick, the Duke of Kent also went into the army but proved so pedantic that he caused a mutiny in Gibraltar. He was recalled from the post and promoted to field marshal. After Princess Charlotte's death he ended relations with his mistress of twenty-seven years, Madame

St Laurent, and married Victoria of Saxe-Coburg with whom, in 1819, he fathered the new heir to the throne, Princess Victoria.

Ernest Augustus, Duke of Cumberland (1771–1851): Trained in the Hanoverian army, the Duke of Cumberland saw much active service and eventually transferred to the British army where he became a field marshal. A brave and able commander, he lost an eye during a battle in 1794 which did not help to endear him to a public already inclined to dislike him. His popularity in Britain was not helped by rumours that he had murdered his valet and fathered a child on his sister Sophia. In 1837 he became King of Hanover by right of heredity and enjoyed popular support in that kingdom until the end of his life.

Augustus Frederick, Duke of Sussex (1773–1843): More interested in books and music than most of his siblings, Sussex was a placid individual, though a staunch liberal and a kind uncle. When his niece, Princess Charlotte, fled from Carlton House to her mother's residence at Connaught Place, after refusing to marry the Prince of Orange, Sussex responded immediately to her cry for help and played a conciliating and supportive role in resolving the issue.

Adolphus, Duke of Cambridge (1774–1850): The youngest of seven sons, Cambridge was also in the military, though with a less colourful career than any of his brothers. Conservative in both his domestic life and his politics, unlike his brothers, Cambridge was restrained in his spending and eschewed keeping a mistress. He did, however, scramble to marry and produce an heir after the death of Princess Charlotte, marrying Princess Augusta of Hesse-Cassell with whom he had two daughters and a son.

Octavius (1779–1783): His father, George III, said of him, 'There will be no heaven for me if Octavius is not there.' Died in infancy.

Alfred (1780–1782): He died in infancy.

Prince Leopold of Saxe-Coburg (1790–1865): Leopold first came to England in 1814 as part of the Russian royal entourage visiting for the Peace Celebrations. A younger son of Prince Francis of Saxe-Coburg, he was a pleasant, serious and handsome man whose lack of fortune did not initially recommend him to the Regent as a suitable husband for his daughter Charlotte. The couple were married in 1816, however, and Leopold was devastated by Charlotte's death the following year. He remained in England for many years but in 1831 was elected King of Belgium. He eventually married Marie-Louise of Orléans, daughter of Louis Philippe of France.

Princess Charlotte and Prince Leopold.

Charlotte Augusta Matilda, the Princess Royal (1766–1828): Known in the family as the Princess Royal (to avoid confusion with her mother from whom she took her name), Princess Charlotte was a shy, quiet woman who endured a constricted childhood in the strait-laced royal household dominated by her dictatorial mother and conservative father. Neither of her parents encouraged her to marry and denied her the opportunity to do so, despite offers from scions of several royal houses. Eventually in 1797, after much delay, she was finally allowed to wed the Prince of Württemberg.

Princess Augusta Sophia (1768–1840): Princess Augusta was a lively and engaging child who captured the affections of those who knew her. She suffered from her parents' repressive attitudes, however, and her hopes for marriage and an independent life were blighted when she fell in love with an English army officer. They never married but maintained a relationship until her lover's death in 1828.

Princess Elizabeth (1770–1840): Known to her sisters as 'Fatima' because of her liking for food, Princess Elizabeth was a plump, spirited young woman who was often ill as a child and probably suffered from a milder form of the family malady. She wanted to be married, but a promising relationship with Louis Philippe, the exiled eldest son of the Duke of Orléans was thwarted by the Queen. She eventually married Frederick, Prince of Hesse-Homburg, established a new home in Europe and lived happily ever after with 'her Fritz'.

Princess Mary (1776–1857): Generally held to be the beauty of the family and known as 'dearest Minny', Princess Mary was a much-loved and caring sister. She was a comfort to her mother which may have been why, of all the royal sisters, Mary gained the Queen's approval of her marriage to her cousin William Frederick, Duke of Gloucester (illegitimate son of George III's brother). Mary was the longest-lived of George III's children; she attended the Great Exhibition of 1851, knew all of Queen Victoria's offspring, and died at the age of eighty.

Princess Sophia (1777–1848): Another of the royal sisters to suffer from the family malady was Princess Sophia. Intelligent and beautiful, she never married. Sophia suffered bouts of ill health and depression throughout her life yet, although she was disliked by her mother, her sweet disposition made her the favourite of many.

Princess Amelia (1783–1810): The youngest of fifteen, Princess Amelia was born after her brothers Octavius and Alfred, both of whom died in infancy. Loved by everyone, she was her father's favourite and her death in 1810 was believed to have contributed to the King's final descent into madness.

Influential Women

Jane Austen (1775–1817): An English novelist, Austen was born in Steventon, Hampshire, the second youngest of seven siblings. Her father was rector at Steventon where they lived until she was twenty-five after which the family moved to Bath and then Chawton. Austen began writing as a child and developed a keen eye for human foibles and the vagaries of English class and society. Her incisive and witty novels about ordinary people have made her one of the world's best-known authors. Four of her six novels were published anonymously before her death in 1817 and the last two appeared posthumously in 1818. Austen died in her sister Cassandra's arms in Winchester on 18 July 1817.

Jane Austen.

Frances (Fanny) Burney, Madame D'Arblay (1752–1840): English novelist and dramatist Fanny Burney's first novel, *Evelina*, was published anonymously in 1778. Her father was a music historian and composer whose ambitions caused him to press his daughter to accept a position in the royal household where she served as second keeper of the robes to Queen Charlotte until ill

Fanny Burney.

health forced her to retire. In 1793 she married a French refugee, General D'Arblay, and travelled with him to France. The D'Arblays were interned by Napoleon from 1802 to 1812 and were in Brussels during the Battle of Waterloo, accounts of which may be read in her well-known *Diaries*. Madame D'Arblay spent some time in Bath where Fanny, Lady Spenborough, encountered her buying ribbons in a shop in Gay Street in *Bath Tangle*.

Mary Anne Clarke (1776–1852): Beautiful and determined, Mary Anne Clarke was the daughter of a London stonemason and became mistress to the Duke of York. He established her in a house in Gloucester Place but also made available a second house at Weybridge—not far from Oatlands where he spent weekends with his wife. The cost of keeping up two households far exceeded her annual £1,000 allowance so Mary began selling army commissions on the side. An untimely end to the affair prompted her to reveal her activities to the Whig opposition and the ensuing public inquiry forced the Duke, in his role as Commander-in-Chief of the army, to resign. An attempt by Mary to capitalise on the scandal with a 'tell all' book entitled *The Rival Princes* was mildly successful.

Maria Edgeworth (1767–1849): She came to fame with the publication of her novel of Irish life, *Castle Rackrent*, published in 1800. Her work influenced Walter Scott, with whom she corresponded, and was also acknowledged by Jane Austen in *Northanger*

Abbey. She wrote a number of other novels and children's stories and was adept in her portrayal of Ireland's people and places.

Margaret Mercer Elphinstone, Viscountess Keith, Countess de Flahault (1788–1867): Close friend and confidante of the heir apparent, Princess Charlotte, Mercer Elphinstone was the only child of one of Nelson's superiors, Admiral Keith. Eight years older than the princess, Mercer supported and advised her by visiting and corresponding over several years. The two women shared similar political views and after 1811 the Prince Regent was inclined to disapprove of Mercer's influence on his daughter. Mercer was one of a handful of people summoned by Charlotte to aid her after she had run away to her mother's home in 1814. She also acted as an intermediary in the Princess's relationship with Prince Leopold. Mercer also corresponded with Lord Byron and in 1814 he gave her his famous Albanian costume. Lady Lynton in *A Civil Contract* scored a great hit when Miss Elphinstone attended her rout party just after Princess Charlotte had run away.

Mrs Fitzherbert, Maria Anne Fitzherbert née Smythe (1756–1837): Already twice widowed when she met the Prince of Wales in 1784, Maria Fitzherbert was a charming, graceful woman with golden hair, a good figure and a comfortable income; she was also a devout Catholic. The Prince became enamoured of her and in 1785 overcame her resistance and married her—an illegal act which contravened both the Act of Succession (forbidding marriage to a Catholic) and the Royal Marriage Act (royal offspring under twenty-five needed the monarch's permission to marry). For several years Mrs Fitzherbert was treated in many respects as the Prince's lawful wife but by 1793 he had become involved with the acerbic and ambitious Lady Jersey and by 1794 his debts were so great that he began casting about for a lawful bride acceptable to the parliament who would increase the annual amount paid to the Prince in the event of such a marriage. Perhaps because of her faith, or because she loved him, Mrs Fitzherbert quietly stood aside when her Prince married Caroline of Brunswick and took him back again after the mismatched couple separated.

The relationship lasted until 1806 when the Prince turned his attention to Lady Hertford. Mrs Fitzherbert eventually withdrew from his life, living quietly in London and Brighton, where a statue of her wearing three wedding rings (one for each husband) was erected after her death in 1837. In *Regency Buck* Mrs Scattergood expressed the opinion of many in the period when she said that she had always felt Mrs Fitzherbert to be the Prince's 'true wife'.

Mrs Fitzherbert.

Isabella Anne Ingram Shepherd, Marchioness of Hertford (1760–1836): One of the Prince's most enduring mistresses, Lady Hertford began her relationship with the heir to the throne in 1807 when she was forty-six and he was still Prince of Wales. The affair continued until 1819 when he transferred his affections to Elizabeth, Countess Conyngham. Lady Hertford was a tall, elegant and attractive woman, whose husband was a wealthy Tory peer. She was disliked by some among the *ton*, including Mrs Dauntry in *Frederica* who thought her an 'odious woman' and worried that in the event of Queen Charlotte's death the Regent might allow his mistress to play host at the Drawing-rooms. The Regent was also good friends with Lady Hertford's rake-hell son, Lord Yarmouth.

Lady Jersey, Frances, 4th Countess of Jersey (1753–1821):
Frances, Lady Jersey was forty-one and a grandmother when she became the Prince of Wales's mistress. She was a friend of his mother's and had known him for years. An attractive, clever woman with an acerbic tongue and ambitions of acquiring royal influence, she deliberately set out to capture the Prince and ruthlessly encouraged him to cast off his morganatic wife, Maria Fitzherbert, in favour of herself. In 1794 she actively encouraged him to marry his unsuitable bride, Caroline of Brunswick—ostensibly to cement her own position as his mistress but also to negate Mrs Fitzherbert's claim to be his lawful wife. In 1796, after the birth of his daughter, the Prince tired of Lady Jersey and ended the relationship.

Mrs Jordan, Dorothea Jordan née Bland (1762–1816): A successful actress for almost thirty years, Mrs Jordan often appeared at Drury Lane theatre to great acclaim and was best known for her feisty comic roles. In 1790 she met the Duke of Clarence (later William IV) and became his mistress. Their relationship endured for over twenty years and they had ten children together, collectively known as the FitzClarences.

Lady Caroline Lamb (1785–1828): Born Lady Caroline Ponsonby, daughter of the Earl of Bessborough, she married William Lamb in 1805. A tempestuous, highly strung and impulsive young woman, Caro Lamb may have been as much a victim of her social context as of her own over-emotional personality. Both her mother and her aunt had affairs (although very discreetly) and she grew up with illegitimate half-sisters and cousins. Her own affairs were wildly indiscreet and

Lady Caroline Lamb.

in 1812 she developed a grand passion for Lord Byron, whom she famously described as 'mad, bad and dangerous to know'. Caroline could be fascinating but the affair lasted less than a year as Byron became disenchanted with her demanding, histrionic behaviour (not altogether unlike his own). Socially damaged as a result of the liaison, she was totally ostracised when, in 1816, she published a romantic novel, *Glenarvon*, in which she had caricaturised several of society's elite.

Ann Radcliffe (1764–1823): Generally considered one of the originators of the Gothic novel, Ann Radcliffe became famous for her tales with a supernatural element. Her first book, *Romance of the Forest* (1791), brought her wide acclaim but it was *The Mysteries of Udolpho* (1794) that established her as a popular writer. She was widely admired by contemporary authors and her work influenced the writings of both Percy Shelley and Byron. It was books like Mrs Radcliffe's which provided the material for Amanda's extraordinary stories in *Sprig Muslin*.

Clara Reeve (1729–1807): Following in the footsteps of Horace Walpole and his famous Gothic novel *The Castle of Otranto*, Clara Reeve won renown for her 1777 book *The Champion of Virtue, a Gothic Story*, later renamed *The Old English Baron*. She also gained acclaim for her enduring study of the evolution of writing from epic to romance to novel in *The Progress of Romance*.

Mary Wollstonecraft (1759–1797): An early feminist thinker and writer, Mary Wollstonecraft worked as a teacher, translator and literary advisor before publishing two landmark texts: *Thoughts on the Education of Daughters* (1787) and *Vindication of the Rights of Women* (1792). In 1792 she went to Paris and met Gilbert Imlay, an American businessman with whom she had a daughter (and who Drusilla Morville in *The Quiet Gentleman* thought she would have liked better than Mr Godwin). They were never married but his infidelities led her to two suicide attempts. The couple gradually moved apart and in 1796 Mary again met William Godwin and they became lovers. They married in 1797 after Mary became pregnant and she died ten days after giving birth to a daughter who would as Mary Shelley, one day, write *Frankenstein*.

Mary Wollstonecraft Shelley (1797–1851): Mary Shelley was best known for her novel *Frankenstein, or the Modern Prometheus* (1818), written in response to a challenge laid down by Lord Byron at a congenial gathering of literary friends during a summer at Lake Geneva. The daughter of the feminist author Mary Wollstonecraft and the writer William Godwin, Mary eloped with the poet, Percy Bysshe Shelley, in 1814, and married him after his first wife's suicide in 1816.

INFLUENTIAL MEN

Lord Amherst, William Pitt 1st Earl of Amherst (1773–1857): Pitt was a diplomat and in 1816 embarked on a diplomatic mission to China. Meg's husband Lord Buckhaven accompanied him there in *Cotillion*. The mission was not a success but in 1823 Lord Amherst was appointed governor-general of India.

Henry Peter Brougham, later 1st Baron Brougham and Vaux (1778–1868): A noted intellectual and lawyer, in 1802 Brougham helped to found the *Edinburgh Review* making regular contributions which helped to establish the journal as one of the foremost political periodicals of the nineteenth century. In 1810 he entered parliament as a liberal Whig with a concern for reform, and spoke out against slavery and in favour of public education and legal reform.

George Gordon Byron, 6th Baron Byron (1788–1824):
Educated at Harrow and Cambridge, Byron received poor reviews for his early work. He travelled extensively in southern Europe, enjoyed a dissipated life, and returned to England with ample new material for his verses. In 1812 he gained overnight fame with the publication of the first two cantos of *Childe Harold's Pilgrimage*. Dark

and handsome, fêted and adored by upper-class society, he became the model for the 'Byronic hero'. In 1815 he married the heiress Annabella Milbanke, from whom he separated the following year. His earlier affair with Lady Caroline Lamb, his rakish lifestyle and rumours of a liaison with his half-sister, Augusta Leigh, eventually saw society turn against him, prompting Byron to leave England, never to return. He died at Missolonghi in Greece.

Lord Byron.

Lord Castlereagh.

Robert Stewart, Viscount Castlereagh (1769–1822): Elected to the Westminster parliament in 1794, Castlereagh became a brilliant war minister who consistently supported the British campaign against Napoleon. He appointed Wellesley (later the Duke of Wellington) to command the army and in 1812 became foreign secretary and leader of the House of Commons. He was married to Lady Castlereagh, one of the patronesses of Almack's.

Coke of Norfolk, Thomas William Coke, 1st Earl of Leicester (1754–1842): Owner of Holkham Hall in Norfolk, Coke (pronounced 'cook') was an agricultural pioneer who invested much of his energy in his estate, to the benefit of both his tenants and his purse. Overcoming stubborn resistance to new farming techniques and crops (he was among the first to grow wheat successfully in Norfolk), in less than forty years Coke increased his annual rental income from £2,000 to £20,000. Eager to share his farming success with others, Coke played host to the Holkham Clippings, an annual three-day event to which many people—including Adam Deveril of *A Civil Contract*—came from all over the world to learn and share ideas about farming. A successful and energetic Whig MP, Coke held his seat in parliament for 57 years.

Samuel Taylor Coleridge (1772–1834): Best known for his poems *The Rime of the Ancient Mariner* and *Kubla Khan*, Coleridge was one of the founders of English Romanticism. He studied at Cambridge and met the poet Robert Southey with whom for a time he became a pantisocrat and (with Drusilla Morville's father in *The Quiet Gentleman*) made plans to create an equitable community on the banks of the Susquehanna. Instead he married Sara Fricker (Southey married her sister Edith) and continued writing.

Coke of Norfolk.

His career as a poet was adversely affected by ill health and an opium addiction, but he continued to write and lecture, producing a weekly paper called *The Friend* as well as critical and theological works, plays and, in 1817, his famous *Biographia Literaria*.

William Godwin (1756–1836): Novelist, philosopher and political writer, Godwin had been a dissenting minister but became an atheist with decided views as to the true nature of man. He believed in the power of reason and that rational behaviour could enable people to live harmoniously without laws or institutions. In 1797 he married the famous writer and feminist Mary Wollstonecraft.

Charles Lamb (1775–1834) and Mary Lamb (1764–1847): Charles and Mary Lamb were brother and sister who spent much of their life together writing plays, poems and prose works. Charles had become responsible for his sister in 1796 when, in a fit of insanity, she had tragically murdered their mother. Mary continued to suffer from intermittent seizures, but was devoted to her brother who also suffered from occasional bouts of madness. The two are best known for their children's book *Tales from Shakespeare.*

Lord Melbourne.

William Lamb, 2nd Viscount Melbourne (1779–1848): The son of the famous Whig hostess, Lady Melbourne, William may have been fathered by the Earl of Egremont. A dutiful son and a kind, amiable husband, William married Caroline Ponsonby in 1805 and quietly endured her affair with Byron and her many other indiscretions. The birth of a mentally disabled son was a personal tragedy and added to his disinclination to deal with harsh realities. The death of his elder brother, Peniston, in 1805, made him heir to the title and he entered the House of Lords as a Whig conservative. He was Queen Victoria's first prime minister.

Sir Thomas Lawrence (1769–1830): A talented artist from his youth, Thomas Lawrence was a renowned portrait painter who, in 1792, succeeded Sir Henry Reynolds as the King's principal painter. He painted many of Europe's most notable figures, including the heroes of the Napoleonic Wars (and also Nell, Lady Cardross, in *April Lady*). He lived for a time at 65 Russell Square where he undertook private commissions at a cost of more than 400 guineas for a full-length portrait. Knighted in 1815, Lawrence became president of the Royal Academy in 1820.

Matthew Gregory 'Monk' Lewis (1775–1818): Lewis became known as 'Monk' after the publication, in 1796, of his popular Gothic novel *Ambrosio, or The Monk*. His writing influenced Walter Scott's early poetry and Lewis collaborated with him and Robert Southey on *Tales of Wonder* (1801). As a liberal he was concerned about the treatment of slaves and twice visited his Jamaica plantation before dying of yellow fever in 1818.

Lord Liverpool, Robert Banks Jenkinson, 2nd Earl of Liverpool (1770–1828): The longest-serving of all British prime ministers, Liverpool entered parliament in 1790 and became prime minister in 1812, overseeing the final years of the Napoleonic Wars, and consolidating the position of his ministry with both the parliament and the people. Although not in favour of many of the reforms proposed during the period, Liverpool was an astute and responsive politician who addressed many of the economic issues of the day. He believed strongly in public order and the rule of law and his government's introduction, in 1819, of the Six Acts in response to the Peterloo massacre was strongly criticised.

Louis XVIII, King of France (1755–1824): The younger brother of Louis XVI, who was executed during the Revolution, Louis XVIII left Paris in 1791 and went into exile, eventually settling in England. When Napoleon was defeated and sent to Elba in 1814, Louis returned to Paris as King. He enjoyed a brief reign before Napoleon's escape from Elba and unopposed entry into Paris—at which point Louis and his family beat a hasty retreat from the city. He regained the throne after Napoleon's final defeat at Waterloo and was the first French monarch to reign with an elected parliamentary government.

Prince William of Orange (1792–1849): Heir to the Dutch throne, William lived in exile during Napoleon's rampage across Europe, spent two years at Oxford and served under the Duke of Wellington (who described him as 'a stupid, untidy and dissolute young man') in Spain, where he was known by the general staff as 'Slender Billy'. In 1813 the Prince Regent, feeling that the Dutch fleet would be a useful addition to the British navy, encouraged his daughter to accept the Prince's marriage proposal. The engagement was broken off, however, and William married the Tsar of Russia's sister, Anna.

Sir Walter Scott (1771–1832): A poet in his early years, Scott enjoyed great popularity with his Scottish border ballads and long narrative poems such as *The Lay of the Last Minstrel* (1805) and *Marmion* (1808). The rise of Byron in 1812 saw Scott turn to novel writing and, drawing on his deep love of Scotland, its history and people, he produced the landmark historical romance *Waverley*. Over the next decade Scott anonymously published a series of best-selling books including *Guy Mannering* (1815), *Rob Roy* (1817), *The Heart of Midlothian* (1818) and *Ivanhoe* (1819) but did not acknowledge authorship until 1827.

Robert Southey (1774–1843): A prolific writer, Southey was a popular poet and biographer who became Poet Laureate in 1813. Best remembered for his biographical works including his *Life of*

Nelson (1813) and *Life of Wesley* (1820), in his day he was admired by the likes of Scott and Byron, and his epic poem *The Curse of Kehama* (1810) was enormously popular. One of the 'Lake Poets', Southey had studied at Oxford where he became good friends with Coleridge with whom he had been a pantisocrat with plans to establish an equitable community on the banks of the Susquehanna. Instead he married Edith Fricker, the sister of Coleridge's wife Sara, and spent much of his life writing.

The Beau and the Dandies

George Bryan 'Beau' Brummell (1778–1840): The subject of countless anecdotes and credited with many famous sayings (such as asking, 'Who's your fat friend?' in reference to the Prince Regent), for many years Beau Brummell stood at the centre of the fashionable world. Born into the middle class, Brummell entered elite circles by way of Eton—where his wit and elegance earned him the nickname 'Beau'—and Oxford. After a short stay at the university he was gazetted a cornet in the Prince of Wales's regiment, the 10th Hussars, and the two became friends. Brummell sold out of the army on his regiment being ordered to Manchester and moved to London where he soon established himself as arbiter elegantiarum, remaining the acknowledged leader of fashion and close friend of the Prince of Wales for more than a decade. Brummell's neat, plain style of dress, his mannerisms and his social decrees were everywhere adhered to and slavishly

Beau Brummell.

copied. In dress he insisted upon personal cleanliness, freshly laundered shirts, a perfectly tied neckcloth and a simplicity of attire that did not draw attention to the wearer. It was Brummell who began the fashion for perfectly cut, dark-coloured coats for evening wear (which continues today in the form of the dinner jacket). Brummell was a leader of society in more than mere clothes, however; he was also admired for his wit and social grace and feared for his satire and insolence. It was said that the Beau could make a man's reputation merely by giving him his arm for the length of the street and could just as easily (it was supposed) blight a person's social career by the lifting of an eyebrow. He exercised a remarkable hold over fashionable society for nearly twenty years, even after falling out with the Regent in 1813. Possessed of a large fortune in his twenties, he had gambled it away by his forties and in 1816 his massive debts forced him into exile in France where he died in an asylum in Caen in 1840.

William, 2nd Baron Alvanley (1789–1849): Universally liked and admired for his handsome demeanour, kindness and lightning repartee, Lord Alvanley was also a noted dresser and one of the leading dandies of his day. The possessor of an immense fortune, he indulged in all the pleasures of the table—both dining and gaming—and thought nothing of paying £200 for a lunch hamper from Gunter's or producing the most expensive dish (a fricassee using thirteen different birds) for a special dinner at White's. He never used cash but lived on credit and famously said of a friend that he had 'muddled away his fortune in paying tradesmen's bills'. Of average height, but well-built, he excelled at sports, was a first-rate huntsman and had seen active service in the Coldstream Guards, attaining the rank of lieutenant-colonel before resigning his commission. Intelligent, well-read and always good-humoured, Alvanley had spent time in many of the European courts and was a popular guest, despite his habit of snuffing his candle with his pillow and requesting that an apricot tart be served to him at dinner every day. Less well-off in his later years, he remained a kind and considerate friend to many until the end of his life.

Charles Stanhope, Lord Petersham, 4th Earl of Harrington (1780–1851): A popular member of the dandy set, Petersham was an elegant dresser with a penchant for inventing clothes. His best-known legacy to the world of fashion was the briefly fashionable Petersham trousers: a loose-fitting form of Cossack pant with wide legs that could be drawn in at the ankle (and thought all the crack by Viscount Desford's younger brother, Simon, in *Charity Girl*). Petersham was also known for eccentric habits such as his refusal to venture out before 6 p.m., his predilection for the colour brown (manifested in his equipage of brown carriage, harness, horses and footmen in brown livery), his passion for all kinds of tea and snuff and his collection of snuff-boxes, reputed to be the finest in England.

The Honourable Frederick Gerald 'Poodle' Byng (died 1871): Allegedly nicknamed 'Poodle' by Georgiana, Duchess of Devonshire, and Lady Bath because of his thick curly hair, Frederick Byng was a serious, somewhat platitudinous young man. He did, in fact, own a French poodle which sat up beside him when he drove his curricle in the park and he endured many jokes on account of his unfortunate sobriquet. In *Arabella*, he took the appearance of Mr Beaumaris's mongrel dog

Poodle Byng.

Ulysses in his master's carriage as a direct insult. Byng spent several years in the Foreign Office, as a result of which he developed the habit of imparting rather tedious bits of trivia to those around him. Although he never gained total acceptance by society's elite inner circle, Byng was present at the marriage of George, Prince of Wales, to Caroline of Brunswick.

Edward Hughes Ball Hughes, 'Golden Ball' (died 1863): The son of Captain Ball, of the Royal Navy, Hughes inherited his vast fortune (£40,000 a year) from his stepfather, Admiral Sir Edward Hughes, whose name he added to his own. Despite being handsome, well-built and always exquisitely dressed, Hughes was never recognised as one of the great dandies nor admitted to the

Golden Ball.

elite inner circle. He irritated some with his peculiar, mincing walk (which made Arabella wonder if he was in pain) and affected lisp, but his cardinal sin was to be judged a *follower* of fashion—one who kept a box at the opera and a stable of hunters, dabbled at sports and went to the races simply to keep up appearances and not because he genuinely enjoyed such pastimes. In fact, Hughes enjoyed a variety of sports and was a great gambler, playing whist for £5 points and often staying up all night to gamble.

APPENDIX 1

A Glossary of Cant and Common Regency Phrases

CANT

During the Regency it became the fashion for upper-class men to integrate into their everyday speech the language of certain of the lower classes. Mainly as a result of the rising interest in sport and the predominance of the horse in this period, many well-born males used boxing cant, racing cant and the vocabulary of the stable hand and the coachman as part of their daily talk. In addition, forays by bored young men into the seedier parts of town saw the inclusion of phrases culled from the extraordinary and colourful slang used in London's underworld. The famous Regency writer and journalist, Pierce Egan, was undoubtedly one of the foremost exponents of sporting cant during the period, and Georgette Heyer enjoyed and made great use of the language in his lively tale of Jerry Hawthorn and his friend Corinthian Tom in Egan's book *Life in London*.

BOXING

a bit of the home-brewed: punching or hitting done by an untrained boxer

bone box: mouth

bottom: courage, guts, stability—in pugilism one who can endure a beating

a bruiser: a boxer

claret: blood

displays to advantage: boxes well, looks good in the ring or in a fight

to draw his cork: to make him bleed—particularly by punching him in the nose

fib him: to beat or hit someone

a mill: a fight, usually a boxing match or fist-fight

a milling cove: a pugilist or boxer

milling a canister: break someone's head

plant a facer: punch someone in the face

Horses

beautiful stepper: a good horse with a fine easy gait

blood cattle: well-bred horses, thoroughbreds

bone-setters: ill-bred horses, inferior horses

bottom: a strong horse with good temperament and endurance

cattle: horses

hunt the squirrel: the often dangerous sport of following closely behind a carriage and then passing it so closely as to brush the wheel. Considered an amusing pastime by stagecoachmen and some sporting gentlemen, the practice often resulted in the victim's carriage being overturned.

neck-or-nothing: a rider who will try anything, a bold daring sportsman or sportswoman

part company: to fall off a horse

prime bits of blood: top quality horses

a screw: a very poor quality horse

a sweetgoer: a horse with an easy action

throwing out a splint: become lame as a result of swelling in the ligament next to the splint bone

DRINKING

a ball of fire: a glass of brandy

blood and thunder: a mixture of port wine and brandy

blue ruin: gin

boosey: drunk

boozing-ken: a tavern or alehouse

bosky: drunk

a bumper: a full glass

daffy: gin

dipping too deep: drinking too much

disguised: drunk

drunk as a wheelbarrow: inebriated

eaten Hull cheese: drunk

an elbow-crooker: a drinker

a flash of lightning: strong spirits, a glass of gin

foxed: intoxicated

fuddled: drunk

half-sprung: tipsy, mellow with drink

heavy wet: porter or stout, malt liquor

in his altitudes: drunk

in your cups: drunk

jug-bitten: tipsy

making indentures: drinking

on the cut: to go on a spree; to get drunk

shoot the cat: to vomit

to cast up one's accounts: to vomit

too ripe and ready: drunk

top-heavy: drunk

FEELINGS AND BEHAVIOUR

a bear-garden jaw: rude, vulgar language; a real talking to

be on the high ropes: to stand on one's dignity; to become very angry; to be excited

blue as megrim: depressed, sad, unhappy

break-teeth words: difficult words, hard to pronounce

buffle-headed: confused, stupid, foolish

corky: lively, merry, playful, restless

cry rope: to cry out a warning

cut one's eye teeth: to become knowing, to understand the world

dicked in the nob: silly, crazy

done to a cow's thumb: exhausted

fagged to death: exhausted

fit of the blue-devils: sad, miserable, depressed, in low spirits

fly up into the boughs: fly into a passion, lose one's temper

Friday-faced: a sad or miserable countenance—derived from the tradition of Friday abstinence which prohibited publicans from dressing dinners on Fridays

high in the instep: arrogant, haughty, proud

a honey-fall: good fortune

in a dudgeon: angry, in a bad mood

in high ropes: ecstatic, elated, in high spirits

kick over the traces: to go the pace; kick up larks; behave in a headstrong or disobedient manner

knocked-up: exhausted

make a mull of it: to mismanage a situation; to fail; to make a muddle of something

mawkish: falsely sentimental, insipid or nauseating

more than seven: to be knowing or wide-awake, experienced in the ways of the world

mutton-headed: stupid

napping her bib: to cry; to get one's way by weeping

ring a peal over one: to admonish or scold someone

set up one's bristles: to irritate or annoy; to offend or make someone angry

spleen: anger

to catch cold: advice to cease or desist; a suggestion that one should cease making threats

to pull caps with someone: to argue

to swallow one's spleen: to curb one's temper

within ames-ace: nearly, or very near

Lying

bag of moonshine: nonsense, a lot of nothing

bamboozle: to deceive, hoax or make a fool of a person; to humbug or impose on someone

Banbury stories: a long-winded nonsense tale, a cock-and-bull story

bouncer: a big lie

Canterbury Tales: a long, tedious story

a clanker: a huge lie

cut a sham: to deliberately trick, cheat or deceive

cut a wheedle: to deliberately lead astray or decoy by flattery and insinuation

doing it much too brown: to go over the top in telling a lie; to lie or cheat thoroughly

faradiddles: a petty lie; originally 'taradiddle'

flummery: false compliments

fudge: nonsense

fustian or fustian nonsense: pompous rubbish

gammon: nonsense, lies; to pretend, lie or deceive

gulled: duped, fooled, tricked

a hum: a falsehood, a deceit, a made-up story

pitching the gammon: to talk plausibly; to hoax someone; to flatter without restraint; to tell grand stories; to deceive merrily

plumper: an arrant lie—possibly from the false cheeks worn in previous centuries

shamming it: to pretend or make things up

slum: to speak cant or talk nonsense

to offer Spanish coin: to flatter with fair words and compliments

toad-eat: to pay compliments or to flatter in the hope of winning a person's favour or approval

whiskers: lies

MONEY

at a stand or a standstill: run out of money and in financial difficulty

blunt: money

brass: money

brought to point non plus: backed into a financial corner with few options for recovery

cheeseparing: miserly, niggardly, mean with money

dibs not in tune: not enough money; in a parlous financial state

dished: financially ruined

drawing the bustle: spending too much money

a dun: a persistent creditor

flush in the pocket or flush with funds: having plenty of ready money

full of juice: wealthy

gingerbread: money

grease someone in the fist: to put money into a person's hand; to bribe someone or give them a monetary incentive

gullgropers: a professional moneylender, especially one who does business with gamblers

hang on someone's sleeve: to rely on someone financially

haven't a sixpence to scratch with: flat broke

high water with him: wealthy; he has lots of money

in deep: in serious debt

in dun territory: in debt

in the basket: to be in financial difficulty—from the practice of putting those who could not pay their gambling debts at a cock-fight into a basket suspended above the pit. The term also relates to those purse-pinched stagecoach travellers who could only afford to travel in the boot—originally a large basket strapped to the back of the carriage.

low ebb or at ebb-water: a lack of money

low water: lack of money

nip-cheese or nip-farthing: a miser

not a feather to fly with: no money, dead broke

note of hand: an IOU

on the rocks: financially ruined, bankrupt

outrun the constable: to overspend; to live beyond one's means

plump in the pocket: to have plenty of ready cash

pockets to let: no money, penniless

purse-pinched: short of money

raise the wind: borrow money

the ready: money, particularly money in hand

recruits: money, often money that is expected

the rhino: money

the River Tick: standing debts

rolled-up: no money and in serious financial trouble

run off one's legs: to have spent all one's money

run on tick: to buy on credit

swallow a spider: to go bankrupt

swimming in lard: very wealthy

tip over the dibs: to lend or give money to someone

to bleed: to extort money either openly or in an underhand way

to fleece: to swindle

to frank someone: to pay their way

to stand huff: to pay the bill in a tavern; to pay for everyone

under the hatches: in debt

vowels: IOUs

well-breeched: having plenty of money in your pockets—a prime target for robbery

well-inlaid: plenty of money

NOT THE THING

a bridle cull: a highwayman

a cursed rum touch: a strange person; an odd or eccentric man who is also annoying

a flat: an honest man; a fool, one who is easily tricked; a greenhorn

fulhams: loaded dice

half flash and half foolish: having a small knowledge of cant and a limited experience of the world

an ivory-turner: one who cheats in dice games

a peep-o-day boy: an unsteady young man always involved in pranks or larks

a rattle: one who talks too much

a rum 'un: a strange person, an odd or eccentric man

a sharp: a cheat who lives by his skill at manipulating the cards or dice

smoky: suspicious, curious

uphills: loaded dice; false dice made to roll to the higher or upper numbers—as opposed to downhills which fall to the lower numbers

PEOPLE

all the crack: in the mode, the height of fashion

an ape leader: a woman beyond marriageable age; an old maid— so-called because of a proverb that says their failure to increase and multiply dooms them to lead apes in hell. Also used by Shakespeare in *Much Ado About Nothing* II.i.41 and *The Taming of the Shrew* II.i.34

awake on every suit: knowing what's going on, understanding the business

a bang-up cove: a dashing man who spends money easily; a good-natured splendid fellow

bang up to the knocker: first-rate; well dressed, turned out in prime style

bang up to the mark: first-rate

bird-witted: thoughtless, brainless, easily imposed upon, gullible, inconsiderate

a bit of muslin: a girl; an attractive female—though usually one who is ready to be seduced or taken as a mistress

bracket-faced: ugly, hard-featured

bran-faced: freckled

a chawbacon: a country bumpkin; a stupid man

a chit: a young girl

a cicisbeo: a married woman's lover or escort

clunch: a clownish person, awkward, foolish

complete to a shade: superbly dressed, dressed in the height of fashion

a diamond of the first water: a remarkably beautiful woman

a dowdy: a plain, ill-dressed female

a downy one: aware, a knowing intelligent person

a doxy: a whore

a green girl: a naive, inexperienced young woman

a hoyden: an active, tomboyish romp of a girl

a hussy: a forward, badly behaved female

a jade: a disreputable woman

a jilt: a woman who cries off from an engagement not long before the wedding

a Johnny raw: a novice, an inexperienced or untried youth

a loose fish: an unreliable person; a person of dissipated habits; a lecher or a drunk

a mort: a woman or wench; but could sometimes mean a harlot

an out and outer: one who is first-rate; a perfect person; excellent in every way

a prime article: a handsome woman, a beautiful female

a romp: a forward girl

a swell mort: an upper-class woman

a tabby: an old maid

a vixen: a shrewish woman

a vulgar mushroom: a pushing, pretentious member of the new rich—the reference being to mushrooms as a kind of fungus which comes up suddenly in the night

a wet goose: a simple or stupid person

SEX AND SOCIETY

an abbess: a procuress of prostitutes, a female keeper of a brothel

barque of frailty: a woman of easy virtue

base-born child: an illegitimate child, a bastard

bird of paradise: a showy prostitute

by-blow: an illegitimate child, a bastard

carte-blanche: monetary support and protection offered to a man's mistress in place of marriage

chère-amie: a mistress—literally 'darling beloved'

crim. con.: short for criminal conversations—a euphemism for adultery

a game-pullet: a young prostitute or a girl likely to become a whore

Haymarket ware: a prostitute

an impure: a woman of easy virtue

incognitas: a masked or disguised prostitute

lady-bird: a lewd or light woman, a prostitute

light o' love: a mistress

lightskirt: a prostitute

loose in the haft: a man of easy virtue and few morals

on-dit: gossip—literally 'one says'

one of the muslin company: a prostitute; a female ready to be set up as a mistress

Paphian: a woman of easy virtue; relating to sexual love

a petticoat-pensioner: one who lives off a woman's ill-gotten earnings, a whoremonger

a rake: a man of great sexual appetite and few morals

side-slips: illegitimate children, bastards

a slip on the shoulder: to seduce a woman, seduction

trollop: a sluttish woman

Marriage

become a tenant for life: get married off, get married

cry off: to change one's mind and call off the wedding

an eligible parti: a suitable marriage partner

leg-shackled: married

make an offer: propose marriage

on the shelf: unmarried and beyond the usual age of marrying

puff it off: announce one's engagement in the papers

riveted: married

set your cap at a man: to try to win a man's favour and a proposal of marriage

smelling of April and May: madly in love

APPENDIX 2

Newspapers and Magazines

By the time of the Regency, newspapers and magazines had become an important part of daily life for many English people—particularly those of the middle and upper classes—although the reading habit was gradually spreading to the servant class and to some among the working class. Although there was no universal education system the efforts of religious groups such as the Methodists to teach the lower classes to read (in order that they might benefit from reading the Bible) helped to create a surprisingly literate population. A large number of newspapers were established in the eighteenth century and, although many did not survive, by the early nineteenth century there were several London dailies and over one hundred provincial newspapers in circulation which offered readers items of general interest, entertaining articles and stories, society news and fashion.

The Times: The most famous of English newspapers, *The Times* was founded in 1785. It was originally called the *Daily Universal Register* but changed its name to *The Times* in 1788 and by the time of the Regency it had established itself as the major London daily newspaper. *The Times* was a broadsheet paper without pictures but with narrow parallel columns of printed articles and advertisements running lengthwise down the page. The front page was generally given over to a wide range of personal and commercial advertisements while the inside pages offered the reader both domestic and foreign news, reports from the war in Europe, obituaries, society news and information about the royal Court.

Morning Post: In 1772 a group of twelve businessmen, including Richard Tattersall (founder of Tattersall's) and James Christie (founder of Christie's auction rooms), established a newspaper, the *Morning Post*, with a view to securing cheaper and more advantageous advertising for their businesses. The famous publisher John Bell was the paper's first main proprietor and Henry Bute its first editor. The *Morning Post* gained early notoriety for its constant criticism of the Prince of Wales (later the Prince Regent) before he bought their support for £1,000 and a promise of £350 a year to refrain from mentioning Mrs Fitzherbert. In 1795 the paper was acquired by Daniel Stuart who radically changed it from a 'ferocious political' journal to a cheerful, entertaining newspaper with a range of literary articles and fashion notes designed to appeal to both men and women. During the Regency it was to the *Morning Post* that the upper class sent their betrothal and wedding announcements.

London Gazette: The first English newspaper, the *London Gazette* was originally called the *Oxford Gazette*, and was published in 1665 during the Great Plague while the royal Court was living in Oxford. A paper rather than a newspaper, the *London Gazette* listed royal activities, official appointments, bankruptcies, military items such as commissions and promotions, and casualty lists in time of war. The *Gazette* continues to be published today.

Gentleman's Magazine: Founded in 1731, the *Gentleman's Magazine* was originally a compilation of previously published articles, reviews, essays and news items. By mid-century, however, original material had become a regular feature as had reports of parliamentary debates. Samuel Johnson wrote for the magazine for some years and by the time of the Regency it was a well-established periodical which included, along with its more serious items, births, deaths and marriages, as well as songs, music, maps and articles of general interest. It survived for nearly two hundred years and finally closed in 1914.

La Belle Assemblée, or Bell's Court & Fashionable Magazine, Addressed Particularly to the Ladies: Established in 1806 by the renowned publisher, John Bell, *La Belle Assemblée* was an elegant monthly magazine with an unusually high standard of production. Larger in size than its competitors, it offered readers both French and English fashion news with two superbly engraved fashion plates with captions indicating the type or style of dress. As well as fashion news the magazine offered readers literary items, articles on science, history and the arts, news from the foreign courts, a gossip column—which was often accompanied by an engraved portrait of a member of the nobility—poetry, political reports, a song and accompanying music, reports on places to visit in London, fashion notes and an embroidery pattern. Each volume finished with a list of notable births, deaths and marriages. *La Belle Assemblée* was expensive, costing 3s. per edition (a general housemaid was earning approximately £8 a year) but it was popular and influential. It remained the leading fashion magazine of its day until its eventual closure in 1832.

Ackermann's Repository of Arts, Literature, Commerce, Manufactures, Fashions and Politics: Founded in 1809, *Ackermann's Repository* was the brainchild of Rudolph Ackermann, a German immigrant from Saxony with a talent for lithography and a sense of the commercial viability of a magazine which offered its readers superb pictures of a wide range of Regency products and fashion. Intended as a kind of cultural guide aimed more at men than women—although it included items designed to appeal to women—the *Repository* was dedicated to the Prince of Wales (later the Prince Regent) and appeared monthly. Every edition carried superb hand-coloured plates depicting furniture, paintings, room interiors, *objets d'art*, silverware and two coloured aquatints showing examples of the latest women's and men's (until 1815) fashions. Intended as a guide to dressmakers and their fashionable clients, the fashion plates included detailed descriptions of the type of costume shown, its style, cut, trim, the fabrics used and their colour and also detailed the style and colour of accessories. Like its competitor, *La Belle Assemblée*, *Ackermann's Repository* maintained a standard of excellence throughout its years of publication. It closed in 1830.

Lady's Monthly Museum or Polite Repository of Amusement and Instruction Being an Assemblage of Whatever can tend to Please the Fancy, interest the Mind, or Exalt The Character of the British Fair: The 'British Fair' was a popular phrase with magazine editors and publishers during the Regency and advertisements and articles frequently spoke of and to 'the British Fair', using the term as a reference to both the female readers and the (mostly mythical) virtuous, elegant and beautiful woman that the magazine assumed each reader aspired to be. It was common for magazines to extol the British Fair as the epitome of womanhood and to exhort readers to dress, think and act in her image. Purportedly published 'by a Society of Ladies', the *Lady's Monthly Museum* was no exception to this rule and actively encouraged women to constantly better themselves. First published in 1798 the magazine was aimed directly at women and contained an appealing mix of articles on fashion (with coloured plates), items of general interest, short biographies of the famous or aristocratic (with accompanying engraved portraits), poetry, essays and a monthly moral tale. The *Lady's Monthly Museum* was one of the first magazines to serialise novels before they appeared as books and maintained a literary section in which it regularly informed readers of forthcoming publications and detailed the latest gossip about people and events in the arts; it also ran one of the early 'lonely hearts' columns.

Lady's Magazine or Entertaining Companion for the Fair Sex: Known as the *Lady's Magazine*, this monthly periodical was founded in 1770 by a Mr Coote and was designed especially to amuse, educate and 'improve' women. Costing only sixpence, it offered a wide range of articles, stories and fashion items and was the first magazine to publish extracts from forthcoming books to tantalise its readers. The *Lady's Magazine* proved popular enough with readers that it continued until the mid-nineteenth century.

APPENDIX 3

Books in Heyer

The publisher and founder of the Minerva Press, William Lane, is generally credited with having initiated the spread of lending, or circulating, libraries to most of the large towns (and many smaller ones) in England throughout the late eighteenth and early nineteenth centuries. Lane's main library was located in Leadenhall Street, in the same building as his Minerva Press which had begun printing novels in about 1790. By setting up his own large lending establishment Lane was able to offer his novels to the borrowing and buying public along with a wide selection of other fiction and non-fiction texts. By the time of the Regency every seaside town and fashionable resort had at least one library—often housed in a shop, assembly room or other publicly accessible building—and London had a number of subscription libraries (over 100 by 1820) ranging from Hookham's in Bond Street (where, in *Regency Buck*, Judith Taverner was able to borrow *Sense and Sensibility*) to Miss Flinders's small shop cum library near Walpole Street. While novels were held by many among the upper classes to be most unsuitable reading matter for young women, they became increasingly popular during the period and the thrilling stories lying between the mottled signature covers of the Minerva Press were to be found in many households. In homes such as the Wraxtons' in *The Grand Sophy*, however, disapproval of novels extended even to the famous works of Ann Radcliffe, Maria Edgeworth and Clara Reeve—and certainly to Lord Byron's poems—whereas Walter Scott's novels and romantic ballads and Jane Austen's stories were considered quite acceptable.

Walter Scott and Lord Byron were both best-selling authors during the Regency.

Jane Austen, *Sense and Sensibility* (1811): The story of two sisters, Elinor and Marianne Dashwood, who, in a reflection of the book's title, react quite differently to the hopes and disappointments of their lives and their love affairs.

Mansfield Park **(1814):** A tale of class and misconception, it tells the story of Fanny Price, a poor cousin who is adopted by her richer relatives and generally treated with condescension. Fanny's natural good sense, modesty and principles support her through various ordeals and she eventually comes to be valued by those she loves while other, less principled characters are eventually shown in their true light.

Lord Byron, *Childe Harold's Pilgrimage* (1812–18): A long poem written in stanzas after the style of Spenser. The first two cantos were published in 1812, followed by the third in 1816 and the fourth in 1818 and together they tell the story of the travels through foreign lands of a disillusioned pilgrim. In the third canto specific links with current events such as the Peninsular War, Waterloo and Napoleon are made and by the fourth canto the poet speaks for himself rather than through the pilgrim.

The Corsair **(1814):** A poem written in heroic couplets, it tells the story of the wicked yet chivalrous pirate chief known as Conrad, his intrigues and battles with Seyd, a Turkish Pasha, and his tragic love affairs with Medora and Gulnare.

Miguel de Cervantes Saavedra, *Don Quixote de la Mancha* (1605 and 1615): Originally published in two parts, the story of the crazy Spanish gentleman who believed himself to be a knight and engaged in acts of chivalry against windmills and sheep, was well known by the time of the Regency and widely read. Begun as a parody of the popular chivalric romance, the book developed a deeper meaning as Cervantes developed the character of the devoted idealist in Don Quixote and the practical realist in his squire, Sancho Panza.

Dante, *Divina Commedia* (early 1300s): Also known as *The Divine Comedy*, Dante's epic poem was his most important work. In it the poet goes on a journey into hell with the spirit of the great Greek classical poet Virgil as his guide. Dante offered readers a vision of the inferno, purgatory and paradise before leading them to God. An allegorical work, it was thought by many to be heretical but the strength of the language, the vision and continual allusions to the human experience gave it universal appeal.

Maria Edgeworth, *Castle Rackrent* (1800): A tale of Ireland and the eventual downfall of the hard-living and reckless Rackrent family as told by the family steward, Thady Quirk.

   ***Tales of a Fashionable Life* (1812):** *The Absentee* was one of the most popular of a series of stories published in six volumes by Mrs Edgeworth from 1809. It tells the story of Lord Colambre and his improvident parents Lord and Lady Clonbrony and the family's eventual return to Ireland at the son's behest.

James Hervey, *Meditations Among the Tombs* (1746–7): Hervey's two volumes of *Meditations and Contemplations* were extremely popular for many years. 'Meditations Among the Tombs' was included in Volume One along with 'Reflections on a Flower Garden' and 'A Descant Upon Creation'. Hervey had an immense appreciation of nature but his writing was often prosy and over-filled with truisms.

Homer, *The Iliad*: The epic Greek poem tells, in twenty-four books of verse, the story of the Trojan War and, in particular, the story of Achilles.

   ***The Odyssey*:** The second of Homer's epic poems, it tells the story of Odysseus (Ulysses) and his many adventures as he travels home to Ithaca after the Trojan War.

Lady Caroline Lamb, *Glenarvon* (1816): Published anonymously, Lady Caroline's first novel was written as a form of revenge against the poet Byron after he ended their affair. The novel caused a scandal with its thinly veiled sketches and caricatures of members of the *haut ton*, including Lady Caroline herself (as the innocent Calantha), her husband, mother and aunt, and Lord Byron as *Glenarvon*. Despite their outrage, members of the upper class pored over the book, looking for portraits of themselves and those they knew. *Glenarvon* went into several editions and even had a key published for easy identification of the various characters.

Matthew 'Monk' Lewis, *Ambrosio, or the Monk* (1796): A story of sin, seduction, murder and a pact with the devil, the Gothic novel made Lewis famous and earned him the nickname 'Monk'.

William Paley, *Natural Theology* (1802): One of several texts by Paley, a fellow of Christ's College, Cambridge, which argued that proof of the existence of God was to be found in the clear design inherent in the natural world and especially in the human body.

Anna Maria Porter, *The Hungarian Brothers* (1807): A popular novel set against the background of the French revolutionary war, it tells the story of the orphaned sons of a Hungarian nobleman who must seek their fortune as officers in the Hungarian army. It was written by the sister of Jane Porter, the popular author of *Thaddeus of Warsaw*, and published in three volumes.

Jane Porter, *Thaddeus of Warsaw* (1803): A popular historical novel in four volumes which tells the story of Thaddeus, a patriotic young man, and his exploits during Poland's struggle for independence. It was reprinted several times during the Regency.

Mrs Radcliffe, *The Mysteries of Udolpho* (1794): The story of Emily de St Aubert, an orphan who is left to the care of her ambitious aunt. The aunt, who is married to the sinister Signor Montoni, has Emily carried off to the castle of Udolpho in the Italian countryside where various apparently supernatural events take place before the heroine is eventually reunited with her lost love.

Clara Reeve, *The Old English Baron* (1777): Originally published as *The Champion of Virtue, A Gothic Story*, and later renamed *The Old English Baron,* the story takes its inspiration from Horace Walpole's *Castle of Otranto,* a Gothic romance with a strong supernatural element. Clara Reeve's novel tells the story of Edmund, a humble hero of obscure origin destined to discover his rightful heritage, overcome temptation and defeat the villain of the piece.

The School for Widows **(1791):** The stories of three women: close friends Rachel Strictland and Frances Darnford, whose husbands are as profligate as their wives are virtuous, and Isabella di Soranzo, a tragic widow.

Colonel David Roberts, *Adventures of Johnny Newcome* (1815): First published by 'an Officer', *The Military Adventures of Johnny Newcome, with an account of his campaigns on the Peninsula, and in Pall Mall* was illustrated with sketches by the famous artist Thomas Rowlandson. A poem in four cantos entitled *Adventures of Johnny Newcome in the Navy* (also with plates by Rowlandson) was published in 1818 under the name of Alfred Burton—aka John Mitford.

Mr Samuel Rogers, *The Pleasures of Memory* (1792): A popular poem of limited literary merit but which was considered 'agreeable verse' during the Regency.

Sir Walter Scott, *Marmion* (1808): A dramatic poem in six cantos, it tells the story of the wicked Lord Marmion and his attempts to win the hand of the wealthy Lady Clare. The fifth canto includes the ballad of Lochinvar, a young hero who rescues the fair Ellen from marriage to a dastardly suitor by swinging her on to his horse and riding off with her in the middle of the bridal feast.

Lady of the Lake (1810): A romantic poem in six cantos. Set in Scotland, it tells the story of a knight and his love for Ellen, the daughter of an outlawed Highland chief. A tale of love and sacrifice.

Waverley (1814): Generally recognised as the first historical novel, it recounts the adventures of Edward Waverley, a romantic young Englishman who travels to Scotland and becomes embroiled in the Jacobites' attempt to restore the Pretender to the throne.

Guy Mannering (1815): Set in Scotland in the reign of George III, it tells the story of Harry Bertram who, as a young child, is kidnapped and taken abroad at the instigation of the evil lawyer Glossin who has designs on the family estate. Bertram's life becomes intertwined with that of Guy Mannering and his daughter Julia whom he loves. Ignorant of his true identity, on his return to Scotland Bertram is again threatened by Glossin's scheming but is saved by the old gypsy Meg Merrilies and the farmer Dandie Dinmont. This was the story which so enthralled Mrs Underhill and her family in *The Nonesuch*.

Mary Shelley, *Frankenstein or the Modern Prometheus* (1818): The story of a young student, Frankenstein, who brings to life a creature he has made from dissected corpses and then abandons it at the moment of its birth. The novel was written as a tale of terror and enjoyed widespread popularity from its first printing. The Duke of Sale could hardly put it down in *The Foundling*.

Mr Robert Southey, *The Curse of Kehama* (1810): A long poem based on Hindu mythology which tells the story of Ladurlad and his daughter Kailyal and the curse placed on Ladurlad by the great Rajah of the world, Kehama, after the death of his son Arvalan.

Felix Lope de Vega (1562–1635): Second only to Cervantes among Spanish writers, Lope de Vega remains the world's most prolific playwright and is considered the founder of the Spanish drama. In addition to plays, he also wrote romantic prose, narrative poetry, parody and historical epics. He was known as the 'Prodigy of Nature' and was so revered by the Spanish that the phrase 'Es de Lope' meant perfection.

Friedrich Augustus Wolf, *Prolegomena ad Homerum* **(1795):** A revolutionary text in that it was the first to focus on the problem of the authorship of *The Iliad* and *The Odyssey*. Wolf addressed the questions of whether Homer actually existed and had written both epic poems, thus establishing the foundation for an important part of modern Homeric scholarship.

Ajax: The original Ajax was a hero of the Trojan War and his deeds are related in Homer's *Iliad*. 'The Unknown Ajax' was a character in Shakespeare's *Troilus and Cressida* in which he was portrayed as a valiant but foolish man and a great fighter.

Venetia: Venetia Digby was born in 1600. A great beauty, she was included in *Aubrey's Brief Lives* and described as 'a most beautiful desirable creature'. Several poets, including Ben Jonson and Aurelian Townshend, wrote verses commemorating her death.

Oedipus: The tragic hero of Sophocles' plays *Oedipus Rex* and *Oedipus at Colonus* who was doomed to kill his father and marry his mother without knowing who they were at the time.

APPENDIX 4

Timeline

1738: George III born.

1744: Charlotte of Mecklenburg-Strelitz born.

1761: George III marries Charlotte of Mecklenburg-Strelitz.

1762: George, Prince of Wales, born (12 August).

1775: Jane Austen born at Steventon (16 December).

1785: George, Prince of Wales, marries Maria Anne Fitzherbert (21 December).

1795: George, Prince of Wales, marries Princess Caroline of Brunswick-Wolfenbüttel (8 April).

1796: A daughter, Princess Charlotte, born to HRH George, Prince of Wales, and Princess Caroline (7 January).

Soho Foundry opened in Birmingham (30 January).

1800: Maria Edgeworth publishes *Castle Rackrent*.

1801: The parliaments of Great Britain and Ireland united in the Act of Union (1 January).

The Prime Minister, William Pitt (the Younger), resigns over the Catholic Emancipation.

The Battle of Alexandria (21 March).

The Battle of Copenhagen.

1802: The Peace of Amiens signed by England, France and Spain.

Gas lighting used for the first time to light the front of the Soho foundry in Birmingham as part of the celebration of the Peace of Amiens.

William Cobbett first publishes his *Political Register* (January).

Walter Scott publishes the first volume of his *Minstrelsy of the Scottish Border*.

Edinburgh Review established (October).

1803: War with France begins again (18 May).

Invasion scare in England.

Samuel Taylor Coleridge publishes his *Poems*.

1804: Pitt again becomes prime minister.

Napoleon proclaimed emperor (May).

1805: Battle of Trafalgar (21 October).

Admiral Horatio Nelson killed at the Battle of Trafalgar.

Battle of Austerlitz (2 December).

Scott publishes *Lay of the Last Minstrel*.

1806: Pitt dies (23 January) and the Ministry of All the Talents takes office.

Lord Grenville becomes prime minister.

The great Whig orator, Charles James Fox, dies (13 September).

1807: Abolition of slavery passed in the House of Lords (25 March).

Gas lighting installed in Pall Mall.

The Whigs are dismissed from Office.

The Duke of Portland becomes prime minister.

Napoleon invades Spain.

Charles and Mary Lamb publish *Tales from Shakespeare*.

Lord Byron publishes *Hours of Idleness*.

1808: The Peninsular War begins.

Covent Garden theatre destroyed by fire (20 September).

Richard Trevithick's early steam engine, the 'catch-me-who-can', runs on a circular track at Euston.

Walter Scott publishes *Marmion*.

1809: Battle of Corunna (16 January).

Drury Lane theatre destroyed by fire (24 February).

The Duke of York forced to resign as army commander-in-chief over the actions of his mistress, Mary Ann Clarke (18 March).

Battle of Oporto (12 May).

Byron goes abroad (2 July).

Battle of Talvera (28 July).

The great engineer, Matthew Boulton, dies in Birmingham aged 81 (17 August).

Canning and Castlereagh fight a duel.

The Duke of Portland dies (30 October).

Spencer Perceval becomes prime minister.

1810: Napoleon marries Marie Louise, daughter of the Emperor of Austria (11 February).

Napoleon annexes Holland (9 July).

Princess Amelia dies (2 November).

George III pronounced insane.

Lady Hester Stanhope travels to the Middle East.

Walter Scott publishes *Lady of the Lake*.

1811: George, Prince of Wales officially becomes Regent (5 February).

The Regent holds his first public levee at Carlton House (26 February).

Battle of Albuera (16 May).

Duke of York reinstated as army commander-in-chief (25 May).

The Regent appoints himself a field-marshal.

The Regent holds a military review of 3,000 troops on Wimbledon Common (10 June).

The Regent holds the great Fête at Carlton House with 2,000 guests (19 June).

Luddites engage in machine breaking in the Midlands.

Nash begins Regent Street.

William Thackeray born (18 July).

Jane Austen's *Sense and Sensibility* published (November).

Percy Bysshe Shelley publishes *Necessity of Atheism*.

Shelley is expelled from Oxford.

London's population passes the one million mark.

Great Britain's population approximately 12.5 million.

1812: Battle of Cuidad Rodrigo (19 January).

Charles Dickens born (7 February).

Parliamentary restrictions on the Prince Regent removed (11 February).

Capture of Badajoz (6 April).

The prime minister, Spencer Perceval, is assassinated in the lobby of the House of Commons (11 May).

Lord Liverpool takes over as head of the Tory government.

Lord Liverpool resigns (21 May).

Lord Liverpool resumes office (8 June).

America declares war on Britain (19 June).

Battle of Salamanca (22 July).

Battle of Borodino (September).

Napoleon begins the retreat from Moscow (19 October).

James Madison elected as US president (November).

London's main streets are lit by gas.

Wheat prices rise dramatically, reaching near-famine prices.

The waltz is danced for the first time in London ballrooms.

Joseph Turner exhibits *Snowstorm: Hannibal and His Army Crossing the Alps* at the Royal Academy.

Byron publishes first two cantos of *Childe Harold's Pilgrimage*.

The Grimm brothers publish their *Fairy Tales*.

Mrs Siddons appears on stage for the last time.

1813: Austen's *Pride and Prejudice* published (January).

Battle of Vittoria (21 June).

Madame de Staël visits London.

Wellington invades France (8 October).

Napoleon defeated at Leipzig (October).

The Methodist Missionary Society is founded.

The Philharmonic Society is founded.

Robert Owen publishes *A New View of Society*.

Robert Southey publishes *Life of Nelson*.

Shelley publishes *Queen Mab*.

Byron publishes *The Bride of Abydos*.

1814: In an extreme winter the Thames freezes over and the great Frost Fair is held (1–5 February).

The Grand Duchess of Oldenburg arrives in London.

The Allies enter Paris (30 March).

Napoleon abdicates and is exiled to Elba (11 April).

Louis XVIII enters Paris as king (3 May).

Wellington created a duke (3 May).

Austen's *Mansfield Park* published (May).

The Allied sovereigns arrive in England (7 June).

The procession of the Allied Sovereigns to Guildhall (18 June).

Military Review in Hyde Park with 12,000 troops (20 June).

Thanksgiving service at St Paul's (7 July).

The Regent holds a grand fête at Carlton House in honour of the Duke of Wellington (21 July).

George Stephenson builds the first working steam locomotive (25 July).

The official Peace celebrations begin in Hyde Park (1 August).

Princess Caroline departs England for an extended tour of Europe.

The Congress of Vienna begins (1 November).

England and America sign the Treaty of Ghent (24 December).

Scott publishes *Waverley*.

Byron publishes *The Corsair*.

Wordsworth publishes *The Excursion*.

The Shelleys leave England.

Edmund Kean appears as Shylock in his debut at Drury Lane.

Cricket is played for the first time by the MCC at Lord's.

1815: Napoleon escapes from Elba.

Napoleon arrives in France (1 March).

Louis XVIII flees from Paris (19 March).

The Hundred Days begins with Napoleon's entry into Paris (20 March).

The Corn Law is passed (23 March).

Anti-Corn Law riots in London (March).

An alliance is formed between Britain, Prussia, Russia and Austria to fight against Napoleon (25 March).

Otto von Bismarck born (1 April).

Anthony Trollope born (24 April).

The Congress of Vienna begins (9 June).

The Duchess of Richmond's ball in Brussels (15 June).

The Battles of Ligny and Quatre Bras (16 June).

Wellington's army defeats Napoleon's troops at the Battle of Waterloo (18 June).

The Congress of Vienna ends (19 June).

Napoleon abdicates (22 June).

The Allies enter Paris (7 July).

Louis XVIII returns to Paris (8 July).

Napoleon is banished to St Helena (17 August).

Humphrey Davy invents the safety lamp for miners.

John Macadam's road-construction technique is adopted in England.

John Nash begins the renovation of the Brighton Pavilion.

Scott publishes *Guy Mannering*.

John Macadam publishes *The Present State of Roadmaking*.

Lord Byron marries Ann Isabella Milbanke.

The Apothecaries Act is passed making it illegal for unqualified apothecaries to practise medicine.

1816: Charlotte Brontë born (21 April).

Princess Charlotte marries Prince Leopold of Saxe-Coburg (2 May).

Beau Brummell leaves England for exile in France (17 May).

Richard Brinsley Sheridan dies (17 July).

Spa Fields Riots (2 December).

The Elgin Marbles are bought by the British Museum.

The Duke of Clarence's mistress, Mrs Jordan, dies.

The Corn Law riots; wheat again approaches famine prices.

Austen's *Emma* published; it is dedicated, by invitation, to the Prince Regent.

William Cobbett publishes his famous *Twopenny Trash*.

John Keats publishes his sonnet 'On Looking into Chapman's Homer' (December).

Coleridge publishes *Christabel and Other Poems*.

Coleridge publishes *Kubla Khan*.

Shelley publishes *Alastor*.

Scott publishes *Old Mortality* and *The Antiquary*.

1817: The Prince Regent is shot at while returning from the opening of Parliament (28 January).

Habeas Corpus is suspended (4 March).

James Monroe becomes fifth president of the US (4 March).

Madame de Staël dies (14 July).

Jane Austen dies (18 July).

Princess Charlotte dies in child-bed (6 November).

Keats publishes his *Poems*.

Coleridge publishes *Biographia Literaria*.

Thomas Love Peacock publishes *Melincourt*.

Blackwood's Magazine founded.

The Scotsman founded.

1818: Habeas Corpus restored (31 January).

Matthew 'Monk' Lewis dies (14 May).

William, Duke of Clarence, marries Adelaide of Saxe-Meiningen.

Edward, Duke of Kent, marries Victoria Mary Louisa, widow of the Prince of Leiningen.

Adolphus, Duke of Cambridge, marries Augusta of Hesse-Cassel.

Mary Shelley publishes *Frankenstein, or the Modern Prometheus*.

Scott publishes *Rob Roy* and *The Heart of Midlothian*.

Keats publishes *Endymion*.

Austen's *Northanger Abbey* and *Persuasion* published posthumously.

Thomas Bowdler publishes his 'sanitised' *Shakespeare*.

1819: Princess Alexandrina Victoria (later Queen Victoria) is born to the Duke and Duchess of Kent (24 May).

The Peterloo Massacre at St Peter's Fields, Manchester (16 August).

James Watt dies at Heathfield aged eighty-three (19 August).

Albert, Prince Consort to Queen Victoria born (26 August).

George Eliot (aka Mary Ann Evans) born (22 November).

British Parliament passes the Six Acts (17 December).

Byron publishes *Don Juan*.

Keats publishes *Ode to a Nightingale*.

Scott publishes *Ivanhoe*.

1820: George III dies at Windsor (29 January).

The Prince Regent is proclaimed King George IV at Carlton House (31 January).

The Cato Street conspirators arrested while planning to murder the Cabinet (23 February).

Five of the Cato Street conspirators executed (1 May).

George IV's wife, Queen Caroline, returns to England from Europe.

Queen Caroline's trial for adultery (June).

Bill of Pains and Penalties against George IV's wife, Queen Caroline, introduced into Parliament (6 July).

Bill against Queen Caroline fails.

Shelley publishes *Prometheus Unbound*.

Keats publishes *Isabella and Other Poems*.

Keats sails for Italy.

1821: Napoleon dies (5 May).

George IV's coronation at Westminster Abbey (19 July).

Queen Caroline is refused admittance to the Abbey.

Queen Caroline dies (7 August).

Pierce Egan publishes *Life in London*.

Thomas Malthus publishes *Principles of Political Economy*.

John Constable exhibits *The Hay Wain*.

Keats dies.

1830: George IV dies (26 June).

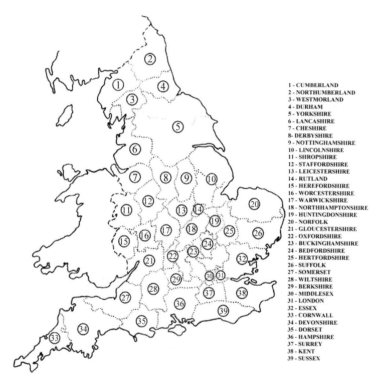

1 - CUMBERLAND
2 - NORTHUMBERLAND
3 - WESTMORLAND
4 - DURHAM
5 - YORKSHIRE
6 - LANCASHIRE
7 - CHESHIRE
8- DERBYSHIRE
9 - NOTTINGHAMSHIRE
10 - LINCOLNSHIRE
11 - SHROPSHIRE
12 - STAFFORDSHIRE
13 - LEICESTERSHIRE
14 - RUTLAND
15 - HEREFORDSHIRE
16 - WORCESTERSHIRE
17 - WARWICKSHIRE
18 - NORTHHAMPTONSHIRE
19 - HUNTINGDONSHIRE
20 - NORFOLK
21 - GLOUCESTERSHIRE
22 - OXFORDSHIRE
23 - BUCKINGHAMSHIRE
24 - BEDFORDSHIRE
25 - HERTFORDSHIRE
26 - SUFFOLK
27 - SOMERSET
28 - WILTSHIRE
29 - BERKSHIRE
30 - MIDDLESEX
31 - LONDON
32 - ESSEX
33 - CORNWALL
34 - DEVONSHIRE
35 - DORSET
36 - HAMPSHIRE
37 - SURREY
38 - KENT
39 - SUSSEX

APPENDIX 5

Reading about the Regency and Where Next?

Aiken Hodge, Jane, *Passion and Principle: The Loves and Lives of Regency Women,* John Murray, London, 1996.

Aiken Hodge, Jane, *The Private World of Georgette Heyer,* Heinemann, London, 1984.

Austen Jane, *Jane Austen's Selected Letters,* Vivien Jones (ed.), Oxford University Press, Oxford, 1994.

Austen, Jane, *My Dear Cassandra*, Penelope Hughes-Hallett (ed.), Collins & Brown, London, 1991.

Bovill, E. W., *English Country Life 1780–1830*, Oxford University Press, London, 1962.

Burgess, Anthony, *Coaching Days of England,* Paul Elek, London, 1966.

Burnett, T. A. J., *The Rise and Fall of a Regency Dandy: the Life and Times of Scrope Berdmore Davies,* Murray, London, 1981.

Burton, Elizabeth, *The Georgians at Home*, Arrow Books, London, 1973.

Cecil, David, *A Portrait of Jane Austen,* Penguin Books, Middlesex, 1980.

Cunnington, C. Willett and Phillis, *Handbook of English Costume in the 19th Century*, Faber and Faber, London, 1973.

David, Saul, *Prince of Pleasure*, Abacus, London, 1999.

Egan, Pierce, *Life in London,* John Camden Hotten, London, 1821.

Ford, John, *Prizefighting: The Age of Regency Boximania*, David & Charles, Newton Abbot, 1971.

Fullerton, Susannah, *Jane Austen and Crime*, Jane Austen Society of Australia, Sydney, 2004.

Girouard, Mark, *Life in the English Country House, A Social and Architectural History*, Yale University Press, New Haven, 1979.

Gronow, Captain, *Selections from the Reminiscences of Captain Gronow*, Nicholas Bentley, ed., The Folio Society, London, 1977.

Hibbert, Christopher, *George IV: Prince of Wales*, Readers Union, Newton Abbott, 1972.

Hibbert, Christopher, *George IV: Regent and King*, Allen Lane, London, 1975.

Hughes, Kristine, *The Writer's Guide to Everyday Life in Regency and Victorian England from 1811 to 1901*, Writer's Digest Books, Cincinnati, Ohio, 1998.

Jago, Lucy, *Regency House Party*, Time Warner Books, London, 2004.

Laudermilk, Sharon and Teresa L. Hamlin, *The Regency Companion*, Garland Publishing, New York, 1989.

Laver, James, *The Age of Illusion*, Weidenfeld and Nicolson, London, 1972.

Laver, James, *Costumes Through the Ages*, Thames and Hudson, London, 1963.

Margetson, Stella, *Regency London*, Cassell & Company, London, 1971.

Palmer, Alan, *The Life and Times of George IV*, Weidenfeld and Nicolson, London, 1972.

Plumb, J. H., *Georgian Delights*, Weidenfeld and Nicolson, London, 1980.

Pool, Daniel, *What Jane Austen Ate and Charles Dickens Knew*, Touchstone Books, New York, 1993.

Porter, Roy and Dorothy, *Patient's Progress: Doctors and Doctoring in Eighteenth-century England*, Polity Press, Cambridge, 1989.

Priestley, J. B., *The Prince of Pleasure and His Regency*, Heinemann, London, 1969.

Quennell, Marjorie and C. H. B., *A History of Everyday Things in England Volume III: 1733–1851*, B. T. Batsford, London, 1961.

Reid, J. C., *Bucks and Bruisers: Pierce Egan and Regency England*, Routledge & Kegan Paul, London, 1971.

Roberts, Henry D., *A History of the Royal Pavilion Brighton*, Country Life Limited, London, 1939.

Rutherford, Jessica M. F., *The Royal Pavilion: The Palace of George IV*, Brighton Arts and Leisure Services, 1995.

Sheppard, Francis, *London 1808–1870: The Infernal Wen*, Secker & Warburg, London, 1971.

Sitwell, Osbert and Margaret Barton, *Brighton*, Faber and Faber, London, 1935.

Stuart, Dorothy Margaret, *Regency Roundabout*, Macmillan, London, 1943.

Summerson, John, *Georgian London*, Barrie & Jenkins, London, 1988.

Thompson, F. M. L., *English Landed Society in the Nineteenth Century*, Routledge & Kegan Paul, London, 1963.

Walrond, Sallie, *Looking at Carriages*, J. A. Allen, London, 1957.

Watkin, David, *The Royal Interiors of Regency England: From Watercolours First Published by W. H. Pyne in 1817–1820,* Dent, London, 1984.

Watkins, Susan, *Jane Austen's Town and Country Style*, Thames and Hudson, London, 1990.

White, Reginald James, *Life in Regency England,* Putnam, New York, 1963.

Wilson, Harriette, *Harriette Wilson's Memoirs,* Century Publishing Co., London, 1985.

WHERE NEXT?

Sally Houghton's excellent Georgette Heyer website: www .georgetteheyer.com

The Georgian Index: www.georgianindex.net

The Republic of Pemberley: www.pemberley.com

Jessamyn's Regency Pages: www.songsmyth.com

Cathy Decker's Regency page has a host of great links: hal.ucr .edu/~cathy/reg.html

The Heyer list: www.heyerlist.org

The Regency Collection: www.homepages.ihug.co.nz/~awoodley /Regency.html

Appendix 6

Georgette Heyer's Regency Novels

Regency Buck (1935)

It is in regrettable circumstances that beautiful Judith Taverner and her brother Peregrine first encounter Julian St John Audley. The man, they both agree, is an insufferably arrogant dandy. But unfortunately for them, he is also the Fifth Earl of Worth, a friend of the Regent and, quite by chance, their legal guardian...

An Infamous Army (1937)

In 1815, beneath the aegis of the Army of Occupation, Brussels is the gayest town in Europe. And the widow Lady Barbara Childe, renowned for being as outrageous as she is beautiful, is at the centre of all that is fashionable and light-hearted. When she meets Charles Audley, the elegant and handsome aide-de-camp to the great Duke of Wellington himself, her *joie de vivre* knows no bounds—until the eve of the fateful Battle of Waterloo...

The Spanish Bride (1940)

Shot-proof, fever-proof and a veteran campaigner at the age of twenty-five, Brigade-Major Harry Smith is reputed to be the luckiest man in Lord Wellington's army. Yet at the siege of Badajos, his friends foretell the ruin of his career. When Harry meets the defenceless Juana, a fiery passion consumes him. Under the banner of honour and with the selfsame ardour he so frequently displays in battle, he dives headlong into marriage. In his beautiful child bride he finds a kindred spirit, and a temper to match. But for Juana, a long year of war must follow.

The Corinthian (1940)

The only question which hangs over the life of Sir Richard Wyndham, notable whip, dandy and Corinthian, is one of marriage. On the eve of making the most momentous decision of his life, he is on his way home, a little the worse for drink, when he chances upon a beautiful young fugitive climbing out of a window by means of knotted sheets—and so finds a perfect opportunity for his own escape.

Friday's Child (1944)

Rejected by Miss Milborne, the Incomparable, for his unsteadiness of character, wild Lord Sheringham flies back to London in a rage, bent on avenging Fate. Vowing to marry the first woman to cross his way, who should he see but Hero Wantage, the young and charmingly unsophisticated girl who has loved him since childhood...

The Reluctant Widow (1946)

Stepping into the wrong carriage in a Sussex village, Elinor Rochdale is swept up in a thrilling and dangerous adventure. Overnight the would-be governess becomes mistress of a ruined estate and partner in a secret conspiracy to save a family's name. By midnight she is a bride, by dawn a widow.

The Foundling (1948)

The shy young Duke of Sale has never known his parents; instead, His Grace Adolphus Gillespie Vernon Ware (Gilly for short) has endured twenty-four years of rigorous mollycoddling from his uncle and valet. But his natural diffidence conceals a rebellious spirit. So when Gilly hears of Belinda, the beautiful foundling who appears to be blackmailing his cousin, he absconds with glee. Only he has no sooner entered his new and dangerous world than he is plunged into a frenzy of intrigue, kidnap and adventure.

Arabella (1949)

An enchanting debutante and the eldest daughter of an impoverished country parson, Arabella embarks on her first London season. Armed with beauty, virtue and a benevolent godmother (as well as a notoriously impetuous temper) she quickly runs afoul of Robert Beaumaris, the most eligible Nonpareil of the day. When he accuses her of being yet another pretty female after his wealth, Arabella allows herself to be provoked—into a deceitful charade that might have quite unexpected consequences...

The Grand Sophy (1950)

When the redoubtable Sir Horace Stanton-Lacy is ordered to South America on diplomatic business, he leaves his only daughter Sophy with his sister's family, the Ombersleys, in Berkeley Square. Upon her arrival, Sophy is bemused to see her cousins in a sad tangle. The heartless and tyrannical Charles is betrothed to a pedantic bluestocking almost as tiresome as himself; Cecilia is besotted with a beautiful but feather-brained poet; and Hubert has fallen foul of a moneylender. It looks as though the grand Sophy has arrived just in time to sort them out, but she hasn't reckoned with Charles, the Ombersley heir, who has only one thought—to marry her off and rid the family of her meddlesome ways...

The Quiet Gentleman (1951)

When Gervase Frant, Seventh Earl of St Erth, returns at last from Waterloo to his family seat at Stanyon, he enjoys a less than welcome homecoming. Only Theo, a cousin even quieter than himself, is there to greet him—and when he meets his stepmother and young half-brother he detects open disappointment that he survived the wars. The dangers of the Lincolnshire countryside could never be more unexpected...

Cotillion (1953)

The three great-nephews of cantankerous Mr Penicuik know better than to ignore his summons, especially when it concerns the bestowal of his fortune. The wily old gentleman has hatched an outrageous plan for his adopted daughter's future and his own amusement: his fortune will be Kitty's dowry. But while the beaus are scrambling for her hand, Kitty counters with her own inventive, if daring, scheme: a sham engagement that should help keep wedlock at bay...

The Toll-Gate (1954)

Captain John Staple's exploits in the Peninsula had earned him the sobriquet Crazy Jack amongst his fellows in the Dragoon Guards. Now home from Waterloo, life in peacetime is rather dull for the huge, adventure-loving Captain. But when he finds himself lost and benighted at an unmanned toll-house in the Pennines, his soldiering days suddenly pale away beside an adventure—and romance—of a lifetime.

Bath Tangle (1955)

The Earl of Spenborough had always been noted for his eccentricity. Leaving a widow younger than his own daughter Serena was one thing, but leaving his fortune to the trusteeship of the Marquis of Rotherham—the one man the same daughter had jilted—was quite another. In a tangle of marriage and manners the like of which even Regency Bath has rarely seen, Lady Serena finds herself involved with her lovely young stepmother, Lord Rotherham and her own childhood sweetheart.

Sprig Muslin (1956)

Finding so young and pretty a girl as Amanda wandering unattended, Sir Gareth Ludlow knows it is his duty as a man of honour to restore her to her family. But it is to prove no easy task for the

Corinthian. His captive in *Sprig Muslin* has more than her rapturous good looks and bandboxes to aid her—she is also possessed of a runaway imagination…

April Lady (1957)

When the new Lady Cardross begins to fill her days with fashion and frivolity, the Earl has to wonder whether she did really only marry him for his money, as his family so helpfully suggests. And now Nell doesn't dare tell him the truth. What with the concern over his wife's heart and pocket, sorting out her brother's scrapes and trying to prevent his own half-sister from eloping, it is no wonder that the much-tried Earl almost misses the opportunity to smooth the path of true love in his marriage…

Sylvester (1957)

Endowed with rank, wealth and elegance, Sylvester, Duke of Salford, has decided to travel to Wiltshire to discover if the Hon. Phoebe Marlow will meet his exacting requirements for a bride. If he doesn't expect to meet a tongue-tied stripling in need of both manners and conduct, he is even more intrigued when his visit causes Phoebe to flee her home. They meet again on the road to London, where her carriage has come to grief in the snow. Yet Phoebe, already caught in one imbroglio, now knows she could soon be well deep in another…

Venetia (1958)

In all her twenty-five years, lovely Venetia Lanyon has never been further than Harrogate, nor enjoyed the attentions of any but her two wearisomely persistent suitors. Then, in one extraordinary encounter, she meets a neighbour she knows only by reputation—the infamous Lord Damerel—and before she realises it, she finds herself egging on a libertine whose way of life has scandalised the North Riding for years.

The Unknown Ajax (1959)

Miles from anywhere, Darracott Place is presided over by irascible and short-tempered Lord Darracott. The recent drowning of his eldest son has done nothing to improve his temper, for now he must send for the unknown offspring of the uncle whom the family are never permitted to mention. None of the beleaguered family are prepared for the arrival of the weaver's brat and heir apparent.

Pistols for Two (1960)

Affairs of honour between bucks and blades, rakes and rascals; affairs of the heart between heirs and orphans, beauties and bachelors; romance, intrigue, escapades and duels at dawn: all the gallantry, villainy and elegance of the age that Georgette Heyer has so triumphantly made her own are exquisitely revived in this book of eleven short stories of the Regency.

A Civil Contract (1961)

Adam Deveril, the new Viscount Lynton and a hero at Salamanca, returns from the Peninsular War to find his family on the brink of ruin and the broad acres of his ancestral home mortgaged to the hilt. It is Lord Oversley, father of Adam's first love, who tactfully introduces him to Mr Jonathan Chawleigh, a City man of apparently unlimited wealth with no social ambitions for himself, but with his eyes firmly fixed on a suitable match for his one and only daughter.

The Nonesuch (1962)

Sir Waldo Hawkridge—wealthy, handsome, eligible, illustrious, and known as 'the Nonesuch' for his athletic prowess—believes he is past the age of falling love. But when he comes north to inspect his unusual inheritance at Broom Hall in the West Riding, his arrival leads to the most entertaining of ramifications.

False Colours (1963)

The Honourable Christopher Fancot, on leave from the diplomatic service in the summer of 1817, is startled to find his entrancing but incorrigibly extravagant mother on the brink of financial and social ruin, and more than alarmed to find that his twin brother has disappeared without trace. The unfortunate Kit is forced into an outrageous masquerade by the tangled affairs of his wayward family—his rigid uncle, Lord Brumby, the surprisingly wily Sir Bonamy Ripple, the formidable old Lady Stavely and Evelyn's betrothed, Cressy—but in the face of Evelyn's continued absence, Kit's ingenuity is stretched to the limit.

Frederica (1965)

Rich, handsome, darling of the *ton*, the hope of ambitious mothers and the despair of his sisters, the Marquis of Alverstoke sees no reason to put himself out for anyone. Until a distant connection, ignorant of his selfishness, applies to him for help. Plunged head-long into one drama after another by the large and irrepressible Merriville family, Alverstoke is surprised to find himself far from bored. The lovely Charis may be as hen-witted as she is beautiful but Jessamy is an interesting boy and Felix an engaging scamp. And, most intriguing of all, their strong-minded sister Frederica, who seems more concerned with her family's welfare than his own distinguished attentions…

Black Sheep (1966)

Charming and wise in the ways of the world, Bath society belle Miss Abigail Wendover has tried hard to detach her spirited niece Fanny from a plausible fortune-hunter. Her valiant efforts on behalf of her relative become vastly more complicated with the arrival of Miles Calverleigh. The black sheep of his family, a cynical, outrageous devil-may-care with a scandalous past—that would be a connection more shocking even than Fanny's unwise liaison with his nephew! But Abby, adept at managing her sweet, silly sister Selina, her lively niece and the host of her admirers among Bath's circumscribed society, has less success in controlling her own unruly heart.

Cousin Kate (1968)

Kate Malvern, rescued from penury by her aunt Minerva, hardly knows what to expect at Staplewood—the grand household is so very different from a life spent following the drum in the Peninsular campaign. But surely, other households are more homelike? Kate's uncle lives in one wing, handsome, moody cousin Torquil in another; though the guests are few, even family dinners are formal. And, when Kate begins to suspect the shocking reason for Minerva's generosity, she has no one to confide in but cousin Philip, who appears to have taken an instant dislike to her...

Charity Girl (1970)

When Fate and a chivalrous impulse combine to saddle Viscount Desford with a friendless, homeless waif named Cherry Steane, to whom else should he turn in such a scrape but his old childhood playmate, Henrietta Silverdale? For all they refused to oblige their parents by marrying, they have always been the best of friends. But as Desford pursues Cherry's lickpenny grandfather and reprobate father around unfashionable watering places and the seedier fringes of society, Hetta is forced to wonder whether he might not, at last, have fallen in love. Without the timely intervention of his scapegrace brother Simon, and Hetta's worthy suitor Gary Nethercott, Desford is in danger of making a rare bumblebroth of his affairs.

Lady of Quality (1972)

Independent and spirited, Miss Annis Wychwood gives little thought to finding herself a suitable husband, thus dashing the dreams of many hopeful suitors. When she becomes embroiled in the affairs of the runaway heiress Lucilla, however, she encounters the beautiful fugitive's guardian—as rakish and uncivil a rogue as she has ever met. Although chafing a bit at the restrictions of Regency society in Bath, Annis does have to admit that Oliver Carleton, at least, is never boring.

Index

Figures in italics indicate captions.

About the Author

During the extensive study and research of Georgette Heyer's work for her Ph.D. thesis, Jennifer Kloester had access to Heyer's private papers and other information made available through the generosity of Georgette Heyer's son and, as a result, has discovered a wealth of new material on a writer who is known to have been an immensely private person. Kloester lives in Victoria, Australia.